The Ages of the Black Panther

ALSO EDITED BY JOSEPH J. DAROWSKI
AND FROM MCFARLAND

*The Ages of The Flash:
Essays on the Fastest Man Alive* (2019)

*The Ages of the Justice League: Essays on America's
Greatest Superheroes in Changing Times* (2017)

*The Ages of the Incredible Hulk: Essays on the Green Goliath
in Changing Times* (2016)

*The Ages of Iron Man: Essays on the Armored Avenger
in Changing Times* (2015)

*The Ages of Wonder Woman: Essays on the Amazon Princess
in Changing Times* (2014)

*The Ages of the X-Men: Essays on the Children
of the Atom in Changing Times* (2014)

*The Ages of the Avengers: Essays on the Earth's
Mightiest Heroes in Changing Times* (2014)

*The Ages of Superman:
Essays on the Man of Steel in Changing Times* (2012)

The Ages of the Black Panther

*Essays on the King of Wakanda
in Comic Books*

Edited by JOSEPH J. DAROWSKI

McFarland & Company, Inc., Publishers
Jefferson, North Carolina

LIBRARY OF CONGRESS CATALOGUING-IN-PUBLICATION DATA

Names: Darowski, Joseph J., editor.
Title: The ages of the Black Panther : essays on the king of Wakanda in comic books / edited by Joseph J. Darowski.
Description: Jefferson, North Carolina : McFarland & Company, Inc., Publishers, 2020 | Includes bibliographical references and index.
Identifiers: LCCN 2020012150 | ISBN 9781476675220 (paperback : acid free paper) ∞
ISBN 9781476639321 (ebook)
Subjects: LCSH: Black Panther (Fictitious character) | Comic books, strips, etc.—United States. | Literature and society—United States.
Classification: LCC PN6728.B519338 A37 2020 | DDC 741.5/973—dc23
LC record available at https://lccn.loc.gov/2020012150

BRITISH LIBRARY CATALOGUING DATA ARE AVAILABLE

ISBN (print) 978-1-4766-7522-0
ISBN (ebook) 978-1-4766-3932-1

© 2020 Joseph J. Darowski. All rights reserved

No part of this book may be reproduced or transmitted in any form or by any means, electronic or mechanical, including photocopying or recording, or by any information storage and retrieval system, without permission in writing from the publisher.

Front cover images © 2020 Digital Vision/Shutterstock

Printed in the United States of America

McFarland & Company, Inc., Publishers
 Box 611, Jefferson, North Carolina 28640
 www.mcfarlandpub.com

To Derek

Table of Contents

Preface
    Joseph J. Darowski   1

The "Secret Origin" of the Black Panther: Literary and Historical Sources of Inspiration
    Liam T. Webb   5

Breaking (Some) Ground While Dodging Politics: How Stan Lee and Jack Kirby Started a Legend
    Cathy Leogrande   20

A Tale of Two Panthers: T'Challa and the Black Panther Party for Self-Defense
    Charles W. Henebry   36

Wakanda Forever! (Except for That One Time…): The Black Panther Party, Apartheid and the Brief Identity Crisis of the Black LEOPARD?!?
    Christopher Maverick   64

Wakanda Speaks: Animals and Animacy in "Panther's Rage"
    José Alaniz   76

Fighting the Long War Against the Klan: The Black Panther as a Symbol of Self-Defense and Social Justice
    Burton P. Buchanan, Ivon Alcime *and* Carlos D. Morrison   99

The Shadow of Apartheid: Analyzing Peter Gillis' Run in the 1980s
    Fernando Gabriel Pagnoni Berns   113

The King of Wakanda and the Emperor of the Useless
  White Boys: Race and Gender in Christopher Priest's
  Black Panther
    JOHN DAROWSKI   125

An Initiative for a More Fantastic Union: Prowling Around
  the PATRIOT Act
    PETER W.Y. LEE   149

Secret Invasions, Lost Technology and 21st Century Learning
  Skills: How Black Panther Saved Wakanda Using
  the "Four C's"
    DANIEL J. BERGMAN   166

Gender in Wakanda: Exploring Intersectionality and
  Hyper-Sexualization in Princess Shuri's Tenure
  as Black Panther
    HOLLIE FITZMAURICE   182

Black Panther, Namor and Mimetic Violence in Jonathan
  Hickman's *New Avengers*
    MATTHEW BRAKE   193

A Different Nation: Continuing a Legacy of Decolonization
  in *Black Panther*
    JULIAN C. CHAMBLISS   204

About the Contributors   221

Index   225

Preface

Joseph J. Darowski

The Black Panther's place in popular culture history is secured even as it is constantly evolving. As the first black superhero in mainstream American comic books, the heroic King of Wakanda is likely to be mentioned in histories of popular culture, particularly comic books. But, as the superhero genre has enjoyed a resurgence in prominence in the entertainment industry with the undeniable success of the Marvel Cinematic Universe, Black Panther's significance has spread beyond the comic book pages. In 2018, Marvel Studios released the film *Black Panther*, which went on to become the top-grossing film at the American box office that year (even outgrossing *Avengers: Infinity War*) after earning more than $700 million. At the worldwide box office, *Black Panther* would earn $1.3 billion. This global popularity is striking, considering the uneven prominence the character has had in Marvel Comics since his first appearance in 1966.

Created by Stan Lee and Jack Kirby, T'Challa is the king of the fictional nation of Wakanda and has become a key participant in the Marvel Universe. With literally thousands of characters that have been created, breaking out in terms of impact and popularity is no small task for Marvel superheroes. Black Panther has had adventures imagined by dozens of creators, with differing takes on the character, themes they explored, and threats to be conquered. This essay collection gathers thirteen essays that explore Black Panther's place in the Marvel Universe, whether his appearances are coming in issues of the *Fantastic Four* or *Avengers*, in his own title, or as part of crossover events. Supporting cast members, such as Everett K. Ross and T'Challa's sister Shuri, are also considered.

The following essays are focused exclusively on Black Panther's comic book adventures, not his appearances in television cartoons or hit movies. The scholars who have written these essays have sought to contextualize Black Panther's printed adventures with the social and political climate at the time the stories were created. This is not to claim that there is a one-to-one symbolism connecting supervillains on the page with real-world figures. Rather, it is an acknowledgment that the creators of our popular entertainment are not disassociated from the hopes and fears of a society or the news-making occurrences that surround them as they produce their art. Comic books are not created in a bubble that is separated from other popular culture phenomena, political events, and social movements. The long-running nature of superhero comic books allows for a unique analysis as adventures of the same character can span hundreds of creators and decades of time.

Liam T. Webb's "The 'Secret Origin' of the Black Panther: Literary and Historical Sources of Inspiration" is an exhaustive identification of existing literary tropes and historical events that share an affinity with the Black Panther's narrative origin. Ranging from Tarzan stories to the real-world "Congo Crisis," Webb acknowledges many of the likely influences that resulted in the creation of an iconic Marvel superhero.

In "Breaking (Some) Ground While Dodging Politics: How Stan Lee and Jack Kirby Started a Legend" Cathy Leogrande examines the first Black Panther stories. Leogrande acknowledges the progressive aspects of the stories while also exploring parts that are problematic for modern readers. Aspects of the 1960s comic book industry and larger social realities that influenced the stories being told in Marvel Comics are acknowledged to provide a thorough understanding of the context in which Jack Kirby and Stan Lee created the Black Panther.

"A Tale of Two Panthers: T'Challa and the Black Panther Party for Self-Defense" provides a thorough discussion of the nearly simultaneous emergence of the Marvel character and Black Panther political party. Charles W. Henebry highlights the likely impact the controversy surrounding the political group had on the tales told with the African king while also analyzing the evolution of Roy Thomas's interpretation of the character.

Christopher Maverick's "Wakanda Forever! (Except for That One Time…): The Black Panther Party, Apartheid and the Brief Identity Crisis of the Black LEOPARD?!?" is unique in this collection as it focuses on a single issue, *Fantastic Four* #119. While many other essays highlight how the creators of Black Panther's comic books are engaging with social issues, this is one instance in which the creators clearly attempt to avoid contemporary concerns. For one issue, Black Panther changes his name to the Black Leopard, and Maverick's analysis highlights the many factors that led to this soon-forgotten moment.

One of the most famous Black Panther stories is "Panther's Rage" by Don McGregor and Rich Buckler. In "Wakanda Speaks: Animals and Animacy in 'Panther's Rage,'" José Alaniz considers several concerns that can alter the interpretation of the story, including contemporary ecological tragedies, the formalist elements of the storytelling, and applying an animist perspective to the imagery of the comic book.

Burton P. Buchanan, Ivon Alcime, and Carlos D. Morrison's essay "Fighting the Long War Against the Klan: The Black Panther as a Symbol of Self-Defense and Social Justice" addresses a different aspect of Don McGregor's writing on the Black Panther: his battle with the Ku Klux Klan. Providing the context for the time it was written, this analysis applies semiotics and metonymy to deepen a reader's understanding of the text.

"The Shadow of Apartheid: Analyzing Peter Gillis' Run in the 1980s" looks at a mini-series that centered on Black Panther's African heritage. Fernando Gabriel Pagnoni Berns analyzes a story written by Peter B. Gillis and drawn by Denys Cowan that addressed the volatile politics around South Africa during its practice of apartheid. After Black Panther had been featured most prominently—but not exclusively—having adventures in America or Wakanda, Gillis and Cowan had the character engage with a neighboring country that practiced a thinly veiled apartheid allegory.

John Darowski's essay "The King of Wakanda and the Emperor of the Useless White Boys: Race and Gender in Christopher Priest's *Black Panther*" looks at a run of comic books from the late 1990s and early 2000s. Christopher Priest wrote *Black Panther* under the Marvel Knights line. Darowski examines this series in light of postmodern expectations of masculinity, including how race affects those expectations.

Though most well known as the King of Wakanda and occasionally as a member of the Avengers, Black Panther did have a brief stint as the leader of the Fantastic Four. In "An Initiative for a More Fantastic Union: Prowling Around the PATRIOT Act," Peter W.Y. Lee provides a close reading of this storyline, contextualizing it with the world political climate post–9/11. As the Marvel Universe was reacting to the *Civil War* events, the superhero community underwent several storylines that deliberately paralleled real-world events. Black Panther is uniquely situated to provide commentary, as a non–U.S. citizen and major political player in the Marvel Universe. Lee highlights the uncomfortable balance that is struck as Black Panther leads the Fantastic Four for six issues written by Dwayne McDuffie.

Daniel J. Bergman writes about one of the many events that have dotted Marvel's publishing history. *Secret Invasion* involved the shape-shifting alien Skrulls taking the place of key characters in the Marvel Universe, and the event touched most titles being published at the time. "Secret Invasions, Lost Technology and 21st Century Learning Skills: How Black Panther Saved Wakanda Using the 'Four C's'" applies modern teaching and education theory to Black Panther's role in the crossover storyline.

"Gender in Wakanda: Exploring Intersectionality and Hyper-Sexualization in Princess Shuri's Tenure as Black Panther" by Hollie FitzMaurice analyzes a storyline in which Shuri took over the mantle of Wakanda's ruler. Applying gender theory allows for new insights into this newer but popular character in the Marvel Universe.

Matthew Brake applies René Girard's theories of mimetic violence to a story written by Jonathan Hickman. "Black Panther, Namor and Mimetic Violence in Jonathan Hickman's *New Avengers*" demonstrates how superhero tales can allegorically engage with real-world concerns, as the cycle of violence depicted in *New Avengers* serves as a warning of an all-too-familiar pattern. Brake's analysis allows Girard's theories to enlighten the thematic underpinnings of Hickman's writing and allows the comic book story to serve as an access point to a theoretical framework.

Julian C. Chambliss considers issues of race, gender, and intersectionality in "A Different Nation: Continuing a Legacy of Decolonization in *Black Panther*." This essay provides a close reading of Ta-Nehisi Coates' run on *Black Panther* and the ways that run acknowledges the legacy of Black Panther comic books while addressing modern concerns and expectations.

Black Panther has a long history in the comic books and a new and very broad fanbase due to his films. The close readings and analysis in this collection demonstrate some of the insights to be gained from a deeper appreciation of the character's adventures. With so many decades of stories and so many possible avenues of analysis, this collection is hardly exhaustive. As more texts are produced and new analyses are performed, the significance of the King of Wakanda in American popular culture will become more apparent.

The "Secret Origin" of the Black Panther
Literary and Historical Sources of Inspiration

Liam T. Webb

The Black Panther debuted in *Fantastic Four* #52 on July 10, 1966. Almost 52 years later, on February 16, 2018, the *Black Panther* movie was released to theaters. Serendipitously, one of the main inspirations for Black Panther was first printed in book form on June 6, 1914, which was a little more than 52 years before *Fantastic Four* #52 went on sale. However, Tarzan's first published appearance was a couple years earlier, in October 1912, in a serialized fiction periodical, *All-Story Magazine*. *Tarzan of the Apes*, written by Edgar Rice Burroughs, is directly alluded to in the Black Panther's first appearance when the Thing calls Black Panther "a refugee from a Tarzan movie" (Lee and Kirby, *Fantastic Four* #52, 2). While Tarzan is a directly acknowledged antecedent of Black Panther, there are many other preexisting genre threads that get woven into the Black Panther's tapestry in the early Jack Kirby and Stan Lee stories. These include Human/Animal hybrids, hidden utopias, science fiction tropes, comic strip characters, and contemporary world history.

Human/Animal Hybrids

It is a common trope in comic book storytelling for characters to blend aspects of humanity with specific members of the animal kingdom. Batman and Spider-Man are perhaps the most famous examples, but the list could fill pages. Of course, the genesis of this idea predates superhero comic books entirely. Storytelling traditions that led to the Black Panther began in medieval times. Jack Kirby, the co-creator of Black Panther, had a significant voice in the first stories in which Black Panther appeared and was a lover of history and legends. He loved the *Prince Valiant* comic strip as well as medieval legends (Groth). Medieval lore includes werewolves, who were "often sympathetic heroes rather than dangerous adversaries" (Zeldenrust), such as the tale of Marrok in the King Arthur cycle of stories. As evidence of the long history of storytellers adapting ideas that came before, Marrok appears to inspired by a French tale about Melion (Hopkins).

Another prominent version of the "man-beast" idea in fiction was in 1865 when George William MacArthur Reynolds of England published his serialized story titled *Wagner, the Wehr-Wolf*. It was a story that took place in "far off" Italy, concerning a man named Wagner who bought wealth and youth from the Devil in exchange for a monthly transformation into a bloodthirsty beast (Reynolds). It was very popular in its time and is likely the cultural catalyst that changed werewolves from benevolent creatures into the monsters we know today. In this respect, Black Panther is a "throwback" to the pre–Victorian idea of man-beast hybrids. Of course, due to American culture generally, it is also near-certain that Kirby knew of the tale of "Beauty and the Beast" originally published in 1740 by Gabrielle-Suzanne Barbot de Villeneuve, which itself reaches back to "Guillaume de Palerne," a French romance poem composed approximately 1200 AD that features a prince changed into a wolf. But even if this isn't the case, movie-loving Kirby would almost certainly have seen one of the many popular werewolf films put out in the 1940s and 1950s by Universal Studios and others. There are clear differences between these stories and Black Panther's appearance in Marvel Comics. In werewolf tales, the moon caused a man to change into a werewolf, and T'Challa would use clothing to become the Black Panther.

In 1896 H.G. Wells published *The Island of Dr. Moreau* about animal-man hybrids made by science, who were at least partly sympathetic characters. This book was, of course, adapted into films and the ideas of such (even without the plot) were incorporated into films which Kirby and Lee could have seen; but even if they did not, Wells was and is such an influence in science fiction culture it is likely Kirby and Lee were familiar with the basic concepts and plot of the story. Wells casts a long shadow within genre fiction, including superhero tales.

In the early 20th century, Howard Pyle's tale of Bearskin from Pyle's book *The Wonder Clock* provides an example of a human character adopting an animal-inspired appearance. This book was published in 1915 and has close parallels to many stories, including Moses, Snow White, and Tarzan. An infant boy is predicted to be king, so the current king takes him and gives him to a woodsman to be killed. The woodsman doesn't kill the boy but puts him in a basket on the river where the baby is adopted by a she-bear and becomes strong, brave, and "the coat he had upon his back was the skin of a bear dressed with the hair on it, and that was why folk called him 'Bearskin.'" (Pyle). Bearskin then defeated a dragon to win the hand of the princess.

In an interview, Kirby acknowledges that the stories he had consumed influenced the stories he told. Kirby said, "I was a student of science fiction and I began to make up my own story patterns, my own type of people" (Groth). While Kirby certainly did make up his own type of people, he, like all artists, was informed by the "people," or characters, that came before. One of the most influential, of those "people," was Tarzan.

Tarzan was first published in October 1912 in *All-Story Magazine*. Tarzan is the orphaned infant son of an English couple in Africa who is adopted by a she-ape, grows up in the ape society, and becomes "king of the jungle" as well as being born the hereditary Lord Greystoke. By the 1960s, when Kirby worked on the creation of Black Panther, Tarzan was an indelible part of book and film culture, and was portrayed as having animal-like powers and affinity for different animals, including being able to reproduce many animal calls in films and story. The impact of the Tarzan story and character was immediate and large. The character captured people's imaginations and it became extremely popular.

Hidden Utopias

Another thread in fiction which Kirby used for Black Panther was that of the hidden utopia. This concept had been used countless times before the advent of Black Panther. It was famously used in Thomas More's 1516 book *Utopia*. More's book was about a rarely-visited island nation somewhere near Brazil. Of course, this idea was used many times after 1516, such as in *Gulliver's Travels* by Jonathan Swift, which was subtitled *Travels into Several Remote Nations of the World*. These books, especially *Gulliver's Travels*, were social commentary and satire. In Samuel Taylor Coleridge's 1816 poem, "Kubla Kahn," the far-off land was introduced as a "stately pleasure dome" instead of political commentary, hearkening to the idea of "cities of gold." This land in "Kubla Kahn" was named Xanadu. Xanadu was, of course, also the name of the estate of "Charles Foster Kane" (a fictional William Randolph Hearst) in *Citizen Kane*. *Citizen Kane* was released in 1941, when a movie-loving Kirby could likely have seen it.

Popular fiction in the late nineteenth and early twentieth centuries continued the tradition of utopias. Of note was H. Rider Haggard's Allan

8   The Ages of the Black Panther

Quatermain books *King Solomon's Mines* and *She: A History of Adventure* in 1885 and 1887 respectively, and Arthur Conan Doyle's *The Lost World* in 1912. Haggard's *King Solomon's Mines* was set in Africa where the characters were looking for a "mysterious kingdom" said to hold the treasures of King Solomon inside of a mountain. The followup book, *She*, was another lost-kingdom-in-Africa's-interior story, this time led by an immortal, mind-reading white queen named Ayesha who reigned over the people as a supernatural being. *King Solomon's Mines* was adapted to film in 1937 and 1950 and to comic books in 1951 and 1952. Film adaptations of *She* were produced in both 1925 and 1935 when Kirby was young, as well as in 1965, a year before the debut of Black Panther. *The Lost World* was adapted for film in 1925 and 1960.

Returning to Tarzan, the character did not only provide an example of a human with animal-like powers, Burroughs also wrote about a hidden world in the heart of Africa. In Burroughs' second Tarzan novel, *The Return of Tarzan* (published in 1913 in the pulps and 1915 as a book), Tarzan and company travel to a lost city deep in the jungle known as Opar. Opar is a lost colony of Atlantis where the local Waziri tribe get their gold. Opar is ruled over by a high priestess named "La," not unlike Ayesha in Haggard's *She*. Also like the plot of *She*, La, the ruler, falls in love upon first meeting the visiting outsider, in this case Tarzan. Tarzan would revisit Opar three more times in his book series (1916, 1923, and 1930).

Not to be overlooked in this tradition is Edgar Rice Burroughs' series about Pellucidar, which started with *At the Earth's Core* in 1914. This series is about a lost Stone Age civilization in the center of the earth. Burroughs had six Pellucidar books published during his lifetime from 1914 to 1944, and a seventh, *Savage Pellucidar*, was published posthumously in 1963, three years before the debut of Black Panther. The fourth book in the series, *Tarzan at the Earth's Core*, was a "cross-over" book where Tarzan visited Pellucidar, and cross-promotional technique that Marvel Comics would use often in its publishing history.

There were 39 Tarzan films from 1918 to 1964, an average of one Tarzan film every 1.2 years. The then-latest Tarzan movie, *Tarzan and the Valley of Gold*, was released the same month as *Fantastic Four* #52, in July 1966. Tarzan also had a daily radio serial from 1932 to 1936 (starting when Kirby was 15) and again from 1951 to 1953. And, of course, most pertinently, Tarzan was made into a comic strip and first published in newspapers on January 7, 1929, as a daily and, in 1931, as a Sunday strip as well; both were in print until 1972 and 2002 respectively.

Science Fiction Tropes

However, unlike the lost lands of Burroughs, More, Haggard, and Doyle, Wakanda was technologically advanced. Kirby and Lee had written science fiction stories previously, and that genre is at the core of *Fantastic Four*. Kirby said, "That was such an innovation to hear the sound of the motor of an airplane flying overhead. I just had to get there in front. I was attracted by everything that seemed to be new and advanced" (Groth). Regarding things like mutation, Kirby said "I was studying that kind of stuff all the time. I would spot it in the newspapers and science magazines. I still buy magazines that are fanciful. I don't read as much science fiction as I did [in my youth]. I was a student of science fiction…" (Groth).

April 5, 1926, the publication of *Amazing Stories*, which codified many of the science fiction tropes for American audiences, began publication. Kirby, a student of science fiction, would likely have been familiar with the late 19th century writers which were often reprinted in those magazines, such as H.G. Wells, Verne, Poe, Burroughs, as well as then-current authors Howard, Asimov, Bester, Bradbury, Williamson, and others.

Wakanda was, of course, right out of a science fiction magazine technologically. In the presentation of Wakanda as outwardly primitive and inwardly advanced, we see how Kirby combined the societies of Haggard and Burroughs with the advancements of Asimov and Williamson. This incongruity of primitive and futuristic is mentioned many times in the course of the three *Fantastic Four* comics that introduce readers to Wakanda. Kirby and Lee's sources for Black Panther then would especially have been the pulps, where Tarzan and much popular science fiction first appeared. One of the best artists of the pulps, known as "the father of modern science fiction illustration," was Frank R. Paul. Paul's art has been described as "a curious mixture of the primitive and the technological" (Haining) which is as apt a visual descriptor for Wakanda as any.

Comic Strip Characters

But what discussion of the genesis of a comic book character would be complete without examining prior events in the comics world? As previously mentioned, Tarzan was made into a comic strip in January 1929, but what of the other influences on Black Panther's conception? First, we turn to two of the all-time greats of comic strip art, Hal Foster and Alex Raymond, two of Kirby's major influences (Evanier 34).

Foster *Prince Valiant* strip has been mentioned, but before creating Prince Valiant, Foster was the first artist on the *Tarzan* strip (Cazedessus).

The first comic strips of Tarzan were adaptations of the novels, but, since there were only so many storylines from the novels, Foster and others who took over were soon required to create their own storylines for Tarzan.

Another comic strip great that had an influence on Kirby was Alex Raymond's *Flash Gordon*. *Flash Gordon* is about an earthman who goes to another planet to fight an evil dictator. Beginning on January 7, 1934, *Flash Gordon* had a character who was a hybrid of lion and man, Prince Thun (who first appeared February 11, 1934), who is another possible "Black Panther" forerunner. The lion men of Mongo were both primitive and highly aggressive, whereas Black Panther and Wakandans are advanced and cultured. However, Black Panther's initial characterization in his debut story is not as dissimilar to Thun's, as Panther is first presented to be a possible adversary to the Fantastic Four instead of clearly a friend. Thun was also first presented as a possible adversary who later allied with the title hero.

The other Raymond strip, *Jungle Jim*, a Tarzan derivative, ran in many newspapers directly above the *Flash Gordon* strip beginning in January of 1934, so it too likely had some influence on the formation of the Panther mythos. Jim was a hunter in Asia, not Africa, and it is possible that his general design of helmet and white suit (with the prevalence of pith helmets on other characters if not the character himself) could very well have informed or even dictated Black Panther's archenemy Klaw's initial appearance. The feature was later made into a comic book by various publishers from 1937 to the end of the 1950s (Goulart 213), and was of course made into films and a television series. Notably, in the films, Jungle Jim was played by Johnny Weissmuller, who also played Tarzan (Goulart 213).

Before Prince Valiant and Tarzan made their comics page debut, there was another influential character in 1929. This character, like Black Panther, was a side character at first and then grew in popularity so much that he became a titular character of a comic. The comic strip the character debuted in was *Thimble Theater*, and the character in question was Popeye the Sailor Man. Popeye and Black Panther differed in that Popeye took over *Thimble Theater* directly and did so quickly, and it took Black Panther seven years to get his own solo feature in *Jungle Action* and another four to have his own self-titled series written and drawn by Jack Kirby.

Popeye is likely significant to the genesis of Black Panther is because Popeye was a strong man but not superhuman and, while he first got "luck" by rubbing the head of a bird, in the Sunday strip of July 3, 1932, he was punched into a garden patch of spinach (having mentioned the benefits of spinach in the strip two weeks before on June 19) (160–2). Popeye eats almost the whole patch, and due to this "wonder food," fights off a gang of big, attacking men (162). Originally, Popeye credits vitamin A in the spinach as the reason for the super-strength. Coincidentally, in this first mid–1932 strip, Popeye beats up this gang of men to prove to a fight manager that he is tough enough to fight a boxer called "Kid Panther"! (162). There's no evidence Kirby or Lee were aware of this, but the idea of ingesting a plant for strength is echoed in the "certain herbs" which T'Challa must eat to gain his "panther power" (*Fantastic Four* #53).

The final comic characters considered here were both created by Lee Falk. The first is Mandrake the Magician's sidekick Lothar, and the other is Falk's The Phantom. Created in 1934, and debuting in papers on June 11, 1934, Mandrake and Lothar appeared together from the very first strip (Robinson 137). Lothar initially spoke broken English (not unlike how Tarzan came to be depicted in film), wore leopard skin, was incredibly strong, and was "Prince of the Seven Nations" who declined to rule and instead travelled around with Mandrake stopping crimes. If not an explicitly stated equal (possibly due to 1930s politics), Lothar was not a sidekick but from the beginning was always a partner to Mandrake. Interestingly, in the 1935 storyline "Kingdom of the Murderers," "Mandrake's female companion was one Rheeta, a … woman [Mandrake] had transformed to human form from a tawny-coated pantheress" (O'Donnell 147).

The Phantom, created in 1936, and debuting on February 17, 1936, in newspapers, was the first costumed superhero of the comics page (Robinson 143), and the first to wear an eye mask that created the "no pupil" look ("Lee Falk"). According to the creator, Lee Falk, "The Phantom is a combination of Tarzan … and also Kipling's Jungle Book" (Abbot). The Phantom was also the first clearly mortal hero for whom dying was a real possibility (Couperie and Horn). Later in the series, in 1954, it is revealed that the current Phantom's first adventure, like Black Panther's, was to catch the man who killed his father ("The Belt"). The role or "title" of The Phantom was conceived at the outset as a position handed down the family line from father to son, much like the title of Black Panther became. The Phantom has a wolf named Devil as a sidekick/partner, and while that isn't in the feline family, it continues the animal association, and could have been what Stan Lee remembered in his recollection of the creation of Black Panther. In an interview, Stan Lee said

> When I was a kid, I loved stories.… I think The Phantom … no, The Phantom had a dog … some character had a black panther, and I thought that was so dramatic when I read those stories, and I liked the name, "The Black Panther." So, I thought, "Okay, that'll be the hero, now what do I do with him?" It occurred to me I'd set the scene … the stories … in Africa [Mitchell].

I was fortunate enough to contact Keith Williams, Sy Barry's inking successor on the daily Phantom comic strip, from 1994 to 2005. I asked him a few questions via email which he graciously answered. Serendipitously, at times we came to the same conclusions.

12   The Ages of the Black Panther

LIAM T. WEBB: [Regarding the above cited Stan Lee quote, I wrote] Phantom had a wolf and horse, and Tarzan and Ka-Zar had lions. Are there any other characters that had panther sidekicks that Lee may have been remembering?

KEITH WILLIAMS: I did a little checking and it seems that Stan might have been influenced by stories he read in the past. Just like any other writer. Kipling's *The Jungle Book*, had Mowgli the orphaned boy in the book, protected and mentored by Bagheera, a black panther. Wakanda being "underground" might have been from Edgar Rice Burroughs, *At the Earth's Core*, the land of Pellucidar. Tarzan even makes an appearance in one of those stories.

LW: In your knowledge of the characters and adventures of the Phantom, is it possible that Phantom was originally derived from Lothar, or "descended" from him? If so, besides marketability to the mostly Caucasian audience, why do you believe Phantom was created as a Caucasian rather than an African?

KW: Well, I never thought of Lothar as ever being related to the Phantom. But it is strange that a "Prince of the Seven Nations" would decide to travel with a magician and be his man servant. His character was a creation of the time Lee Falk lived in. As for the Phantom, he is possibly like Edgar Rice Burroughs's Tarzan.

LW: [I provided an image of Kirby's original character design, called "The Coal Tiger" next to an image of the Phantom] Looking at the costume designs, especially the trunks and belt (and details on the wrists of Phantom's costume) do you believe that my hypothesis that Kirby was influenced by Phantom's costume in designing the Coal Tiger is correct? If so, why?

If not, what other information do you have (that I do not) that supports your hypothesis?

Also, since as a rule Marvel heroes don't wear capes, why do you believe Kirby added one to Coal Tiger? To indicate royal station, or some other reason?

KW: It's possible that the original Black Panther costume may have taken some of its notes from the Phantom's. The stripe part in particular. But also remember that he was called Coal Tiger for a while and tigers do have stripes. I guess we may never know for sure what was on the minds of Lee and Kirby. The cape I'm sure was to show royalty being that he was a prince of a kingdom. But the cape did disappear later on. I like it better without the cape.

LW: Open-ended question: As you have much more familiarity with the Phantom than I do, what other similarities do you see between the Phantom and Black Panther as Kirby originally created him? (*Of course, both in a lineage of heroism passed from father to son and are "leaders" in their areas).

KW: Of course there are the similarities of lineage and heroism. They also wear superhero costumes. The Phantom was the first to have the white eye mask. Black Panther the same. Both live in a partially unknown country. They have family that they are very close to. Both are rich. They will go to the ends of the earth to help someone in trouble.

Finally, I should note that Marvel's publishing group already had its own Tarzan knock-off in Ka-Zar, who had a sabretooth tiger sidekick (though still not a panther). Ka-Zar was originally printed in a three-issue pulp series by Martin Goodman (who was later the publisher of Timely/Marvel) in 1936 and 1937. These pulp stories were reprinted in comic format in *Marvel Comics* (Goulart 251) and future issues, and the character was revived (but as another person) in *X-Men* #10 by Kirby and Lee, which was printed in March of 1965. In this X-Men comic, Ka-Zar now lived in the fictional Savage Land, a hidden prehistoric land in Antarctica (the original pulp character resided in the Congo area); *X-Men* #10 was printed just 17 months after "Savage Pellucidar" was first printed in *Amazing Stories* in November 1963.

It took (and takes) approximately six months for a comic to be published, so that brings the inception of the "Savage Land" to just eleven months after "Savage Pellucidar" was printed. Both the pulp and comic Ka-Zar had an animal familiar who either directly or indirectly helped raise him; in the pulp it was Zar the lion and in the comics it was Zabu the sabretooth tiger, both felines.

Contemporary World History

But literature and films were not the only inspiration for the Black Panther, or at least for the struggle Wakanda finds itself in with Ulysses Klaw in the first story arc. The conflict between Wakanda and Klaw seems to have been inspired by then-recent historical events. From 1960 to 1965 the "Congo Crisis" raged. The Congo Crisis was the internecine strife and warfare between political groups in the newly-independent Congo, and the exacerbation of such by both the Soviets and Americans, who used the People's Republic of the Congo (later named Zaire and later the Democratic Republic of the Congo) as a proxy for a Cold War battle. The main reason why the superpowers were so interested in the Congo was due to its supply of rich uranium, which America was purchasing since World War II (Williams).

Incredibly rich uranium, "the purest concentration in the world," was discovered at a low hill in the Congo in 1915 by Robert Sharp (an employee of a foreign company) (Marnham). At the time the international supply was limited and the ore was highly valuable. Colonel Kenneth Nichols wrote that the Shinkolobwe mine "represented a freak occurrence in nature. It contained a tremendously rich lode of uranium pitchblende. Nothing like it has ever again been found" (Nichols). Uranium is "is a dense, silvery-white, slightly paramagnetic, radioactive metal. It is also ductile and malleable. ... Its radioactivity ... has led to uranium's use in energy generation, both for civilian and military purposes" ("Uranium..."). It was also called "the most important deposit of uranium yet discovered in the world" by intelligence reports (Williams).

Black Panther's vibranium is also found under a tall hill/small mountain and is a rarely-found, ductile, malleable, highly valuable, energy-reactive (here, energy-absorbing) metal, and in *Fantastic Four* #53 it is colored as silvery-white. In the comic, vibranium is treated as more of a positive than as a negative item, and this fits the 1960s "Jetsons"-era positivity about energy sources and the future. Klaw wants to control the vibranium so that he can use it for his "super-science" experiments, as well as for its financial value. The Congo Crisis ended in late November 1965 ("The Congo…") and *Fantastic Four* #52 was printed in July 1966, meaning approximately mid–January 1966 was when the story was being plotted, just two months after the Congo Crisis ended.

Conclusion and Timeline

The Black Panther, like most comic book superheroes, was not a completely original invention. The character follows in a long literary tradition of characters that had similar elements, but Kirby and Lee reworked those elements and combined them into something new. What follows is a succinct and orderly timeline for easy reference of several of the most identifiable cultural antecedents to the Black Panther. I have not included every Tarzan novel nor the majority of Tarzan movies for clarity; I have only mentioned pertinent books and the first film, first talking film, and film movie closest to Black Panther's debut. I believe that by looking at the events in a direct timeline will make where and when the "pieces of the Black Panther puzzle" clearer or more digestible.

- 1200—*Guillaume de Palerne* published featuring a benevolent werewolf. Unknown, dedicated to literary patron Countess Yolande of Flanders (Sconduto).
- 1268—Story of Melion printed featuring a benevolent werewolf. Unknown.
- 1485—*Le Mort d'Arthur* (Marrok) published featuring a benevolent werewolf. Unknown.
- 1516—*Utopia* published. Sir Thomas More.
- 1726—*Gulliver's Travels* published. Jonathan Swift.
- 1740—"Beauty and the Beast." Traditional, published by Gabrielle-Suzanne Barbot de Villeneuve.
- 1816—"Kubla Kahn" published. Samuel Taylor Coleridge.
- 1865—*Wagner, the Wehr-Wolf* is published featuring a nefarious werewolf. GWM Reynolds.
- 1885—*King Solomon's Mines* published. H. Rider Haggard.
- 1887—*She: A History of Adventure* published. H. Rider Haggard.
- 1895—*The Jungle Book* published. Rudyard Kipling.

- 1896—*The Island of Dr. Moreau* published. H.G. Wells.
- 1904—*Green Mansions: A Romance of the Tropical Forest* published. WH Hudson.
- 1912—*The Lost World* published. Arthur Conan Doyle.
- 1925—*The Lost World* film released.
- 1912, October—*All Story Magazine*, first appearance of Tarzan. ER Burroughs.
- 1913—*The Return of Tarzan* published. ER Burroughs.
- 1914—*At Earth's Core* published (Pellucidar). ER Burroughs.
- 1914, June 6—*Tarzan* novel, first printing. Edgar Rice Burroughs.
- 1915—*Pellucidar* novel published. ER Burroughs.
- 1915—*The Wonder Clock* containing "Bearskin" published. Howard Pyle.
- 1915—Uranium discovered in the Congo by Robert Sharp.
- 1916—*Tarzan and the Jewels of Opar* published (Tarzan visits Opar). ER Burroughs.
- 1917, August 28—Jack Kirby (Jacob Kurtzberg) born in New York.
- 1918—First *Tarzan* film released, silent movie.
- 1919—Uranium valued at $3 million per ounce.
- 1922, December 28—Stan Lee (Stanley Leiber) born in New York.
- 1923—*Tarzan and the Golden Lion* published (Tarzan visits Opar). ER Burroughs.
- 1925—*She* filmed is released.
- 1926, April 5—*Amazing Stories* is first published. Hugo Gernsback.
- 1929—*Tarzan at the Earth's Core* published (crossover Tarzan and Pellucidar). ER Burroughs.
- 1929—*Tanar of Pellucidar* novel published. ER Burroughs.
- 1929, January 7—*Tarzan* daily newspaper comic strip debuts. RW Palmer and Hal Foster.
- 1929, January 17—*Thimble Theater* newspaper strip introduces Popeye. EC Segar.
- 1930—*Tarzan the Invincible* published (Tarzan visits Opar). ER Burroughs.
- 1931—*Tarzan* Sunday newspaper comic strip debuts. RW Palmer and Rex Maxon.
- 1932 to 1936—Tarzan's first daily radio serial.
- 1932—First talking *Tarzan* movie released.
- 1932—*Island of Lost Souls* movie released; based on *The Island of Dr. Moreau*
- 1932, July 3—Popeye first eats spinach.
- 1934, January 7—*Flash Gordon* and *Jungle Jim* newspaper strips begin. Alex Raymond.

- 1934, February 11—*Flash Gordon* newspaper strip introduces Thun. Alex Raymond.
- 1934, June 11—*Mandrake the Magician* newspaper comic strip begins. Lee Falk.
- 1935—New *She* film released.
- 1935—Kirby begins to work on Popeye cartoons for Fleischer Studios.
- 1936, February 17—*The Phantom* newspaper comic strip begins. Lee Falk.
- 1936, October—*Ka-Zar* pulp magazine first published.
- 1937—*King Solomon's Mines* is released as a film.
- 1937—*Back to the Stone Age* published (Pellucidar). ER Burroughs.
- 1937, February 13—*Prince Valiant* debuts. Hal Foster.
- 1939, January 12—Timely Comics founded by Martin Goodman (would become Marvel Comics).
- 1939, October—*Marvel Comics* #1 released by Timely.
- 1941, September 5—*Citizen Kane* released to theaters. Orson Welles.
- 1944—*Land of Terror* published (Pellucidar). ER Burroughs.
- 1950—New *King Solomon's Mines* film released.
- 1951—*King Solomon's Mines* becomes a comic book.
- 1951 to 1953—Tarzan's second daily radio serial.
- 1952—*King Solomon's Mines* becomes a comic book again.
- 1959—*Green Mansions* film released.
- 1960—New *The Lost World* film released.
- 1960 to 1965—The "Congo Crisis" occurs. America and the Soviet Union involved.
- 1961, August 8—*Fantastic Four* #1 released. Kirby and Lee.
- 1963—*Savage Pellucidar* novel published. ER Burroughs.
- 1965—New *She* film released.
- 1965, March—*X-Men* #10 is released featuring the revised Ka-Zar and the new Savage Land. Kirby and Lee.
- 1966, July—*Tarzan and the Valley of the Gold* film released.
- 1966, July 10—*Fantastic Four* #52. Black Panther debuts. Kirby and Lee.
- 1966, August—*Fantastic Four* #53. Second part of first Black Panther story arc. Kirby and Lee.
- 1966, September—*Fantastic Four* #54. The denouement/wrap up of the first Black Panther story arc. Kirby and Lee.

Works Cited

Abbot, James. "Master Magicians and Phantoms: An Interview with Lee Falk." *The Jade Sphinx.blogspot.com.* February 25, 2014. Web. 22 May 2019. http://thejadesphinx.blogspot.com/2014/02/master-magicians-and-phantoms-interview.html.

"African Lions." NationalGeographic.com. n.d. n.p. Web. 20 May 2019. https://www.nationalgeographic.com/animals/mammals/a/african-lion/.
Athenæum Journal. No. 3027. "Novels of the Week." *The Athenæum Journal of Literature, Science, the Fine Arts, Music, and the Drama.* July to December 1885. London: John C. Francis, 1885. 568. Web. 20 May 2019. https://babel.hathitrust.org/cgi/pt?id=njp.32101077276432;view=1up;seq=362.
"The Belt (Sunday Story)." *Phantomwiki.org.* n.d., n.p. Web. 22 May 2019. http://www.phantomwiki.org/The_Belt_(Sunday_story).
Burroughs, Edgar Rice. *Tarzan of the Apes.* October 1912. n.p. *American Literature.com.* Web. 15–24 May 2019. https://americanliterature.com/author/edgar-rice-burroughs/book/tarzan-of-the-apes/summary.
———. *The Return of Tarzan.* Illus. J. Allen St. John. New York: A.L. Burt Company; Great Britain: A.C. McClurg & Co., 1915. Print.
Cazedessus, Camille E., Jr. "Lords of the Jungle." *The Comic-Book Book.* Eds. Don Thompson and Dick Lupoff. New Rochelle, NY: Arlington House, 1973. 256–289. Print.
"The Congo, Decolonization, and the Cold War, 1960–1965." n.d., n.p. *Office of the Historian.* Department of State (United States). Web. 20 May 2019. https://history.state.gov/milestones/1961–1968/congo-decolonization.
Couperie, Pierre, Maurice C. Horn, Proto DeStefanis, Edouard François, Claude Moliterni and Gérald Gassiot-Talabot. *A History of the Comic Strip.* Trans. Eileen B. Hennessy. New York: Crown Publishers, Inc., 1974. Print.
DeForest, Tim. "Marvel Comics." n.d, n.p. *Encyclopedia Britannica.* Web. 15–24 May 2019. https://www.britannica.com/topic/Marvel-Comics.
Degg, D.D. "First and Last—Tarzan Comic Strip." *The Daily Cartoonist.com.* July 13, 2018. n.p. Web. 15–24 May 2019. https://www.dailycartoonist.com/index.php/2018/07/13/first-and-last-tarzan-comic-strip/.
Evanier, Mark. *Kirby: King of Comics.* New York: Harry A. Abrams, Inc., 2008. Print.
"Fallout Shelters." n.d. n.p. U-S-History.com. Web. 21 May 2019. https://www.u-s-history.com/pages/h3706.html.
Gifford, Dennis. "Obituary: Lee Falk." *The Independent (UK).* March 19, 1999. n.p. Web. 22 May 2019. https://www.independent.co.uk/arts-entertainment/obituary-lee-falk-1081509.html.
Goulart, Ron. *Comic Book Encyclopedia: The Ultimate Guide to Characters, Graphic Novels, Writers, and Artists in the Comic Book Universe.* New York: HarperCollins Publishers Inc., 2004. Print.
Great Books Foundation. *Beauty and the Beast.* n.p. Chicago: The Great Books Foundation. 2011. Web. 15–25 May 20919.
Groth, Gary. "The Jack Kirby Interview." *The Comics Journal* 134 (Feb 1990): n.p. *The Comics Journal Archive.* Web. 15–25 May 2019. http://www.tcj.com/jack-kirby-interview/.
Haggard, H. Rider. *King Solomon's Mines.* Illus. Walter Paget. New York: Modern Library, 2002. Print.
Haining, Peter. *The Classic Era of American Pulp Magazines.* Chicago: Chicago Review Press, Incorporated, 2000. Print.
Holloway, Clark J. "Ka-Zar the Great." *The Holloway Pages: Pulp Heroes Page.* 2000. n.p. Web. 15–24 May 2019. http://webarchive.loc.gov/all/20061101035428/http://home.comcast.net/~cjh5801a/Ka-Zar.htm.
Hopkins, Amanda, ed. and trans. *Melion and Biclarel: Two Old French Werewolf Lays.* n.p. Liverpool: University of Liverpool, Dept. of French, 2005. Web. 15–25 May 2019. https://www.liverpool.ac.uk/media/livacuk/modern-languages-and-cultures/liverpoolonline/Werwolf.pdf.
Hudson, W.H. *Green Mansions: A Romance of the Tropical Forest. Gutenberg.org.* July 26, 2008. n.p. Web. 21 May 2019. http://www.gutenberg.org/ebooks/942.
"Jungle Jim—Fury of the Congo (1951)." Youtube.com. n.d. n.p. Web. 20 May 2019. https://www.youtube.com/watch?v=F1MxtB2TEB4.
Kenton, Erle C. "The Island of Lost Souls." Criterion.com. n.d. n.p. Web. 20 May 2019. https://www.criterion.com/films/27861-island-of-lost-souls.

"King Solomon's Mines (1951) comic books." MyComicsShop.com. n.p. Lone Star Comics Inc., 1996–2019. Web. 20 May 2019. https://www.mycomicshop.com/search?TID=353311.

Kodi-Lists. "Tarzan: Huge List of Tarzan Based Movies." IMDB.com. 1990–2019. n.p. Web. 15–20 May 2019. https://www.imdb.com/list/ls021548826/?sort=release_date,desc&st_dt=&mode=detail&page=1.

"Lee Falk." *NewWorldEncyclopedia.org*. June 24, 2018. Web. 22 May 2019. http://www.newworldencyclopedia.org/entry/Lee_Falk.

"Lee Falk's Phantom-1: Origins of Ghost Who Walks." Comicology. April 17, 2009. n.p. *Comicology.in*. Web. 15–24 May 2019. http://www.comicology.in/2009/04/lee-falks-phantom-1-origins-of-ghost.html.

Lee, Stan (w), and Jack Kirby (a). "X-Men #10." March 1965. *Marvel Masterworks Volume Three: X-Men*. Eds. Tom DeFalco and Bob Budiansky. New York: Marvel Entertainment Group, 1987. Print.

Lee, Stan (w), Jack Kirby (a) and Joe Sinnot (i). "Fantastic Four #52." July 1966. *Marvel Masterworks: Fantastic Four Vol. 6*. Joe Sinnott, inker. Ed. Cory Sedlmeier. New York: Marvel Publishing Inc., 2004. Print.

_____. "Fantastic Four #53." August 1966. *Marvel*.

Marnham, Patrick. "Tracing the Congolese Mine That Fuelled Hiroshima." *The Telegraph (UK)*. 4 Nov 2013. n.p. Web. 20 May 2019. https://www.telegraph.co.uk/culture/10416945/Tracing-the-Congolese-mine-that-fuelled-Hiroshima.html.

Masterworks: Fantastic Four Vol. 6. Ed. Cory Sedlmeier. New York: Marvel Publishing Inc., 2004. Print.

_____. "Fantastic Four #54." September 1966. *Marvel*.

_____. Ed. Cory Sedlmeier. New York: Marvel Publishing Inc., 2004. Print.

_____. "Fantastic Four #13." April 1963. *Marvel*.

Masterworks Volume Two: Fantastic Four. Steve Ditko, inker. Ed. Cory Sedlmeier. New York: Marvel Publishing Inc., 1988. Print.

Merriam-Webster Dictionary. "Xanadu." n.d. Web. 15–25 May 2019. https://www.merriam-webster.com/dictionary/Xanadu.

Mitchell, Maurice. "The Secret History of Black Panther by Stan Lee." TheGeekTwins.com. Feb 14, 2018. n.p. Web. 22 May 2019. http://www.thegeektwins.com/2018/02/the-secret-history-of-black-panther-by.html.

More, Saint Thomas. *The Utopia of Sir Thomas More*. Ed. William Dallam Armes. New York: MacMillan Company, 1912. Web. 15–25 May 2019. https://archive.org/details/TheUtopia/page/n11.

Nichols, K.D. *The Road to Trinity*. 44–47. Morrow: New York. 1987. Print cited in https://en.wikipedia.org/wiki/Shinkolobwe. Web. 18 May 2019.

O'Donnell, Dick. "It's Magic." *The Comic-Book Book*. Eds. Don Thompson and Dick Lupoff. New Rochelle, NY: Arlington House, 1973. 144–173. Print.

OTRCat. "Tarzan Radio Show." OTRCat.com. 2001–2019. n.p. Web. 20 May 2019. https://www.otrcat.com/p/tarzan.

Overstreet, Robert M. *The Overstreet Comic Book Price Guide, 43rd Edition*. Hunt Valley, MD: Gemstone Publishing, Inc., 2013. Print.

"The Phantom." n.d. n.p. ComicsKingdom.com. Web. 15–24 May 2019. https://www.comicskingdom.com/phantom/about.

Pyle, Howard. *The Wonder Clock, Or, Four & Twenty Marvelous Tales, Being One for Each Hour of the Day*. Illus. Howard Pyle. New York: Dover Publications, Inc., 1965. Print.

Raymond, Alex. *Flash Gordon (Vol. 1)*. West Carrollton, OH: Checker Book, 2005. Print.

"The Return of Tarzan 1913 Synopsis." EdgarRiceBurroughs.com. 2019. Web. 15–24 May 2019. https://www.edgarriceburroughs.com/series-profiles/the-tarzan-series/the-return-of-tarzan/.

Reynolds, G[eorge] W[illiam] M[acArthur]. *Wagner, the Wehr-Wolf*. Illus. Henry Anelay. Ed. E.F. Bleiler. New York: Dover Publications, Inc., 1975. Print.

Robinson, Jerry. *The Comics: An Illustrated History of Comic Strip Art*. New York: G.P. Putnam's Sons, 1974. Print.

Sconduto, Leslie A. *Guillaume de Palerne: An English Translation of the 12th Century French Verse Romance.* Texas: MacFarland, 2004. Print.

Segar, E.C. *Popeye Volume One.* Seattle: Fantagraphics Books, Inc., 2006. Print.

_____. *Popeye Volume Two.* Seattle: Fantagraphics Books, Inc., 2007. Print.

Superfriends Wiki. "Rima." n.d. n.p. *Superfriends Wiki.* Web. 23 May 2019. https://superfriends.fandom.com/wiki/Rima.

Swift, Jonathan. *Gulliver's Travels.* Eds. Peter Dixon and John Chalker. London: Penguin Books, 1967. Web. 15–25 May 2019. https://archive.org/details/gulliverstravels00jona_1/page/n5.

Syracuse University. *Harold R. (Hal) Foster: An Inventory of His Papers at Syracuse University.* n.p. Syracuse: Syracuse University. n.d. Web. 15–25 May 2019. https://library.syr.edu/digital/guides/f/foster_hr.htm#d2e151.

"Tarzan and the Valley of the Gold (1966)." IMDB.com. 1990–2019. Web. 15–20 May 2019. https://www.imdb.com/title/tt0061067/?ref_=ttls_li_tt.

"Tarzan Movies Through the Years...." IMDB.com. 16 May 2014. Web. 15–20 May 2019. https://www.imdb.com/list/ls058415951/.

Tollin, Anthony. "A Visit with Lee Falk." n.d., n.p. Phantomwiki.org. Web. 22 May 2019. http://www.phantomwiki.org/A_Visit_with_Lee_Falk.

"Uranium Element Facts." Chemicool.com. n.d. n.p. Web. 21 May 2019. https://www.chemicool.com/elements/uranium.html.

Von Ruff, Al. "Publication: Amazing Stories, November 1963." Isfdb.org. 1995–2019. n.p. Web. 15–24 May 2019. http://www.isfdb.org/cgi-bin/pl.cgi?56607.

Williams, Keith. Personal interview via email. 20–21 May 2019.

Williams, Susan. "Congolese Uranium, Nazi Germany and the Race to Build the A-Bomb." *Newsweek.* 18 June 2016. n.p. Web. 19 May 2019. https://www.newsweek.com/congolese-uranium-nazi-germany-and-race-build-bomb-471167.

Wright, Nicky. *The Classic Era of American Comics.* Reprint 2008. London: Prion Books Limited, 2000. Print.

Zeldenrust, Lydia. "Becoming Beast: Marvel's New Black Panther Movie Has a Surprising Medieval Connection." n.p. *Ancient Origins.* Web. 15–25 May 2019. https://www.ancient-origins.net/news-history-archaeology/becoming-beast-marvel-s-new-black-panther-movie-has-surprising-medieval-021821.

Breaking (Some) Ground While Dodging Politics
How Stan Lee and Jack Kirby Started a Legend
Cathy Leogrande

In a time of political and social turmoil, an African king emerged from the imagination of two white Jewish men from New York City who were no doubt balancing a business acumen with social consciousness. T'Challa's origin story has been told and retold, but it is one that continues to provide a means of examining storytelling as a product of its time as well as a platform for future readers and creators. This essay addresses the factors that combined to make 1966 the year of the first Black superhero in mainstream comic books.

The Comic Book Industry in the 1960s

The Golden Age of comic books is generally seen as the introduction of the archetype of the superhero. Around the period before and after World War II, characters such as Superman and Captain America became popular. Superhero popularity began to falter after the war, partly due to the connections between the stories of good versus evil and world situations (Gavaler 80).

As the industry shifted in response to audience changes, there were more non-superhero comics with characters such as Archie and Dagwood, and stories from other genres like Westerns, romance, horror and detective stories. The claim that these darker, more adult themes in comics contributed to juvenile delinquency, and the establishment of the Comics Code Authority also helped slow the sales of comic books, with fewer new superhero characters. In addition to negative publicity, publishers had to deal with competition from television and social stigma of comic books as childish entertainment (Genter 955).

What has now become known as the Silver Age of Comics brought back superheroes, beginning with DC stories featuring the Flash and the Justice League of America. The Justice League team idea was very well-received, and they became part of the resurgence in comic books. Marvel comics, under Martin Goodman, wanted to compete, so writer Stan Lee and artist Jack Kirby were given the assignment to create a comic book with a similar group of superheroes. At the time, DC owned National, the company that distributed Marvel Comics, so Kirby and Lee had to be careful with the degree to which their team was like JLA. As Simcha Weinstein writes:

> Since DC superheroes were typically costumed and masked and had secret identities, Kirby and Lee were obliged to work outside these firmly established conventions and come up with something highly original yet enough like the Justice League to piggyback on its success. The result? The Fantastic Four, a team of superheroes unlike any other before [72].

The origin of the Fantastic Four is important context for Black Panther, since his first appearance was in *Fantastic Four* #52. Stan Lee wanted characters who were real people. Like Batman, they were "normal" people that had something happen to them. Reed Richards (scientist), Ben Grimm (pilot), Susan Storm (Reed's fiancée), and Johnny Storm (Susan's younger brother) were on board a spaceship when they were hit by cosmic rays. When they returned to Earth, the impact of the rays affected each of them differently. They became Mr. Fantastic (Richards), the Thing (Grimm), Invisible Girl (Susan), and the Human Torch (Johnny).

The Fantastic Four set the stage for T'Challa in several ways. They did not have secret identities or disguises. When they did don costumes in *Fantastic Four* #3, it was not to hide their identities but a business decision in order to demonstrate their unity as a team (8). Others in society knew who they were on a human level as well as a superhero. Reed and Susan married, just as they would have if they had not been changed. The line between the person and the superhero all but vanished. Lee and Kirby also put more typical personality traits into these characters. They bickered, blamed each other, and basically appeared to be more like their readers. They had the normality of Bruce Wayne with the powers of Superman. Readers loved them.

Stan and Jack and Jewish Aspects of Comics

The fact that Stan Lee and Jack Kirby were Jewish men from New York City permeated their creations, beginning with the Fantastic Four and eventually including Black Panther. Danny Fingeroth explored these connections, including the humor and dialogue that overtly echoed Stan and Jack's own backgrounds and experiences. They were not alone. Much has been written about the number of individuals of Jewish background in the Silver Age of comics. Many of the men who founded and built the industry were from immigrant families and shared a common Eastern European Jewish background. A number of them attended the same high school, DeWitt Clinton, in the Bronx. Fingeroth stated: "That the comics industry was simply coincidentally founded and peopled by Jews was, as comics pioneer Will Eisner and many others feel, mostly a matter of coincidence—that Jews and publishing were centered in New York and that more established fields like advertising were closed to them—is a credible point of view" (17). Fingeroth nevertheless goes on to explain how the New York Jewish experience that was a large part of popular entertainment during the late 1950s and early 1960s was the "cultural milieu" from which the Fantastic Four emerged. He writes: "That the tenor of the times allowed for, if not a direct statement of Jewish themes and subjects in The Fantastic Four, then for at least a less disguised version of Jewish-influenced sensibility to make its way into the comics" (96).

What were those sensibilities? First and foremost was family. At a time in society when divorce was becoming more common and women were taking on new roles outside the home, the concept of a group of people not necessarily related by blood but functioning as a family was appealing. In fact, "their success against a series of supervillains was dependent upon the solidity of their relationships" (Genter 957). The bickering, sometimes playful and sometimes closer to an argument, was a feature in many immigrant families. It was acceptable to fight among relatives, but a united front must be presented to all outsiders in order to survive. The use of humor to counter problems and build acceptance was another aspect. Dialogue that blurred lines between friend and enemy using joking to hide or reveal true feelings was also evident. Early stories of the Fantastic Four included themes such as grappling with difficult decisions, problems with no easy solutions, and being forced to choose between differing opinions of loved ones and trusted advisors. The heavy mantle of carrying the responsibility for the survival of the loved ones and neighbors is regularly featured in the stories. This was no Justice League; this was a family.

Jack Kirby has identified the many links between himself and Benjamin Jacob Grimm, born on the East Side of Manhattan and a member of a gang (Weinstein 75). In later stories, the connections were more overt, with examples of exodus from slavery, Yiddish phrases and stories of guilt and redemption. Kirby always felt this obligation to bring forth the stories of those outside the mainstream in order to educate and promote tolerance and acceptance.

One can assume that these feelings were also in play when he helped create T'Challa and Wakanda. Stan Lee has often been quoted as saying he wrote the kind of stories he himself would want to read. Most creative artists imbue their characters and stories with parts of themselves. Where Kirby was more overt, Lee downplayed the Jewish values and aspects in the comics he helped create:

> We never thought about it, never talked about it, never even seemed to be aware of it. We were story tellers and artists, trying to entertain, amuse and trill our readers. Religion never really entered the picture as far as we were concerned. In fact, speaking for myself, the one thing I always tried to emphasize was the common bond between people, the fact that we were all passengers on Spaceship Earth, and our ship was never divided into different classes [Fingeroth 9].

However, Julian Chambliss discussed how their Jewish background influenced the stories these men told:

> The fantastic nature of superhero comics allowed Jewish creators to incorporate social commentary into their work. Captain America's first appearance punching Adolf Hitler predates U.S. involvement, but expressed Jewish sentiments toward Nazi Germany. In the aftermath of the war, Jewish creators, many like Kirby veterans of the armed forces, continued to celebrate the freedom, opportunity, and agency represented by United States. For Kirby and his contemporaries, the United States was a haven that welcomed minorities with opportunity and defended the oppressed everywhere.

There seems to be a connective thread from the traits and backgrounds of these men and the characters and stories they created at the beginning of the Silver Age and resurgence of comic books. The "outsider" story was soon extended to include an African prince from a secret nation.

Civil Rights, a New Hero, and Controversy

The Fantastic Four were a product of their times. They reflected the Cold War, the space race with Communist Russia and fears about the rise of technology. Robert Genter explores how the Cold War culture helped shape Marvel comics using Reed Richards as the embodiment of the scientists upon whom American hopes were pinned. "Reed's major commitment throughout the series is to use his scientific knowledge to help the United States defeat the Soviet Union" (961). Marvel had shifted to adult themes and stories and characters with typical problems and anxieties facing society in the 1950s. Genter states, "Not simply a meaningless product directed toward young children, Marvel comic books were now consumed by young adults and college students and consequently became one of the most popular cultural expressions of the twentieth century, selling millions of copies each month throughout the 1960s" (954).

24   The Ages of the Black Panther

A more adult audience opened the door for Lee and Kirby to address other social issues. One of these was civil rights and the changes related to Blacks in America. The Supreme Court ruling in the case of *Brown v. Board of Education* of Topeka, Kansas, in 1954 had ruled that segregation was illegal in public schools. That did not mean that change happened swiftly or easily. Between 1961 when the Fantastic Four debuted and 1966 when T'Challa emerged as a new character, racial problems rivaled the Vietnam War as the issue most dividing Americans. A year after the Brown decision, Rosa Parks was arrested after refusing to give her seat to a white passenger on a Montgomery, Alabama, bus. The Montgomery bus boycott followed, as did sit-ins and demonstrations. Jim Crow laws in the Southern states were under attack, and many people in Northern states supported change. In 1961, the Freedom Riders challenged segregation laws in rest rooms and lunch counters, and were met with violence, arrests and even death. The Civil Rights Act of 1964 was passed and enforced by the Justice Department. Martin Luther King, Jr., won the Nobel Peace Prize in 1965 for his efforts to make change through nonviolent means. Problems were far from over. In 1965, to bring attention to voter registration problems, King led a march from Montgomery to Selma and the peaceful marchers were met with violence when they tried to cross the Edmund Pettus Bridge. This is the America in which Lee and Kirby, two liberal white Northern sons of immigrants, debuted T'Challa.

T'Challa seemed the perfect superhero for the times. The term Black had begun to replace Negro. More and more African Americans were exploring their roots and learning about nations from which their ancestors were forcibly taken. Black students were part of colleges all across America, not just at historically Black college and universities. Blacks were becoming a growing political force in government. T'Challa was a well-educated and gifted ruler, who could be a fierce fighter but sought to keep peace where possible. Their new character embodied strong intelligent African culture and helped break the stereotypes that still existed.

Many continue to celebrate Marvel for publishing this breakthrough at such a time. Gerard Jones and Will Jacobs described T'Challa as "a heartfelt conception from creators who clearly supported Black people's struggle for power and dignity… [the characters is] a scientist, a warrior, and a gentleman, drawn as all muscle and Blackness by Jack and finely scripted by Stan" (105). Julian Chambliss, however, raises questions about the degree to which the character and origin story were groundbreaking:

> Recognizing that 1960s' social aspirations questioned establish norms, Marvel thus incorporated this shifting landscape into their stories. This philosophy was not revolutionary. Lee wrote, and Kirby drew heroes that demonstrated through action the values the United States strived to achieve. Thus, the Black Panther, the first black superhero offered a model of heroic action identical in substance, yet diverse in

appearance. The Black Panther provides the visual cue of difference that broke the barrier of white heroic privilege, but not the cultural perspective that created it. Removed from the U.S. experience by national identity, personal history, and individual motivation the Panther's appearance did not directly address the stifling effect of racial prejudice. The Panther looked different, but like Kirby, his actions affirm his right to inclusion.

Micah Peters also notes that despite the fact that "the inception and early stewardship of the character is very much the work of white guys," there was still enough fantasy to allow readers who were not supportive of progressive change to enjoy the comic. He states, "Neither for nor against neatly explained the Black Panther's politics at the time. Making the character be from a futuristic country in Africa was groundbreaking. But it also allowed the Black Panther character a certain distance from the civil rights movement that— wittingly or not—the series capitalized on."

This essay does not address in depth the conflicting stories about whether or not it was Stan or Jack that originally birthed the character or if the idea was deliberate response to the horrors that were televised nightly as change came uneasily to the South. Stan gave his version in an interview from 2005 published by Roy Thomas in *AlterEgo #104*. In that discussion, he details specific aspects of the character that were designed to break racist stereotypes of the times. Lee told and embellished T'Challa's origin story often, usually describing it as part of a larger sociopolitical plan:

> At that point I felt we really needed a black superhero.... And I wanted to get away from a common perception. So, what I did, I made I made him almost like [Fantastic Four's] Reed Richards. He's a brilliant scientist and he lives in an area that, under the ground, is very modern and scientific and nobody suspects it because on the surface it's just thatched huts with ordinary "natives." And he's not letting the world know what's really going on or how brilliant they really are [Osteroff].

Kirby fans and historians like Rob Steibel and Stan Taylor bristle at the idea that Lee was the creative spark and note that Jack created a first sketch for a character called the Coal Tiger. With yellow and black striped gloves and suit over grey tights with no mask covering his face, he bore more resemblance to Superman than the character that appeared in *Fantastic Four* #52. Most likely it was a mix of noble idealism and business planning. Stan was always looking at ways to extend his stories and sales beyond what others were doing, and he and Jack were both clearly involved.

The Black Panther Appears

When T'Challa finally arrived on the page in 1966, he was a blend of expectations and surprises. As Evan Narcisse states, "From the first time the reader sees and hears Wakanda, the fictional country is a mix of paradoxes. It's super-advanced, has never been colonized and hides from the rest of the world. It's almost as if Lee and Kirby knew they had to temper the idea of a black super-society with the element of making it hidden and doubling down on nativism" ("Politics"). The very first panel finds the Fantastic Four heading for Wakanda in a magnetic flying ship that is far beyond ordinary machines. Reed explains it was a gift from an African "chieftain" called the Black Panther. Ben questions this in a comment that builds on the image most people had of Africa and its natives at the time: "How does some refugee from a Tarzan movie lay his hands on this kinda' gizmo? And why would he give it to you" (3)? Like Ben, most readers thought of Africa as the "Dark Continent." Their concept was of a monolithic landmass; there was almost no understanding of distinct countries and cultures. These were all blurred together, inhabited by scantily-clothed savages straight out of *National Geographic*. The natives were tribal, had few modern conveniences and little connection with Western nations and "civilized" customs.

The idea that a technologically advanced nation could exist in the middle of the jungle, ruled by an educated leader who *chose* to stay isolated from the western countries because of their antagonistic and selfish ways was as much a fantasy as Kryptonite. Evan Narcisse notes that Ben's statement includes the assumption that the only way an African chieftain could have a ship like this would be to obtain it by some more sophisticated individual or culture ("Politics"). "Lay his hands on" almost sounds like T'Challa stole the ship. When Reed describes how the ship operated on a "brand new principle" Johnny reinforces Ben's point and says, "Now I know you're connin' me! How does an African chieftain latch on to a plane that flies by magnetic waves?" (7). Narcisse credits the creators: "Now, it should be noted Lee and Kirby were doing their job as storytellers here, crafting a set of expectations for the reader that they'd upend for a surprise later in the issue. It would turn out that T'Challa is in fact a genius on par with Reed Richards and cunning enough to trap and nearly defeat the Fantastic Four in battle" ("Politics"). So, the first Panther stories are both remarkable and archaic.

Upon their arrival in Wakanda, T'Challa defeats the Fantastic Four one by one, although they manage to survive. The second part of the story, in *Fantastic Four* #53, reveals a calculated plan by T'Challa to use the four heroes as a test to prepare him for the fight against Ulysses Klaw, the man who killed his father. The Fantastic Four, the most powerful superhero team at the time, are pawns in the Panther's long-range plan rather than the white saviors found in most stories set in Africa. To have a black character best the super smart Reed Richards and super powerful Thing, and then befriend them and join forces against a greater (white) villain was groundbreaking.

Like many other comic characters, part of T'Challa's origin story is based on mythology that combines reality with the supernatural and spiritual. T'Challa is royalty, a king due to his family bloodline. It is a hereditary position but must also be earned in trial by combat by defeating other Wakandan tribal champions as part of the succession rite. T'Challa is a chieftain, head of the Panther tribe. He follows cultural traditions of his tribe. A mixture made from special heart-shaped herb is part of the assumption of power. The herb results in a type of vision quest and also enhances his physical abilities. The herb was a gift from the Panther God Bast but was enhanced by the vibranium meteorite that is the source of Wakanda's advanced technology. After he consumes the herb, he gains powers such as enhanced speed, agility, strength, endurance, and the ability to see in the dark and track by scent much like his animal namesake.

T'Challa is also different from other superheroes of that time. Black Panther is not an alter ego or secret identity. He is officially king of the nation of Wakanda. Although his powers are metaphysical in origin, he has many aspects that are grounded in reality. He is head of state but not an elected president or prime minister. He is a skilled diplomat and politician. He is wealthy, but so is his country. He has a Ph.D. in physics from Oxford University. He is proficient with technology, but he is also a great hunter and tracker without the use of inventions. Similar to Bruce Wayne, he has aspects of an unusual but ordinary person along with characteristics that are more related to fantasy. Adilifu Nama writes, "The character and comic series melded science fiction iconography with African imagery" (42). T'Challa is majestic, other worldly, and normal at the same time. As Vann R. Newkirk II wrote, the hereditary role of the Black Panther is "empowered by a combination of divine blessing, biological enhancement, and cutting-edge technology."

Wakanda is also unique. The country has achieved economic and political independence and is respected by other nations around the world. It has chosen its own path, that of seclusion, in order to resist outsiders who would colonize it because of vibranium, its priceless and exclusive natural resource. Like Atlantis, the country endorsed a policy of isolation for survival. Questions of identity and responsibility to others become critical issues for all. While these lofty attributes seemingly separate Wakanda from the standard portrait of African nations, dialogue and illustrations seem to reinforce stereotypes. The dancers at the heroes' ceremony that opens *Fantastic Four* #53 are frantically jumping while Ben says, "Sheesh! A bunch'a Fred Astaires they ain't" (2)! Drums, spears and headdresses are part of the tableau. Wakandans operate technological dashboards yet are dressed in loincloths. This is explained by Reed, "They are not the ordinary native tribe they seem to be. Though the Wakanda tribe lives in the tradition of their forefathers, they possess modern, super-scientific wonders we can only marvel at!" (2). When

T'Challa is telling his background story in *Fantastic Four* #53, Ben yawns and says he saw this story in a million jungle movies, perpetuating the stereotypical ideas held by most readers.

The two-part introduction of the Black Panther in 1966 is both a product of its time and a story of possibilities. Stan Taylor presents the duality:

> Some have complained that the concept was weakened by making the Panther a super-rich, European educated, African monarch, instead of an American from the inner city. Others disagree saying that making T'Challa an African was even braver by introducing a new hero from the emerging continent of Africa, rather than making him an American. Africa had never had a particularly positive image in American culture. More of an after-thought used mostly for Tarzan movie backgrounds where the black populace was useful for carrying bags and feeding the lions. Lee and Kirby transformed Tarzan into a black native—the equal to any white hero.

There is no denying the fact that T'Challa was a different type of superhero. As Jamil Smith writes, "Supernatural strength and agility were his main features, but a genius intellect was his best attribute."

Why T'Challa Means So Much

There is more to T'Challa's origin story than just the plot. In the 1960s, political turmoil and racial unrest were happening on a national and global level. African nations that had been colonized by European countries were fighting for independence. Leaders like Jomo Kenyatta in Kenya and Patrice Lumumba in the republic of the Congo were helping form independent nations in Africa. The road to freedom were not easy and carried much economic and political unrest. Assassinations, coup d'états, and dictatorships were sad realities during the struggles. The Marvel stories took these facts into account. Early Black Panther stories have elements of both Pan Africanism and Afrocentrism.

The Pan African movement was part of the civil rights discussion in America in the 1960s. Pan-Africanism is generally defined as a philosophy that seeks to create solidarity and connections among people of African descent. Omotayo Oloruntoba-Oju describes some of the core ideas of the movement as the validation and emancipation of Africa and a belief in a distinct African personality and Black identity (191). Beginning as early as the 18th century, anti-slavery groups and others began to form a political movement that promoted the values of African cultures and worked against slavery and colonialism. Pan Africanism was a result of several factors, including the African diaspora, dehumanization of Africans as part of the slave trade and European imperialism (Campbell 29). In 1957, Kwame Nkrumah became the first president of an independent Ghana and advocated for the unity of one collective Africa. Malcolm X in America espoused these ideas, and although they may not have been central to Lee and Kirby's plans, readers were able to see connections between the stories and the philosophy. Like these real-life leaders, T'Challa embodied the hopes of his people and like-minded American Blacks (Nama 43).

Art is often a way to spread ideas and reach people on a more emotional level. The Black Panther comics can be seen as part of cultural, literary and aesthetic representation of concepts of Pan-Africanism. Crystal Z. Campbell described a model for African artists that would promote pride and reduce negative media messages. She points to the Harlem Renaissance as an example of a celebration of all sides of the Black experiences (34). While Campbell discusses the need for African art created by African people, others have described the powerful impact of any positive view of Africa and its people, no matter who the producers. Speaking of the first Black Panther comics, Jamil Smith writes:

> It was a vision of black grandeur and, indeed, power in a trying time, when more than 41% of African Americans were at or below the poverty line and comprised nearly a third of the nation's poor. Much like the iconic Lieutenant Uhura character, played by Nichelle Nichols, that debuted in Star Trek in September 1966, Black Panther was an expression of Afrofuturism—an ethos that fuses African mythologies, technology and science fiction and serves to rebuke conventional depictions of (or, worse, efforts to bring about) a future bereft of black people. His white creators, Stan Lee and Jack Kirby, did not consciously conjure a fantasy-world response to [Stokely] Carmichael's call, but the image still held power. T'Challa was not only strong and educated; he was also royalty. He didn't have to take over. He was already in charge.

Even with flaws, the early Black Panther stories provided a positive view of Africans.

The vibranium aspect of the story also ties T'Challa to reality and Pan Africanism. Lee and Kirby had both served in World War II and were aware of many aspects of the nuclear and space age. The Fantastic Four, the Hulk, Spider-Man and the X-Men were all products of their knowledge and understanding of science and technology. T'Challa's story centers on the most powerful element in the world, the fight over who will control access to it and whether it will be used for good or evil. In the 1940s, Einstein identified the source of high-quality uranium in the Shinkolobwe mine in the (then) Belgian Congo. Thomas F. McDow writes, "In 1945 uranium from Shinkolobwe was used in the atomic bomb dropped on Hiroshima and protecting the mine during and after the Second World War had involved deep espionage." He goes on to describe the political activities surrounding military and industrial interests in the aftermath of that country's independence in 1960. The true story of assassinations and UN involvement sounds like something off the pages of Stan and Jack's comic books. As McDow says, "So the origin story of Black Panther introduced in 1966 looks like what would have happened if Batman/Bruce Wayne's parents had been Patrice Lumumba and Malcolm X. In the face of their murder, the loyal son dons a mask and uses the wealth at his disposal to avenge his parent's death."

Another aspect that made Black Panther stories powerful was their connection to Afrocentrism. This may not seem obvious, since the idea encompasses a validation and study of African cultural elements, and these were superficial in the early Marvel issues. However, the idea that there was value in the tribal traditions, even for a modern ruler, demonstrated the worth of maintaining ties with past beliefs and customs. Black Panther is black; he is African, not African American with all of the baggage that goes with that label and experience. Several writers have discussed the importance of this, not only when T'Challa was first drawn into existence, but throughout his Marvel run over the years.

Kristen Page-Kirby discussed the impact of the recent Black Panther film in terms of identity. She points out, "It is an opportunity for those who have the advantage of thinking that skin color doesn't matter to recognize why and how it does. To think of Black Panther's race as an aside, as happenstance—the way it is with most white superheroes—is to dismiss the very core of the character. It's not only a matter of color; it's a matter of identity." She describes the way other superhero characters have in some cases had changes in race, the most recent being Miles Morales as Spider-Man. Their whiteness can be "shrugged off" or reclaimed because "when you're white, it's easy to pretend race is unimportant." Page-Kirby tells the story of her Scottish-Irish-English-Swedish-German son wanting to be Black Panther for Halloween, something Kirby and Lee could never have dreamed of back in those early days. That is something that never could have happened in 2019 if T'Challa had not been given strong roots in 1966.

Page-Kirby goes further: "When my son pulls off his Halloween mask, he'll re-enter a country where every president save one, over 90 percent of CEOs and all of the original movie Avengers (when one of them isn't green) share his skin color. That experience will not be the same for a black kid." Mikhail Lyubansky, while also discussing the recent film, finds the Afrocentrism that was there in the comics all along, despite the early stereotypic aspects:

> There is really no white superhero equivalent. There cannot be, given this country's (and this world's!) racial politics. For T'Challa, his blackness and his Wakandan heritage are a source of pride. Other superheroes can exhibit national pride (hello, Captain America), but white pride is off limits for heroes, just as it is off limits for us mere mortals, at least those of us who value being part of the cultural mainstream. This is as it should be. For T'Challa, for other Africans, and for African Americans,

racial pride is legitimately earned by overcoming or even just surviving an oppressive history and reality.[...] T'Challa is aware of his blackness and is unapologetically proud of it.

Todd Steven Burroughs discussed fan reaction to this new character as found on the Fantastic Four Fan Page (6). In Issue #55, Ken Greene of Washington, D.C., praised the increasing quality of the illustrations, and then added, "But the main thing that made my heart sing is the latest in your concerted effort to bring comic literature to a more adult level by portraying members of races other than white." He applauds not only the Black Panther, but Wyatt Wingfoot, the American Indian character. Greene adds that he is partially of American Indian ancestry and is happy to see a "modern Indian" shown as being more than a relic of the past. He notes, "Wingfoot's pride, his skill, and his dignity are in keeping with the real tradition of the past" (22). It was another affirmation that characters were more than just drawings on a page. Individuals took notice of the power of identity and the ability of an art form to change perceptions.

Stan's Soapbox & Legacy

The controversy over the Marvel Method and credit for character and story creation will never end. Family, friends and fans of the men involved continue to spin details and provide what they consider solid proof of the truth (Taylor). One special component that does provide some proof of Lee's ideas and Marvel history is *Stan's Soapbox*, part of the *Bullpen Bulletins* news and information page that appeared in most Marvel comics. Beginning in 1965 grown out of the letters page, the monthly piece gave fans previews of upcoming comics, a peek behind the scenes at staff members and their work. In 1967, "Stan's Soapbox," Lee's monthly platform for his thoughts and opinions, became part of the feature. In the column, Lee talked directly to his readers in a conversational and humorous tone, joking about competitors and a fictional staffer named Irving Forbush. Forbush even had a Black Panther connection. On the first page of *Fantastic Four #53*, the native dance troupe is identified in the credits as the "Ballet Forbush Terpsichorean Troupe."

In September 1968, Stan told readers that over the years, staff had received many letters asking editors' opinions about real world issues, including the war in Vietnam and elections. Lee indicated that there was no consensus on any issue (except mother love and apple pie), but did tell readers:

> As for Yours Truly, and a few others, we prefer to judge the person, rather than the party line. That's why we seek to avoid editorializing about controversial issues—not

because we haven't our opinions, but rather because we share the same diversity of opinion as Americans everywhere. But, we'd like to go on record about one vital issue—we believe that Man has a divine destiny and an awesome responsibility of treating all who share this wondrous world of ours with tolerance and respect—judging each fellow human on his own merit, regardless of race, creed, or color. That we agree on and we'll never rest until it becomes a fact rather than just a cherished dream! [Lee, 15–16].

In response, readers flooded the company with letters, most asking him to editorialize more. The letter cited in Stan's Soapbox October 1968 from Achille Dibacco stated, "Marvelism is fast becoming a philosophical movement.... Marvel Comics are the voice of a new breed of intellectual. Therefore, editorializing is virtually a necessity" (16). Lee responded that this meant he had a "magnificent mandate" to speak his mind and, "let the chips fall where they may." He teased the next column with the tag line, "What is a bigot?" The November 1968 column was Lee's now famous commentary that bigotry and racism are among the deadliest social ills plaguing the world today. That column was written mere months after the assassination of Dr. King. Tom Brevoort, longtime Marvel staffer and current Executive Editor, wrote about his personal feelings regarding Stan's Soapbox pieces in an essay called "True Believers" in the collection of columns. He wrote about the credibility of Stan's words, stating, "It just smells of the groovy, '60s, this middle-aged editor being moved by the activism of the times to try to speak out and teach his young readers, to make a difference in their lives" (17).

Jason James wrote after Lee's death from a different perspective. As a child of the 1990s, he came to Marvel comics decades after those first Fantastic Four stories. James gives his version of Stan's impact. "And while at the time the Martin Luther King Jr. holiday was still up for debate, Al Sharpton was considered controversial and Public Enemy wasn't played on 'mainstream' radio—in a strange way all of that comic reading gave me a racial and political education that my lily-white suburban Virginia life never did." James is speaking not just about Black Panther but the wider Marvel catalog. In his words, it provided, "a curriculum for black kids like myself when public schools and all other forms of pop culture summarily shut us out." James describes his emotional reaction when reflecting on how much joy and validation he felt when reflecting on his feelings as a black child in the 1980s and '90s back when comic books were considered a "white" thing, but Lee's characters "put blackness and the black experience at the forefront." His tribute notes that Stan's activism was rooted in his background, " a Jewish guy born to Romanian immigrant parents in New York who hated bigotry." He notes that Lee fought bigotry, "in comic pages when mainstream newspaper editorials were still deciding if black folks should be able to live where they wanted." James, now a comics scholar and professor at Morgan State University, is testimony to the long-lasting influence of Stan, Jack and others at Marvel who sought to sell ideas along with comic books. "The fact remains that Stan Lee was steadfast in his belief that super-heroes should look and sound like the world around us; that they needed to reflect the best in people while tackling the worst of human instincts."

How and why did two middle-age Jewish male storytellers from New York City decide that 1966 was time for a black superhero king from a technologically advanced country that was unfamiliar and potentially scary to the demographic of their audience? It is clear that there were both progressive aspects as well as good business sense at work. Evan Narcisse sums up the situation:

> Given the times that he was created in, it's very plausible that The Black Panther was Lee and/or Kirby's way of saying that a black person was as capable of being a hero as their white characters. Even more daring, the Panther seemed to be more cunning and intelligent than some other heroes. Yet, making him African gave Marvel license to call on the exoticization of non–American black people. T'Challa wasn't like the black folk American readers were used to and this notional distance kept the Panther away from the marches, murders and discrimination in the United States. In the early part of his publishing history, he'd be a character that funneled escapism more than commentary ["Politics"].

As recently as October 2017, Lee posted a video on YouTube with a message about the deliberate inclusivity in the Marvel Universe: "The only things we don't have room for are hatred, intolerance and bigotry." That seems to have been part of the Marvel philosophy from the beginning, and those conditions helped birth T'Challa. Narcisse wrote about the later stories, where the Black Panther joins the Avengers, and how that spoke to him, a child of the '70s and '80s, as a Haitian immigrant:

> As I've thought about the stew of ideas that might have been in Lee's and Kirby's heads when they cooked up Wakanda, I've wondered how much their experiences as Jewish-American men in the early 20th century might have influenced them. On the African continent, former colonies were fighting to become their own sovereign countries. Here in America, the civil rights movement swirled all around Lee and Kirby, who themselves hailed from a persecuted group that had stereotypes flung it. All of these motifs seemed to be in play in the Panther's early stories, and it felt like Lee's stentorian scripting was specifically designed to pull me in ["Wakanda"].

Narcisse has gone on to write current Black Panther stories. He is not oblivious to the problems with the earliest Panther appearances, but he is comfortable with the way those opened the door for those like him who felt marginalized. He summed the complexity up by saying, "T'Challa is evidence that Stan Lee, his co-creators, and the writers and artists who followed in their footsteps knew that black people existed in a fuller way than was often shown in comics. Some of their well-meaning efforts were clunky and embarrassing, but they were gesturing in the right direction. That was enough for me" ("Wakanda").

WORKS CITED

Abad-Santosalex, Alex. "Marvel's comic book superheroes were always political. Black Panther embraces that."*Vox*, 22 Feb 2018. www.vox.com/2018/2/22/17028862/black-panther-movie-political.
Burroughs, Todd Steven. *Marvel's Black Panther: A Comic Book Biography, From Stan Lee to Ta-Nehisi Coates*. Diasporic Africa Press, 2018.
Campbell, Crystal Z. "Sculpting a Pan-African Culture in the Art of Negritude: A Model for African Artist." *The Journal of Pan African Studies*, vol. 1, no. 6, 2006, pp. 28–42.
Chambliss, Julian. "Blank Panther?: Jack Kirby, Blackness and the American Dream." *Popmatters*, 16 Feb 2011, https://www.popmatters.com/137258-blank-panther-jack-kirby-blackness-and-the-american-dream-2496076219.html.
Couch, Aaron. "'Black Panther' Flashback: When T'Challa (Briefly) Became the Black Leopard."
Englehart, Steve. "Avengers #105." *Avengers*, vol. 1, no. 105, Marvel, November 1972.
Fingeroth, Danny. *Disguised as Clark Kent: Jews, Comics, and the Creation of the Superhero*. Bloomsbury Academic. 2007.
Gavaler, Chris. *Superhero Comics*. Bloomsbury Academic, 2017.
Genter, Robert. "'With Great Power Comes Great Responsibility': Cold War Culture and the Birth of Marvel Comics." *Journal of Popular Culture*, vol. 40, no. 6. 2007, pp. 953–978.
The Hollywood Reporter, 14 February 2019, www.hollywoodreporter.com/heat-vision/black-panther-flashback-tchalla-became-black-leopard-1185811.
Hornshaw, Phil, and Ross A. Lincoln. "No, 'Black Panther' Was Not Named After the Black Panther Party." *The Wrap*, 20 February 2018, www.thewrap.com/black-panther-name-black-panther-party/.
Jones, Gerald, and Will Jacobs. *The Comic Book Heroes: The First History of Modern Comic Books—From the Silver Age to the Present*. Prima Lifestyles, 1996.
Lee, Stan. "A Message from Stan Lee." *YouTube*, uploaded by Marvel Entertainment, 5 October 2017, www.youtube.com/watch?v=sjobevGAYHQ.
_____. "Fantastic Four #52." *Fantastic Four*, vol. 1, no. 52, Marvel, July 1966.
_____. "Fantastic Four #53." *Fantastic Four*, vol. 1, no. 53, Marvel, August 1966.
_____. "Fantastic Four #55." *Fantastic Four*, vol. 1, no. 55, Marvel, October 1966.
_____. *Stan's Soapbox: The Collection*. The Hero Initiative, 2008.
"Lowndes County Freedom Party (LCFP)." *Digital SNCC Gateway*. www.snccdigital.org/inside-sncc/alliances-relationships/lcfp/.
Lyubansky, Mikhail. "The Racial Politics of Black Panther." *Psychology Today*, 20 February 2018. www.psychologytoday.com/us/blog/between-the-lines/201802/the-racial-politics-black-panther.
McDow, Thomas F. "Searching for Wakanda: The African Roots of the Black Panther Story." *Origins: Current Events in Historical Perspective*, 15 February 2018. www.origins.osu.edu/connecting-history/searching-wakanda-african-roots-black-panther-story.
Nama, Adilifu. *Super Black: American Pop Culture and Black Superheroes*. University of Texas Press, 2011.
Narcisse, Evan. "The Politics of Marvel's Black Panther." *Kokatu*, 5 May 2016. www.kotaku.com/the-politics-of-the-black-panther-1766701304.
_____. "Wakanda Was the Way Stan Lee Spoke to Me." *Polygon*, 16 November 2018. www.polygon.com/comics/2018/11/16/18098440/stan-lee-black-panther-wakanda.
Newkirk, Vann R. II. "The Provocation and Power of Black Panther." *The Atlantic*, 14 February 2018. www.theatlantic.com/entertainment/archive/2018/02/the-provocation-and-power-of-black-panther/553226/.
Oloruntoba-Oju, Omotayo. "Pan Africanism, Myth and History in African and Caribbean Drama." *Journal of Pan African Studies*, vol. 5, no. 8, 2012, pp. 190–209.
Osteroff, Joshua. "Marvel Comics Icon Stan Lee Talks Superhero Diversity And Creating

Black Panther." *Huffington Post*, 1 September 2016. www.huffingtonpost.ca/2016/09/01/stan-lee-marvel-superhero-diversity_n_11198460.html.
Page-Kirby, Kristen. "Black Panther Is More Than a Name. It's an Identity." *Washington Post*, 16 February 2018. www.washingtonpost.com/express/wp/2018/02/16/black-panther-is-more-than-a-name-its-an-identity/?utm_term=.5d5e493c5564.
Peters, Micah. "The Evolution of Marvel's 'Black Panther.'" *The Ringer*, 14 February 2019. www.theringer.com/pop-culture/2018/2/14/17012374/marvel-black-panther-comics-history.
Smith, Jamil. "The Revolutionary Power of Black Panther." *TIME*, 11 February 2018. www.time.com/black-panther/.
Steibel, Rob. "Stan Lee: 'I Created the Black Panther.'" *Kirby Dynamics*, 24 April 2012. www.kirbymuseum.org/blogs/dynamics/2012/04/24/9165/.
Taylor, Stan. "Bullpen? Bullshit!!" *Looking for the Awesome #20*, 10 February 2019. www.kirbymuseum.org/blogs/effect/.
Thomas, Roy. "Avengers #99." *Avengers*, vol. 1, no. 99, Marvel, May 1972.
_____. "Fantastic Four #119." *Fantastic Four*, vol. 1, no. 119, Marvel, February 1972.
_____. "Stan Lee's Amazing Marvel Interview." *AlterEgo*, vol. 3, no. 104, 2011. pp. 3–45.
Weinstein, Simcha. *Up, Up, and Oy Vey: How Jewish History, Culture, and Values Shaped the Comic Book Superhero.* 2009, Barricade Books.

A Tale of Two Panthers

T'Challa and the Black Panther Party for Self-Defense

Charles W. Henebry

On January 14, 1970, wealthy New Yorkers gathered at the home of Leonard and Felicia Bernstein for a cocktail party fundraiser on behalf of 21 Black Panthers who were jailed and awaiting trial on possibly trumped-up charges. In 2017, writing recently in response to widespread criticism of Colin Kaepernick, Jamie Bernstein recalled the firestorm that greeted her parents' advocacy of the Panthers. According to Ms. Bernstein, her mother was the driving force behind the fundraiser, but contemporary press coverage in the *Times* society section insisted on placing her father center stage, archly describing how the world-famous conductor debated party philosophy with Black Panther leader Donald Cox in front of 90 guests before "hugging one another, agreeing that they were brothers, and having dinner together" (Curtis). The *Times*' editorial staff followed up a day later, condemning the "group-therapy plus fund-raising soirée" as "elegant slumming" that "mocked the memory of Martin Luther King, Jr." ("False Note...").

For the next few weeks the Jewish Defense League picketed the Bernsteins' building, but the incident would likely have been forgotten if not for the version that emerged five months later from the clattering typewriter of Tom Wolfe. Republished shortly afterward as the first half of *Radical Chic and Mau-Mauing the Flak-Catchers*, Wolfe's *New York Magazine* article commented sardonically on the presence of radicals sporting black leather jackets, dark glasses, and giant afros in a duplex apartment on the Upper East Side: "Wonder what the Black Panthers eat here on the hors d'oeuvre trail? Do the Panthers like little Roquefort cheese morsels wrapped in crushed nuts this way, and asparagus tips in mayonnaise dabs, and meatballs petites au Coq

Hardi, all of which are at this very moment being offered to them on gadrooned silver platters by maids in black uniforms with hand-ironed white aprons..." (ellipsis in original, here and elsewhere, except when marked by square brackets). But if Wolfe cast a sidelong aspersion at the supposedly Maoist Panthers enjoying the fruits of capitalist decadence, he reserved his real venom for the Bernsteins and their set. Ticking over a long list of recent liberal fundraisers in "this season of Radical Chic" (three parties for the Black Panthers, one for the Chicago Eight, and still others for grape workers, Irish activists, and the Young Lords), Wolfe perceived not the workings of social conscience but social competition, what right-leaning critics today call "virtue signaling."

Curiously, Wolfe's satirical recounting of the Bernsteins' fête found its way into in the August 1971 issue of *The Incredible Hulk*. The comic opens with the Hulk turning up in New York Harbor and deciding to take a nap in the crook of Lady Liberty's arm. He's spotted soon afterward, and the military mobilizes—but holds off from approaching for fear of damage to the famous statue. At news of this standoff, a pair of wealthy Manhattan socialites spring into action: "Malicia my pet, it would appear that our social fortune is made. [...] Everyone who is anyone this season has given at least one fund-raising party for some socially-oppressed group. The Panthers, the grape-pickers, even the friends of the Earth. They've all been done. We are going to give such a party for ... the Hulk!" What follows is a reenactment of the Bernsteins' fundraiser, with the Hulk standing in for the Panthers as a primal threat to the social order that nonetheless rouses liberal sympathies: "I just don't see how the army can go on persecuting him that way," says one woman, to whom another replies "Yes—just because he tears down an old building now and then!" (Thomas, "They Shoot Hulks..."). Readers likely agreed with this sentiment, since the Hulk of this era was a monster deserving sympathy: enormously destructive, yes, but innocently so. Yet these cultured fools plainly take sympathy too far when they attend a party menaced by that great green engine of destruction. Thus the comic turns up the heat of Wolfe's satire, from wry irony to outright ridicule. And even as it accuses Manhattan's elite of being clueless, the comic insinuates something far darker in choosing to affiliate the Black Panthers with a creature of brooding rage.

What motivated writer Roy Thomas to take the Hulk on a one-issue detour into pointed political commentary? As a first clue, we might note that Thomas scripted this issue just a few months after sending T'Challa, Marvel's Black Panther, home to Wakanda, thus ending the character's three-year stint on the Avengers' active roster. Thomas wrote every *Avengers* issue from 1968 through 1971, during which period the Black Panther Party was very much in the national spotlight. Fan scholar David Jefferson has probed the odd coincidence that the Black Panther, the world's first black superhero, was created in 1966, the same year that the Black Panther Party formed in Oakland, California. But while Jefferson concludes that Jack Kirby and Stan Lee acted independently of Huey Newton and Bobby Seale, he does not consider how the Party impacted the hero once its local chapters spread across the nation and its legal troubles rendered it a cause célèbre.

As we shall see, by the time Black Panther joined the Avengers, writer Roy Thomas could hardly avoid addressing the issue of race in America. To Thomas's credit, race is explicitly referenced in about half of *Avengers* comics from this period and is central to four story arcs. By contrast, Women's Lib is addressed in just one, highly satirical issue (#83), while Vietnam receives no mention whatsoever. Yet Thomas' treatment of race in this period focused far more on the failings of black radicals than on the systematic injustices those activists sought to overcome. This, then, is the tale of two panthers, birthed independently but frequently confused with one another. Both radiated "cool" even as they burned hot with idealism, and both looked to Africa as a once-and-future black utopia. Yet their conflicting visions of America set them in mutual opposition.

The Cold-War Politics of Post-Colonial Africa

In the early days of 1966, activists from the Student Nonviolent Coordinating Committee (SNCC) began organizing "all-Negro" slates of candidates to run for local office in Mississippi and Alabama counties where voter registration drives had succeeded in giving blacks the majority of votes (Roberts, "2 Rights Groups"). Pointing to the failure of a biracial government in Tuskegee, Alabama, these radicals argued that real change required toppling the power structure by replacing all officials with black candidates (Roberts). SNCC had been an important ally of the NAACP and Martin Luther King's SCLC in the early 1960s, but its embrace of Black Power under the leadership of Stokely Carmichael placed it at loggerheads with those centrist civil rights organizations. Those groups managed to defeat SNCC in the November elections, but not before its Lowndes County Freedom Organization had adopted the black panther mascot of a local black university as its political emblem, a fierce black cat pouncing outward from its leaflets and posters (Cushing).

The superhero known as Black Panther made his debut on the cover of the July 1966 issue of *Fantastic Four:* an agile, black-garbed human figure springing triumphantly above the titular characters, who were busy exploring a strange and tangled jungle of circuitry. It's possible, as Sean Howe suggests (85), that Lee or Kirby read about the LCFO's black panther mascot in a January 23 *New York Times* article. But the article, unillustrated and buried deep in the newspaper, made only passing reference to the party's mascot. Nor do we find any reference in the comic's plot to the struggle to end Jim Crow by dominating the ballot box. Rather, the story revolves on themes of imperialism and American diplomacy in the developing world. At its outset, an emissary greets the Four with the gift of a marvelous aircraft and an invitation to come to Wakanda where they will be honored by his chieftain with "the greatest hunt of all time" (*FF*#52, 3). But it turns out the mighty chieftain plans to hunt *them*—in the guise of the Black Panther. By means of this strangely villainous treachery, the Panther captures each of our four heroes before the tables are turned by an unexpected fifth guest, Johnny Storm's Native American college roommate, Wyatt Wingfoot. In the following issue, T'Challa recounts how he won the title of chieftain years earlier by driving off a European adventurer named Klaw, who sought control of the mineral riches of Wakanda's "Sacred Mound" (FF#53, 7). He somewhat lamely explains the "great hunt" of the previous issue as a personal test of his readiness—at which point an alarm sounds. Sure enough, Klaw is back, and in the battle that follows the Fantastic Four face off against bright-pink African wildlife created by Klaw from pure sound, while the Panther hunts down and defeats the nefarious European in his lair.

While this narrative of a proud African ruler has no immediate relevance for the Civil Rights struggle in the Deep South, that isn't to say it lacked all significance. "I wanted to create the first black super-hero," Stan Lee claimed in a 2005 interview, "but I wanted to avoid stereotyping" (38). Lee's insider stories of early Marvel history are sometimes colored by wishful thinking, but in this case his recollection is corroborated by the script he wrote in 1966. The working-class Thing, Ben Grimm, repeatedly tries to pigeonhole the Panther, calling him a "refugee from a Tarzan movie" (*FF* #52, 2) and dismissing his origin story as a Hollywood cliché: "I know the rest by heart! Everything wuz hunky dory until the greedy ivory hunters made the scene!" (*FF* #53, 6). But events prove the Thing wrong; the Panther defies easy categorization. Far from being a superstitious native, T'Challa made a fortune by selling just a small fraction of the Sacred Mound's vibranium, reserving the rest to use in crafting a multitude of wonders, from flying machines to sensor arrays. This portrait of a wise and canny leader led David Jefferson to celebrate Jack Kirby for defying contemporary racial stereotypes (215–16). Jefferson is right to focus on Kirby's role in creating the Panther, given how inventively the comic's visuals juxtapose the tropes of darkest Africa with those of high technology: men in native dress wield strange devices (*FF* #52, 3); thick jungle canopy gives way to reveal a labyrinth of circuitry (*FF* #52, 8); most vitally, barbaric ritual combines with modern wizardry in the great panther totem that rises out of the ground at T'Challa's command (*FF* #52, 4).

But if the story and artwork defy racist preconceptions, they do so in service of an equally powerful belief-system, American Exceptionalism. Taking as premise America's unique nobility among nations, in the first decades of the Cold War, American presidents from both parties sought to forge a new world order based on the liberal ideals of democracy and self-determination (Holm vi). This meant an end to global imperialism. In place of the economic and cultural subjugation of the prior age, America would lead the way through international loans, grants and advisors. The Kennedy Administration was particularly keen in its embrace of Modernization Theory, founding not only the Peace Corps but USAID, and thus committing not only American youth but American dollars to the cause of bringing democracy and prosperity to the developing world. So it isn't surprising that Lee and Kirby staged their critique of racial stereotypes in Africa, rather than reckoning with the legacy of slavery in America. A wave of liberation swept across Africa in the postwar period, from Ethiopia in 1944 up through Botswana and Lesotho in the year the Black Panther first appeared—some 36 nations in just 23 years. Klaw, the story's villain, wears a pith helmet during his initial foray into Wakanda, and bears a name that is reminiscent of Kurtz, from Conrad's *Heart of Darkness,* and redolent of the clawing, rapacious character of European imperialism. Meanwhile, the titular heroes play the role not of liberators, but rather allies of a fiercely independent local chieftain. And in this endeavor they are helped by Wyatt Wingfoot, as if to suggest the happy resolution of America's own history of subjugating its native population.

None of this is to say that Wakanda perfectly fits the 1960s narrative of a developing nation. Far more typical is a feature article that ran in *Life* magazine when Nigeria gained independence from Britain in 1960. On one two-page spread, under the subheading "A Modern World Springing from Mud Huts," the layout editor set a large image of village tribesmen directly across from smaller photos showing the shiny ductwork of a canning factory and workers on a Unilever assembly line. This layout anticipates Kirby's juxtapositions of tribesmen and technology, but in a way that highlights the developmental gap in Africa rather than erasing it: "In a farm village," reads the first photo caption, "Habe tribesmen lounge about the compound while their women do most of the heavy work in the fields, cultivating" (64). In the course of modernization, we gather, these tribesmen will have to abandon their leisurely folkways and become more like Americans, working long hours in dull factory jobs. By contrast, Kirby imagines a people who have mastered technology, yet still live in grass huts, wear elaborate headdresses, and dance to honor their chieftain. Kirby's Wakanda seems thus to have achieved modernity without disrupting social norms. This utopian quality would later prove fertile soil for Afrofuturism (Brown et al.).

But the Wakanda of this first Black Panther story wasn't quite a utopia.

Something savage lurked at its heart: a great black idol that T'Challa summoned forth to initiate a barbaric attack on his unsuspecting guests: "Raise the totem! Let the ritual begin! The time has come for the Black Panther to stalk once more!" (*FF* #52, 4). T'Challa was never more terrifyingly Other than in that first scene, surrounded by bloodthirsty followers wielding spears and machine-guns. This proud chieftain rules through shows of strength. Hemmed in by primitive notions of the Great Man, T'Challa could not simply ask the Fantastic Four for help against Klaw. Instead, he plied them with gifts to demonstrate his magnanimity, then unexpectedly attacked them to show his prowess in battle. Only after making those gestures could he tell them his moving story, lest they respond with pity and not heroic camaraderie. This lends significance to the Four's effort at story's end to persuade T'Challa not to retire his Panther costume after defeating Klaw. Though his father has been avenged and his nation made safe, that's "no reason for the Black Panther's career to come to an end! The world will always have need of a dedicated, powerful fighter against injustice!" With these words Reed Richards encourages T'Challa to reframe his identity as something different from culture-hero to his people. The chieftain responds, somewhat reluctantly, by pledging henceforth to dedicate his powers "to the service of all mankind" (*FF* #53, 20). Similar to the way that *Life* imagined Habe tribesmen taking jobs on an assembly line, this ending suggests that, despite his mastery of technology, T'Challa still needed to give up his narrow, culture-specific notion of heroism. It's a typical 1960s fantasy: a group of idealistic Americans (whether from the Peace Corps, the Pentagon, or a superhero group) travel to a developing nation to inspire a local leader to embrace the universalist ethos of American liberalism.

Integrating Marvel's Fictional Lineup

Judging from letters published in *Fantastic Four* #55–57, Marvel's fans were enthusiastic about the Black Panther. But the emphasis these readers placed on the hero's race re-cast Lee and Kirby's fable of international development as a vital step in the ongoing saga of desegregation in America. Praising the creators for having already "broken all the precedents of your profession" by including Gabe Jones in the cast of *Sgt. Fury,* Henry B. Clay of Detroit reported that after reading *FF* #52–53 he was "doing flip-flops and walking around in a daze" at the sight of "a real live Negro super-hero!!!" Washington, D.C., reader Ken Greene predicted that the Panther "would turn out to be the first great Negro hero-villain in comic book history" after having read just the first half of the two-issue story. Greene went on to remark, "Being partially of American Indian ancestry," he was also "gratified at the introduction of Wyatt Wingfoot" as a notable break with stereotype. New Orleans reader Linda Lee Johnson, who went so far as to share the comic with her mother, was equally unstinting in her praise: "you are the first, the very first to create and introduce a Negro super-hero who is as brilliant as he is handsome to team up with your already fantastic heroes."

While plainly proud of these readers' accolades, Stan Lee responded somewhat cagily to their framing of the Panther as a vital milestone in the history of race relations. He made a particular point of rebuffing Henry Clay. Paraphrasing an oft-quoted line from Martin Luther King's Dream speech, Lee insisted that the Panther should be judged on the content of his character and "not on the color of his skin": "We too are fond of the Black Panther—not because he's a Negro—but because he's a right Joe!" Lee also maintained a pretense of color-blindness in his response to Johnson, setting her proposal that the Panther join the Fantastic Four on par with "countless similar suggestions" regarding heroes like the Silver Surfer and the Inhumans. These responses weren't ambivalent so much as canny. To claim credit for "desegregating" superhero comics would have meant acknowledging how little the industry had done up until that point—not to mention how much remained to be done. Marvel's bullpen was even whiter than its roster of heroes; the company hired its first black artist six years after the Black Panther's debut, and its first black editor some six years after that.[1] What's more, to claim credit would have meant acknowledging the ugly history of segregation and the continuing problem of racism in America—a history that Lee and Kirby had hoped to dodge by setting their tale in far-off Wakanda. So, instead of claiming credit, Lee indirectly accepted it. Even as he asserted a color-blind opposition to any form of racial quota, he selected for publication a series of congratulatory letters from fans—fans whose names, cities of origin, and tone of personal excitement marked them as likely African Americans.

Imitating an American Classic

Two years later, Linda Lee Johnson would get a variation of her wish when the Black Panther signed on with the Avengers. In the interval, the Panther had two appearances in *The Fantastic Four,* followed by an extended, four-issue guest role fighting alongside Captain America—a role that immediately preceded his first *Avengers* issue. The frequency and timing of these appearances suggests something about the new hero's popularity. Lee was a master of cross-promotion decades before the technique had a name; through this sequence of guest spots, each one longer and more involved than the last, Lee built a following for the Panther in advance of his launch in *The Avengers,* even as he drew on that nascent following to promote other titles.

The first, very brief, appearance came at the end of the November 1966 issue (*FF* #56) in which Lee ran Henry Clay's letter along with other pro–Panther fan mail. The second, a year later in *Fantastic Four Annual* #5, featured not just the Panther but another of Kirby's popular creations, the Inhumans. Perhaps most significant, though, was the third and longest role, during Captain America's January to April 1968 transition from sharing space with Iron Man in *Tales of Suspense* to heading up a title of his own. Lee and Kirby pulled out all the stops to promote that vital story arc,[2] employing, in addition to the Panther, Cap's longstanding nemesis Baron Zemo.

The Panther's team-up with Captain America was more than just a promotional exercise, however. Eight months earlier, in May 1967, the Black Panther Party for Self-Defense stepped decisively into the national spotlight when a group from its Oakland chapter entered the California State Capitol, fully armed, to protest a proposed change in gun regulations. They made it as far as the floor of the Assembly chamber before being disarmed and escorted from the building. Party members would later claim that the group did not intend to commandeer the legislative process that day, but merely took a wrong turn on their way to the visitors' gallery (Stern 187).

Blunder or not, the optics of an armed coup were irresistible to the news media: "Capitol Is Invaded," ran the full-width banner headline on the *Sacramento Bee's* front page. A day later the story was reported in the front sections of newspapers nationwide. Founded with a mission of counter-balancing Oakland's all-white police force, the Panthers had been taking advantage of California's longstanding open-carry law to arm neighborhood patrols. Leather jackets, wraparound sunglasses, and black berets could only do so much; as co-founder Huey Newton told a New York Times reporter (paraphrasing Mao), "Political power comes through the barrel of a gun" (Turner). Such revolutionary language did little to assuage the fears of those unsettled by the sight of paramilitary patrols on city streets. Judged as a political action protesting a bill to revoke the open carry law, the Panthers' trip to the State House was a public-relations disaster, doing much to ensure that bill's passage. Judged, however, as political theater, the event was a fantastic success, imprinting on the nation's consciousness a new breed of black radical, a gun-toting paramilitary activist in sunglasses and black beret, prowling urban neighborhoods and speaking the language of revolution: "Black people realize," Newton told a reporter, "that they are already at war with the racist white power structure" (Stern 188). Thus, while the organization had already spread to Detroit and New York City,[3] it was the action in Sacramento which catapulted the Panthers to national prominence.

The Party's prominence likely played a role in Marvel's decision to add the hero to the Avengers' roster. As we will see, *Avengers* writer Roy Thomas was eager to comment on the problem of race in America, a task made easier by a hero who shares his name with a group in the headlines. Yet that overlap also threatened to sow confusion, given that the Party's radical ideology was at odds with Marvel's liberal ethos. Put simply, the Black Panthers made white folks uncomfortable, a discomfort still evident years later in Lee's 2005 interview:

> It was a strange coincidence because ... there was a political party ... called the Black Panthers. And I didn't think of that at all. It had nothing to do with our character, although a lot of people thought there was some tie-in. And I was really sorry—maybe if I had it to do over again, I'd have given him another name, because I hate that confusion to be caused [38].

So an important function of the four-issue team-up with Captain America was to lay the groundwork for the Panther's debut in the pages of *The Avengers*. Lee and Kirby reasserted their original character concept in the face of the Black Panther Party's conflicting brand image, repeating key beats from the hero's first appearance in the pages of *Fantastic Four:* Cap is summoned to Wakanda in a futuristic flying vehicle and unexpectedly attacked by his host upon arrival, after which the two heroes join forces against an old foe—this time a nemesis of the American rather than the Wakandan hero. In this way, Lee and Kirby reminded readers that their Panther was a denizen of distant Wakanda and the legitimate, royal ruler of his people, not a radical fomenting revolution in the "asphalt jungles" of the inner city. The hero, according to this narrative, had nothing to do with the Party.

Yet the story still offered an indirect commentary on black radicalism. For in rehashing the earlier story's plot, Lee and Kirby also reprised its central theme, dramatizing the Panther's conversion from tribal hero to super-hero. At the story's outset, T'Challa still thinks of himself as the defender of *his* people in particular: "Again we are menaced by those who would destroy us! And again we shall strike back—and fight till victory—or death!" (*ToS* #97, 4). Just as he had done with the Fantastic Four, he seems testy about calling on an outsider for help (*ToS* #97, 10), and once again he makes an unprovoked attack on his guest as a "test" (*ToS* #98, 3). But at the story's crisis, the Panther turns away from insularity. When Zemo threatens to use an orbital death-ray to "wipe out the United States," T'Challa springs to the defense of his American ally's homeland, explaining his action by reference to a universal principle: "That leaves us no choice, Avenger! Better to die as men—than to live—as slaves!" (*ToS* #99, 9). With these words T'Challa abandons the mantle of tribal hero to adopt the ethos of Captain America. Lee points the moral at the story's end, when T'Challa refers to Wakanda not as a tribe or as a people but as a nation of laws, offering to Zemo's surrendering henchmen "The justice of Wakanda" (*CapA* #100, 19).

In the *Fantastic Four* story from 1966, a similar version of this plot read as a celebration of America's selfless intervention in foreign conflicts. Two years later, though, the focus had shifted from the American to the Wakandan hero's willingness to make common cause. Not coincidentally, in this period many black radicals had begun to question their allegiance to American interests and ideals. In February 1966, Muhammad Ali had responded to news that he might be drafted to fight in Vietnam by declaring that, as a Black Muslim, he had "no quarrel with them Vietcong" ("Clay Plans"). In furious reaction, an upcoming title bout was relocated at the last minute from Chicago to Louisville, then cancelled altogether in favor of a fight with a relative unknown in Toronto, outside the United States altogether (Eskenazi). And while much of the immediate news coverage presented Ali as a blowhard,[4] over time his opposition to the war came to be seen in ideological terms, consonant not merely with the antiwar movement but—more particularly—with the separatism of black militancy. SNCC's Stokely Carmichael expanded on Ali's phrase to explain why the descendants of slaves might be unwilling to fight a war in Southeast Asia: "Why should black folks fight a war against yellow folks so that white folks can keep a land they stole from red folks? We're not going to Vietnam. Ain't no Vietcong ever called me n—r!" (quoted in Bingham and Wallace 119).

Nor was the disaffection of black radicals limited to American foreign policy in Southeast Asia. In the summer of 1966, SNCC expelled whites from its membership. This announcement caused a great deal of consternation, as witnessed by *New York Times* coverage on August 5: a front-page article, along with excerpts from an internal SNCC position paper and a profile of Carmichael, the organization's newly elected chairman ("Black Power Idea," "Excerpts," and "Black Power Prophet"). Six weeks later, the *Times* ran a lengthy profile of SNCC's history in its *Magazine,* taking care to note, right at the outset, the declared opposition of Martin Luther King to all calls for "violence and black power" (Roberts, "Story of Snick" 242). For context, SNCC had played a vital role in the civil rights struggles of the early 1960s, placing young activists on the front lines during lunch-counter sit-ins, the Freedom Rides, and the rallies of Mississippi's Freedom Summer. As suggested by its logo, an interracial handshake, in that period the organization welcomed whites to join its pickets (Carson 17). But now SNCC was abandoning the ideals of that storied past in favor of racial exclusion, a move that struck white liberals as tantamount to racism. Carmichael insisted in interviews with white reporters that the new policy was not "racism in reverse," explaining "the Negro wanted 'to build something of his own, something that he builds with his own hands. And that is *not* anti-white'" (Carson 205). But despite giving space to Carmichael's account, mainstream news tended in the end to focus on the plight of whites excluded by SNCC's new policy, as for example the anecdote with which the *Times* ended its profile of the young leader:

> He recently addressed a racially mixed audience here and, with several whites of long acquaintance in the room, declared that he had never known a white person he could trust. A young white man who had considered himself Mr. Carmichael's friend rose from the audience. "Not one, Stokely?" he asked. Mr. Carmichael looked directly into his eyes and replied, "No—not one" ["Black Power Prophet"].

This narrative, of black radicals betraying not merely the cause of racial comity but the personal feelings of their erstwhile comrades-in-arms, was to have a lasting influence on the politics of race in America.

Against this backdrop, then, Lee and Kirby staged the Black Panther's team-up with Captain America. The story emphasizes the likeness between the two heroes, each the champion of his people. The Panther's brief skirmish with Cap proves not merely that they are evenly matched, but that they share the same combat style, overcoming foes through speed and skill, not brute strength. Both are also demonstrably brave, plunging into danger even when they know that their enemy has likely laid traps for them. Indeed, Kirby repeatedly posed the two heroes as mirror images: charging forward into battle (*ToS* #98, 11 panel 1 and *ToS* #99, 9 panel 6), plotting against their common enemy (*CapA* #100, 7 panel 1), punching mooks to left and to right (*CapA* #100, 9 panel 1), or the slightly more complicated harmony of Cap striking three foes with an uppercut followed by the Black Panther striking three others with a downward slap (*ToS* #98, 8 panels 1-2; for a similar instance, *ToS* #99, 4 panels 1-2). The significance of this shadow-play is revealed on the story's final page, when Captain America announces that he's no longer an active member of the Avengers, and invites the Panther to take his place. Plainly the Panther is physically capable of filling Cap's shoes; the question is whether he's willing to forsake the narrow claims of Wakanda for the liberal, globalist vision of the Avengers. At a time when black radicals were traveling—and even emigrating—from America to the newly independent nations of Africa, Lee and Kirby lauded the African T'Challa for making the opposite journey, to join up as an Avenger in New York City.

Coming to America

At the end of that trip, the Black Panther passed into the hands of a new writer. Two decades younger than either Lee or Kirby, Roy Thomas had come of age in the Civil Rights Era, and, as we will see, he was far more willing to highlight America's shortcomings than the character's creators had been. By situating the world's first black superhero abroad, Lee and Kirby had managed to dodge the problem of race in America, turning the occasion into a celebration of American Exceptionalism. Thomas, by contrast, would seize upon the character as an instrument of critique. For the first time, readers encountered the urban blight of a racial ghetto in a mainstream American comic-book. Through the lens of the Black Panther, Thomas portrayed a nation riven by racism and—what's more—by the desperate, idealistic urge to do something about it. But this earnest ambition left Thomas with little room to maneuver and open to criticism from all sides. Even as his stories depicted the fracturing of the liberal consensus, the comic's letters page resounded with that same loss of comity. By 1971, the experiment was over; stripped temporarily of his controversial heroic moniker, T'Challa was shipped back to Africa.

Roy Thomas' ambitions for the Panther are evident in the story with which he introduced the character in May 1968. T'Challa doesn't arrive to diplomatic fanfare or even the warm welcome of his new teammates, but to suspicion, false accusations, and, on two separate occasions, police gunfire (*Av*#52, 12–13, 19). Avengers Mansion is locked, its windows dark, and so as the book opens the Panther is clambering over its roof like a cat-burglar. Choosing to investigate with "a stealth such as none but the Panther can achieve" (1), he enters through a high-tech skylight, then fights his way past the building's automated defense systems only to discover the dead bodies of Goliath, Hawkeye, and the Wasp—at which point Shield Agent Jasper Sitwell enters, gun trained on the Panther, and accuses him of murder. To clear himself of this crime, the Panther breaks free from police custody and returns to Avengers HQ to find the real villain, the Grim Reaper, holed up in the group's vault-like meeting room. Learning in the course of the ensuing battle that the three Avengers are not really dead but merely in a state of suspended animation, the Panther takes the Reaper's techno-scythe to the hospital where the bodies had been sent. At the climax, he dodges a hail of police gunfire while using the scythe to bring the dead Avengers back to life—upon which Hawkeye drives home the Panther's innocence by pinning the offending officers to the wall with a volley of carefully aimed arrows.

In the present era of #BlackLivesMatter, it's easy to see this story as commenting on the suspicious gaze that white America directs toward black bodies. Working with artist Sal Buscema, Thomas had modified the Panther's mask to show the lower half of his face. By revealing his race, the modified mask leant political significance to his treatment by the police: T'Challa may be a king in his own land, but in the United States he's a criminal until proven otherwise.

In fact, the scene echoes the inciting incident of 1967's Oscar winner for Best Picture, *In the Heat of the Night*. Sidney Poitier stars as a black Philadelphia police detective, Mr. Virgil Tibbs, who's arrested on suspicion of murder while passing through a small town in Mississippi. But whereas the movie contrasts racial tension in the Deep South with a fantasy of racial comity in Philadelphia, Thomas set his story of racial stereotyping in New York City.

In so doing, he ratcheted his critique a notch closer to the version given by Huey Newton when he spoke of the police in Northern cities as an "occupying army": "Black people realize ... that they are already at war with the racist white power structure" (quoted in Stern 220 and 219). Roy Thomas may have read Sol Stern's profile of the Panthers, which ran in *The New York Times Magazine* in August 1967. If not, he likely ran across similar coverage elsewhere in the months leading up to launching the comic book hero in the May 1968 issue of *The Avengers.* In an evocative quote from that same *Times Magazine* article, Bobby Seale invoked the Party's animal mascot to explain how its ideology of self-defense might entail "executing racist cops": "It is not in the panther's nature to attack anyone first, but when he is attacked and backed into a corner, he will respond viciously and wipe out the aggressor" (quoted in Stern 219). This line may well have inspired Thomas—though if so he made a crucial change, for when cops corner the Black Panther in *Avengers* #52 he responds by using the Grim Reaper's scythe not to kill but to *restore* life. In sum, in his first Avengers story the Panther ventured into the political maelstrom of late-60s politics. In close parallel to the Black Panther Party for Self-Defense, he suffers the unjust suspicion of a racist police state—but like Virgil Tibbs he responds with restraint, suggesting thereby a means of healing the body politic.

This analysis of the comic-book story ignores one crucial detail, however: the script fails—or, rather, refuses—to represent racial prejudice openly, fatally undermining the resonance of the Panther's forbearance toward New York City's Finest. The arresting officer in Stirling Silliphant's screenplay for *In the Heat of the Night* calls Mr. Tibbs "boy" no fewer than four times in the space of a 70-second scene. That bit of ugliness sets the stakes for when Tibbs' boss (reached by telephone a few minutes later) asks him to help the cops who arrested him find the true culprit. By contrast, the police in Thomas' comic call T'Challa "laughing-boy," an odd bit of 1940s slang that was a staple of early 60s Marvel Comics banter (see for example FF#18, 6, FF#20, 13). This peculiar manner of defanging a racist epithet likely betrays the editorial intervention of Stan Lee. In his history of Marvel Comics, Sean Howe describes Lee as "master of the middle ground," crafting comics stories that felt grounded in real world issues but which were "so ambiguous in their political subtext that Marvel was embraced by both the far left and the far right" (94). Whether imposed by Lee or merely inspired by his example, the erasure of both race and racism was thoroughgoing. Despite the visible outrage of an innocent black man fired upon by cops, the story stipulates that those officers, like the automated defense systems of Avengers Mansion, were acting merely in response to circumstances. The Black Panther's cold welcome in the U.S. is further obscured by the issue's cover, which gave pride of place to the Grim Reaper's vengeful quest. For the crowning touch, the story quietly dropped

"Black" from the hero's name, reducing him to the spare "Panther." The result is a story with far too much plot and far too little thematic coherence, fraught with symbolism but lacking an emotional core.

Stan Lee's chary treatment of racial themes is also exemplified by an exchange on the letters page two issues later. Echoing his response to Henry Clay years earlier, Lee once more sought to celebrate the racial milestone of the Panther joining the Avengers while denying that the move was politically motivated. At some point prior to the publication of *Avengers* #52, Lawrence Isaacson wrote in suggesting, "As there is never too much that can be done to lessen the tensions between the races, why not introduce a black Avenger to the lineup?" Isaacson wasn't a teenage enthusiast; he identified himself in his signature as a teacher at Brooklyn's P.S. 189. Lee responded by claiming race had never been a consideration: "Just for the record, we ought to make it clear that we didn't have our African Avenger sign up because he was a Negro.... In our eyes the important thing is whether or not an individual member adds something to the group, not what color his skin happens to be." But even as we note Lee's cagy manner of taking credit for integrating the Avengers, we should also note the changing context in which he did so. For questions of representation were just then coming to a boil in Brooklyn's public schools. An experiment in "local control" in Ocean Hill–Brownsville, a largely black neighborhood just east of Isaacson's P.S.189, promoted African American history, art, and literature, celebrating the notionally "black" values of mutuality and cooperation in the face of meritocratic "white" culture (Podair 96, 7). This new pedagogy was anathema to the vast majority of teachers in the district, many of whom (like Stan Lee himself) were immigrants or the children of immigrants who had made good on the meritocratic promise of New York City's public schools (Podair 13–14). The teachers staged a walkout in May 1968, likely just around the time that Lee was selecting Isaacson's letter for publication; a month-long citywide strike followed in September. As historian Jerald Podair notes, the controversy left a lasting scar on the city: while it "did not itself create 'two New Yorks'—one black, one white, divided politically, socially, and culturally," Ocean Hill–Brownsville was "their most visible, palpable symbol" (8).

The Panther and His People

Stan Lee's squeamishness was, however, just one challenge that Thomas faced in his effort to engage the problem of race in America. His hero's exotic origin posed a different one: how could an African chieftain evoke the difficult legacy of slavery? Or bear witness to the crime and poverty of black urban neighborhoods? This problem's magnitude can be sensed from Thomas' heavy-handed efforts to affiliate the Black Panther with black Americans. Three issues into the Panther's run in *The Avengers,* he's shown shackled like a fugitive slave (*Av*#54). Two of his white teammates are similarly bound, but later issues dispensed with any pretense that these bindings weren't about T'Challa's race. *Avengers* #74 and #78 both feature the Panther alone in captivity, chained in manacles and a neck collar. As a means of invoking the African American experience, the iconography of slavery must have struck Thomas as less controversial than police racial bias—though from the perspective of the present day it's certainly in worse taste. An ultimately more significant adjustment was T'Challa's move to Harlem, where he took up lodgings, acquired a romantic interest, and became a schoolteacher (*Av*#78, 9, #74, 20, #77, 12). Given our brief synopsis of the Ocean Hill–Brownsville teachers' strike, the Panther's new job seems particularly significant: in the June 1970 issue T'Challa, dressed in tribal robes, inspires his young charges with tales of their African heritage, presenting it as "a birthright that lays as great a stress on courage [...] as Medieval Europe did on chivalry" (*Av*#77, 13). T'Challa's students respond by turning the conversation to a modern-day inspiration—amusingly, not the Black Panther but the Falcon, the African American hero introduced by Stan Lee and Gene Colan in September 1969 (*CapA*#117). On some level the scene is corporate self-congratulation, but it's notable to find Thomas espousing a pedagogy of representation strikingly at odds with his editor's official stance.

Thomas had initiated the Panther's move to the ghetto some two years earlier, in a troubled monologue delivered by T'Challa on a rainy evening, walking through the city in civilian clothes: "Had to get out of the Avengers' mansion! Only here, in the open air, can the Black Panther be free to think—think about his life—or what passes for his life! I was a prince in far-off Africa … of a hidden kingdom possessed of matchless wealth! But, I found my throne an empty, hollow mockery…! Thus I became an Avenger … hoping to find fulfillment in ridding society of those who would ruthlessly destroy it! Yet even that is not enough! I must do more—" at which point his rumination is cut off by cries of "Help…. Police! Robbery" (*Av*#57, 7). Slipping invisibly into costume, the Black Panther makes short work of the thieves, one black and two white men. Everyone else in the scene is black, from the man who called for help at the outset to the officer who arrives in its aftermath, and with this we realize just how far the Panther has travelled, from the posh Upper East Side of Avengers Mansion into the bustle and squalor of Harlem: just two miles north but a world apart. Echoing the hero's earlier self-critique, the policeman praises the Panther for making the trip: "Glad to see you Avengers have time to do something besides save the Earth from super-villains once in a while!" (*Av*#57, 9). In the same panel a young teen enthuses, "Man, that Black Panther is somethin' else! We could sure use 'im on my block!" And of course T'Challa takes this to heart, musing "Something in that youngster's voice may just have given me the answer I've been seeking" (*Av#57*, 9).

Running just a panel beyond two pages, this scene in *Avengers* #57 succeeds in replacing the emotional center that had been edited out from the Panther's inaugural story five issues earlier. While neither issue mentions race explicitly, #52 fatally undercuts its potentially hard-hitting critique of police prejudice, whereas #57 has a neighborhood cop criticize the Avengers for ignoring urban blight. Interestingly, even though this criticism applies to the whole team, the story only demands a response from T'Challa. By way of contrast, in the same issue Hawkeye and the Black Widow struggle to integrate romance with their heroic identities (*Av*#5, 6–7)—and Hank Pym tries to find the courage to propose to Janet van Dyne (2). These white heroes enact a familiar drama counterposing the demands of public calling and private life. Only the Black Panther is forced to reconcile competing visions of his calling; he alone must consider who his community really is. We saw earlier how Reed Richards and Steve Rogers challenged T'Challa to reconceptualize himself as more than merely the tribal hero to Wakanda: by taking up the mantle of Avenger, he could fight on behalf of all mankind. But once T'Challa set foot in New York City, Roy Thomas demanded that he reinvent himself a second time, as the hero of black urban America.

This new character concept found expression in a recurrent visual motif: the Panther on the prowl, creature of the asphalt jungle. The title page for *Avengers* #58 depicted the Panther crouching on a wall with an (unrelated) brickwork title, "Even an Android Can Cry." Six months later, the May 1969 issue of *Daredevil* bore the evocative title "The Night of the Panther!" and featured a two-page spread of the Black Panther moving silently over rooftops, Daredevil's kinetic double (#52, 2–3). A similar montage followed in the February 1970 issue of *Avengers*, except this time images of the prowling hero were surmounted by a figurative representation of the Panther's urban identity: a great black cat, big as a building, stalking across the city's skyline, lit by the full moon (#73, 18). Where Kirby's Panther totem in *FF*#52 gave technological expression to primitive superstition, this new spirit-animal suggested a noble beast transplanted to a modern cityscape—implicitly rewriting the character's central paradox without reference to technology. True, the Panther continued to appear in his former guise of science-hero. He also made several visits to his homeland and delivered a speech before the UN General Assembly in ceremonial dress (*Avengers* #59, 6). But when fighting for the soul of the inner city, he eschewed both the gadgetry and the pageantry that were his due as ruler of Wakanda.

More than that, though, on those missions the Panther fought without the help of his white teammates, a thematic echo of the separatist impulse of the Black Power movement. On one particularly memorable occasion from February 1970, T'Challa claimed a special kinship with New York City blacks, denying the moral right of the other Avengers to serve as champions of "his" people: "Those are my people that the Serpents have been beating... killing! And I claim my right to take them ... alone!" (Av#73, 16). With this declaration, T'Challa completed his transformation from Wakandan prince to Harlem activist. We saw earlier how Lee and Kirby sought to counter the expulsion of whites from SNCC with a team-up between T'Challa and Captain America—a team-up that Lee re-created in 1969 when he added the Falcon as a regular in *Captain America*. Thomas took a more daring approach, affiliating the Black Panther with the activities, the cause, and to some extent the ideology of the Black Panther Party—all in order to spotlight moments when the fictional hero dramatically renounced that ideology.

Race, Racism and Division

In this connection, three story arcs stand out from the Panther's stint in *The Avengers*. The first, from March 1969, is by far the least direct in its political messaging. Indeed, its villain, Man-Ape—a hulking black man dressed in the skin of an albino gorilla—sounds and looks like a crude racist caricature. Set in Wakanda, the issue centers on the treachery of M'Baku, a warrior that T'Challa left to rule in his stead. Unsatisfied with mere stewardship, the traitor seizes on an unexpected visit from his liege to put his plan into action. Drugging the other Avengers to get them out of the way, M'Baku assumes the identity of "Man-Ape" by clothing himself in the "forbidden guise of the white gorilla—in our legends the most savage ... most merciless of beasts!" (Av#62, 8). His aim is to defeat the Black Panther before the assembled Wakandan populace and then destroy T'Challa's technological Panther totem, inaugurating a new era of barbarism under the watchful gaze of a giant Gorilla idol hewn from blocks of white stone.

Physically imposing, Man-Ape offers multiple points of contrast with the Black Panther: a strong rather than an agile fighter, a tyrannical rather than enlightened ruler, someone eager to restore "darkness [...] to the primeval jungle" (18). He gives his soldiers standing orders to shoot outsiders, and he accuses T'Challa of having "sold yourself to our white-skinned enemies" (10). Given his name, M'Baku was almost certainly intended as commentary on the wave of brutal dictators seizing power from democratically elected governments across Africa, starting in the mid–1960s with Congo's Mobutu. From this angle, M'Baku's perverse decision to clothe himself in a racist stereotype calls out Mobutu for proving correct the racists who opined that Africans weren't ready to rule themselves. This doesn't account, however, for the unusual color of the animal's fur. Himself a racist, M'Baku dons an ideology lifted from white racists but with the colors reversed. His villainous moniker, "Man-Ape," makes the same point, insofar as it inverts the heroic moniker of Tarzan, that racist fantasy of colonial Africa. Thomas thus complicated Lee and Kirby's utopian vision by using Wakanda to depict the curdling of the postcolonial dream. But the story of Man-Ape likely had a broader resonance, with M'Baku embodying the folly of those so determined in their struggle against "white skinned enemies" that they adopted those enemies' savage hatred: what liberal critics liked to call the "reverse racism" of black radicals.

A year later, Thomas followed up with a Panther-centered story set squarely in the United States—one with a far clearer application to contemporary debates about race. The two-issue arc reprised the Sons of the Serpent, a villainous group created by Stan Lee in 1966 for *The Avengers* #32–33. Mixing elements of the KKK with Hitler's Brownshirts, the Serpents preached hatred of minorities, concealing their identity behind green and orange masks. Lee's story focused on the danger posed to a pluralistic society when ordinary citizens remain silent in the face of intolerance. Despite its powerful message, the story was something of an anachronism. It came to a climax at a well-attended public gathering reminiscent of the anti-Semitic, isolationist America First rally held in Madison Square Garden back in 1941, when Lee was just 18 years old (*Av*#33, 13). Thomas' story updated Lee's midcentury morality tale, replacing its echoing public arena with the echo chamber of a television studio where the rights and wrongs of race are debated between hot-headed black radical Montague Hale and snarling white conservative Dan Dunn. Far from healing the national rift, their debate only exacerbates it, as tracked over the course of the story in the reactions of two cameramen, each of whom only hears the logic of arguments he agrees with (*Av*#73, 5, *Av*#74, 6). We watch this rift spread even into the ranks of the Avengers; the group sits down together to watch Hale debate Dunn, but afterward the Black Panther explodes with anger, insisting (as noted earlier) that the protection of the people of Harlem is his responsibility alone (16). In offering this astute critique of the media, Thomas' point of reference was likely the appearance of Black Panther leader Eldridge Cleaver on William F. Buckley's *Firing Line* on November 13, 1968.

Yet Thomas blamed the media only for exacerbating this rift, not for creating it. His two-part story has an impressively tight structure, with the second issue not merely resolving the tension of the midpoint cliffhanger, but offering new insight into the nature of the problem confronting America. The first issue places the spotlight on the Serpents' racist thuggery—but also on the failure of the white mainstream to take that threat seriously. From their secret lair, a gigantic mechanical snake hidden in the ocean's depths, the Serpents send out teams to beat up black New Yorkers walking alone late at night (*Av*#73, 6). But the victims simply don't seem credible to most whites. We hear this first in the words of professional troll Dan Dunn ("Now, Mr. Hale, tell us more about this alleged assault ... from which you received such microscopic bruises," *Av*#73, 4) but it happens again when the police arrive after an attack on African American singer Monica Lynne ("Take it easy, lady ... no need for hysterics now!" *Av*#73, 14). Even Avenger Janet van Dyne is susceptible, dismissing Hale for failing to speak politely about the outrages he's suffered: "To tell the truth, T'Challa, I found Montague Hale something less than civil!" (*Av*#73, 15).

In these moments, *Avengers* #73 voices a common complaint among 1960s black activists: whites could not perceive or would not acknowledge the sheer magnitude of racism, and this failure was itself a form of oppression. No wonder T'Challa blows up at his teammates. Though they express concern about the Serpents' return, they're still monitoring the situation from their mansion headquarters when the Serpents strike for the second time—an attack that would have succeeded if not for the Panther's protective presence on the streets of Harlem. Hale drives the point home in his effort to radicalize Lynne: "After what the Establishment's done to our people ... after what the Sons of the Serpent did to me...!" (*Av*#73, 5). In much the same way, Eldridge Cleaver dismissed both Democrats and Republicans as "criminal conspiracies against the people" in his televised interview with Buckley ("The Black Panthers" 09:27–09:41). For Hale, as for Cleaver, the structural racism of mainstream society is no different from the outright violence of self-declared racists.

This diagnosis proves premature, however, because the following issue forces a retrospective re-evaluation of everything that happened in *Avengers* #73. The Serpents turn out to have not one but two leaders—none other than Dan Dunn and Montague Hale. The two radicals had been secretly in league all along, for in Thomas' vision extremism feeds upon the outrages perpetrated by its opponents. Seen from this perspective, the real threat to society isn't racism but the loss of the political center. While the story's first issue focuses on T'Challa, his dramatic capture on its final page makes him, in retrospect, not a hero but a tool. With the real Panther chained and fettered in their underwater lair, the Serpents put an ersatz version on the streets in *Avengers* #74 to play the part of a fully radicalized black superhero. In deliberate reference to the revolutionary provocations of the Black Panther Party, this lawless "hero" undertakes retributive attacks on businesses owned by known sympathizers to the Serpents' cause, thereby contributing to the narrative of a nation riven in two.

In place of the angry heroism of Black Power, *Avengers* #74 thus posits the heroism of the political center. Its dispassionate nature is embodied most clearly by the Vision, who, when informed by a mob that he must choose sides, sinks wordlessly into the pavement, choosing to walk in the sewers rather than "walk among" those he hopes to save from their folly (*Av#74*, 7–8). The heroism of the political center is also cooperative, a quality typified by the Avengers' distinctive contributions to their victory in the final conflict: Goliath holds off the mooks, Vision sets the real Panther free, T'Challa unmasks the false Panther, and Wasp and Yellowjacket unmask Hale and Dunn. Even singer Monica Lynne plays a part, knocking Hale and Dunn off-balance, providing T'Challa with an opening for a pair of knockout kicks.

A Lesson in Civil Discourse

As witnessed in the letters page, Marvel believed this story offered serious insight into a pressing political problem and would engender meaningful conversation among fans. Working as series editor, Lee published a letter from reader Keith Pollard in the issue immediately preceding *Avengers* #73 as a teaser for the "bombshell" to follow. The following month Lee attempted to kick off future political discussion of the story by including a lengthy analysis of the ethics of the Black Panther's heroism by reader Esau Simmons. Chances are likely that both letters were received months earlier and had been set to one side in anticipation of Thomas' reworking of the Sons of the Serpent. In his choice of Simmons' letter, Lee showed an unusual openness to wide-ranging political debate, for Simmons offered an implicitly Marxist critique of Marvel's characters: given that "Superheroes, like the police, protect the 'haves' against the 'have-nots,'" why should the Black Panther fight to defend the corrupt American legal system rather than the "real equality" of the "socialist state" that is Wakanda? Lee replied by reaffirming the Panther's faith in the liberal internationalist vision of the Avengers, but he went on to acknowledge the new direction that Thomas had given to the character, suggesting that racism was a greater threat than economic inequality and declaring that the Panther "was born to fight foes like the Sons of the Serpent." This exchange seems to have had its intended effect, inaugurating a debate that dominated the letters column for multiple issues.

Anthony Albensi challenged Simmons' claim that the Panther's duty lay in Wakanda, agreeing with Lee's notion of T'Challa as "a defender of all nations." Many more readers engaged with the political questions raised by Thomas' story, with Lee taking care to publish a diversity of viewpoints. Eric Hayden celebrated *Avengers* #73 for giving credence to the arguments of Montague Hale, signing off with a winking reference to Hale's real-world counterpart: "Yours until T'Challa meets Eldridge Cleaver." For an opposing view, Air Force Sergeant Michael Kuhne objected to issue #73 for its apparent attack upon the political center: "Lay off this 'Establishment business, will ya? The so-called 'Establishment' hasn't done a thing to [Hale's] people since 1965"— a reference to the passage of the Civil Rights Act. From a shade further to the right, Dave Puckett of Cave City, Kentucky, averred that while he was "all against racism" he was tired of all the focus going to the hatred of blacks by whites when there were so many other invidious prejudices in need of attention. Responding to the story's second half, Cecil Hutto praised Thomas for providing a hopeful message, so different from newspapers: "the personifications of bigotry and hate vanquished by your heroes."

In this way, Lee transformed the fanmail page of *Avengers* #77 and #78 into a forum for the discussion of serious issues, with the two parts of Thomas' story functioning something like the assigned reading in a high-school Civics class. If, in the pages of that story, we witness a society torn nearly in two by intemperate debate, on the letters page Lee was proud to showcase Marvel readers contributing to the healing of that national rift through reasoned discussion. As he said in his response to Albensi, "Thanks ... for explaining a part of our viewpoint to reader Simmons. Didn't we say that Marveldom Assembled can defend us better than we can do it for ourselves?" In its echo of the series' battle cry, "Avengers Assemble!," Lee's phrasing suggests a fundamentally heroic conception of the work being done on the letters page. But it also gives away that Lee believed there were right and wrong answers to the questions raised by the comic. Like any good Civics class of that era, seemingly open-ended discussion was intended to reach a predetermined conclusion by the end of class.

The challenge of this approach is that a student will sometimes surprise the teacher just five minutes before the hour. And students in 1970 weren't afraid to challenge the authority of their teachers and professors, having instigated shutdowns of university administration buildings across the nation just two years earlier. To his credit, when Lee received a long letter from one Philip Mallory Jones cataloguing the racist subtext of key lines and images from *Avengers* #74, he published it in full (with the exception, he noted, of a single expletive). Yet the special treatment Lee gave this letter had something in common with the supercilious politeness with which Buckley listened to Cleaver on *Firing Line*. For while Lee gave Jones space to express his views— the entire letters column of *Avengers* #79—Lee refused to meaningfully engage with what Jones had to say, leaving that task to Thomas, whose reply was put off until the next issue.

Jones, who at the time was enrolled in Cornell's MFA writing program (Jones, "About"), seems to have envisioned his letter to Marvel as an offbeat job application. He opened by identifying himself as "a black writer and a long-time reader of your often very sophisticated magazines," and ended by declaring his readiness to come work for the company, to help Lee and

Thomas "bust out of your Middle American Myth bag." Pointing to Thomas' portrait of a black radical in the person of the "clean," well-spoken Montague Hale, Jones suggested that the writer had only created another avatar of "America's mythic negro," a character who "thinks like a white man would imagine he would think if he were black." Though brusque in his phrasing, Jones was almost certainly right that a lack of diversity on its creative staff made it hard for Marvel to engage the deep differences of perspective that defined the racial divide in America. Two years later, Marvel hired African American artist Billy Graham and put him to work on *Luke Cage, Hero for Hire*, and in 1974 the company brought in another black artist, Keith Pollard—the same Keith Pollard whose letter was published in *Avengers* #72. So it's interesting to imagine the alternate timeline that might have unfolded if, during the period of ferment and new hires following his 1972 promotion to Editor-in-Chief, Thomas had taken Jones up on his offer—or recruited some equally outspoken young black writer. But it's also difficult to imagine that happening—not just because the letter's format made it seem like an unending litany of complaints. The fundamental problem was the gulf of perspective that separated Jones' pessimism from Lee's idealized vision of America. Responding to Goliath's outraged exclamation, "The Panther's bein' framed!" (*Av*#74, 2), Jones wrote "True. But assumes that the judicial system is legitimate," after which he went on to question Goliath's faith in the ideal of justice after the "recent conviction of the Chicago Seven and Bobby Seale, not to mention the national repression of the Black Panther Party." The writers that Thomas wound up hiring (all of them young, white, and male: see Howe 125–27) went on to question America's involvement in Vietnam in the pages of *Iron Man* and to depict altered states of consciousness in *Strange Tales*. But it would never have occurred to them to posit the fundamental injustice of the American legal system.

  This gulf of perspective led Lee and Thomas to respond to Jones' admittedly arrogant job application as if it were a systematic critique of the ideological underpinnings of their story. Lee made great show of giving Jones' "thought-provoking" letter its due, printing it in full and enjoining readers to "mull it over" while they waited for Thomas' reply in the following issue. Thomas took a similar tack, opening with a sentence fragment as if to convey his extreme shock in discovering that a black writer had found fault with his sedulously even-handed political vision: "Mixed emotions—and a time of soul-searching." But Thomas did not so much engage with Jones' criticisms as enact a theatrical performance of the wounded artist, speaking "as a, yes, white writer whose sympathy for the justice of the black cause was the major raison d'etre of *Avengers* #73–74." Thomas leapt to the defense of his hard work and good intentions against what he insisted was an unjustified attack: "You assume that you—but not I, who am obviously wallowing in my Middle

American Myth bag, arms a-flutter—have been able to gain such a superior perspective upon the world that you are able to pass unfailing judgment upon matters which are still troubling the hearts and minds of countless Americans of all creeds and colors." From the distance of half a century, this response represents the wholesale breakdown of the intellectual forum that Lee had inaugurated in *The Avengers* letters page just a few issues earlier. Far from offering a haven from the angry recriminations of the Hales and Montagues of the world, the letters page had, in a supremely ironic twist, come to resemble the moment when those two characters nearly fell to blows, shouting accusations past one another: "Communist!" "Racist!" (*Av*#74, 6).

The Decisive Break

In the wake of Jones' letter, Thomas retreated from his ambition to use the Panther to engage with black radicals in the hope of healing the national rift. His ambition was initially stymied by Stan Lee's anxious editorial meddling lest Marvel be perceived as taking sides with the Black Panther Party on the question of police harassment. Later efforts, likely coordinated with his editor, worked to affiliate the hero with uncontroversial elements of both the Black Panther Party and the larger Black Power movement: in particular, their focus on addressing urban blight and improving education in neighborhood schools. This set up the drama of the Sons of the Serpent, with the Black Panther functioning in two distinct ways as a commentary on black radicalism. On the one hand, T'Challa's insistence on fighting the Serpents alone suggested the seductive folly of the Black Panther Party's divisive ideology. On the other hand, T'Challa's pointed dismissal of Black Panther Party stand-in Montague Hale suggested that righteous anger over instances of outright racism need not result in wholesale conversion to the Panthers' way of thinking. In sum, by acknowledging the reality of racism in *Avengers* #73, Thomas sought to appeal to readers sympathetic to the Panthers, setting them up to recognize, in the following issue, the danger posed to society by radicalism. But Jones' letter confronted Thomas with a reader whose radicalism made him immune to the blandishments of this morality play. For all the points of critique that Jones listed, his letter stood itself as evidence of a far more fundamental shortcoming, the comic's failure to bridge the gulf between its liberal white writer and a radical black reader.

So Thomas stopped trying to reach people sympathetic to the radical vision of the Black Panther Party. His last major Panther-centric story ran in *Daredevil* #69, just two months after Jones' letter ran in *Avengers* #79. T'Challa undertook this side-mission while his teammates split up to tackle other challenges. That split-up, in *Avengers* #80, was itself thematically significant, an effort to demonstrate how self-righteous idealism can threaten the unity of a group—or, indeed, a nation. Alongside Thomas' response to Jones ran a story largely taken up with infighting among the heroes over the question of which one of several perils most deserved the group's attention. Iron Man testifies about the menace presented by Zodiac, a world-spanning supervillain group that "none but the Avengers can hope to stop" (6). This appeal to reason is countered by an appeal to emotion delivered by the Black Panther: organized crime is "waging battles every day for the minds—the bodies—the very souls of kids like the ones I teach!" (7). Into the midst of this disagreement enters a hero likely inspired by the American Indian Movement, founded in 1968: Red Wolf seeks to avenge himself upon Cornelius Van Lunt, a millionaire who killed his parents and stole his ancestral lands. If the heroes' range of ambitions evokes the variety of causes embraced by the New Left, the heat of their discussion references the fraught politics that increasingly divided those young activists in the late 1960s and early 70s. Debate quickly gives way to personal attacks and recriminations, as when Goliath suggests that organized crime is really a job for the police and the Scarlet Witch counters by questioning the giant's heroism: "The Panther is right! It's a job for everyone—or are you so high up that you don't care about such things any longer?" (7). There is even a hint of the problematics raised by Jones in his letter. Vision had earlier prevented Red Wolf from killing in the name of vengeance; when he pledges to "help you bring [Lunt] alive to justice," the young man snarls, "Justice? The white man's justice?" (17) As the spirit of altercation reaches fever pitch, Captain America steps in to suggest that each Avenger should follow his conscience (18). But while this prevents the group from coming to blows, it raises the troubling possibility that the Avengers will part ways, never to reunite (20). Like America itself—but unlike the Fantastic Four or the X-Men—the Avengers were bound together by little more than a shared vision. As Thomas observed toward the end of his letter to Jones, the great "question of the 70s—the question which might well decide the fate of the nation in this decade—was 'Will the center hold?'"

A different crisis occupied the Black Panther in the pages of *Daredevil*. T'Challa described his target as "organized crime" in *Avengers* #80, but the criminals turned out to be the Thunderbolts, a "hate-crew" (5) plainly modeled on the Black Panther Party. Sporting sunglasses and toting automatic rifles, its members spout divisive rhetoric, wielding the epithet "Uncle Tom" like a truncheon (on page 5—artist Gene Colan gave this metaphor visual expression). Whereas in earlier episodes Thomas had placed his Black Panther in somewhat ambiguous relation to the Party, here at last T'Challa directly confronts a black paramilitary organization. The contrast could not be more explicit. The Panthers—or, rather, the "Thunderbolts"—despise the Panther no less than he despises them: "Well well well, if it aint—the Panther!

The original Establishment Black Man himself!" to which T'Challa replies, "Don't try to palm off that 'Establishment' jargon on me, friend! I'm old enough to tell the difference between a dissenter and a criminal!" (18). With that ringing condemnation, Thomas turned a vital corner in his treatment of black radicalism.

The Thunderbolts of *Daredevil* #69 lack a meaningful ideology; their distinct perspective on the world is really just jargon—words and phrases used to condemn anyone with the courage to stand up to their willful criminal acts. Back in *Avengers* #73 Thomas had made an effort to explore what ordinary black citizens like Monica Lynne found attractive in the ideology of radicals like Montague Hale. *Daredevil* #69, by contrast, presents the Thunderbolts in a wholly unattractive light: criminals who pay off night watchmen so they can steal from a warehouse (3); bullies who win new members through intimidation (8). As T'Challa comments, "Those vermin aren't interested in Black Power—only in Thunderbolt power!" (11). In fact, though, T'Challa himself no longer seems interested in Black Power. Whereas in a June 1970 story he was teaching schoolchildren about their proud African heritage (*Av*#77, 12), just four months later in this October 1970 story he's still working in that all-black school, but now he's doing a unit on the Mayflower Pilgrims (*DD*#69, 11–12).

A Fresh Start

This was indeed a period of rapid change for Marvel's Black Panther. Six months further on, the April 1971 *Avengers* #87 reprised his 1966 origin story by way of valediction. The issue's ending was somewhat ambiguous, with the hero trying to decide between remaining a "ghetto teacher and crime-battling Panther" in Harlem or returning to rule as the "true heir" in Wakanda. But its title signaled which choice would be imposed upon him, urging "Look Homeward, Avenger!" After that, T'Challa dropped out of sight for almost a year, eventually cropping up in Thomas' script for the February 1972 *Fantastic Four* #102. That story's fictional setting, Rudyarda, may have been a stand-in for Rhodesia, though the focus on T'Challa's unjust imprisonment suggests a reference to the celebrated cause of Mandela and other ANC leaders in South Africa. Either way, with this story Thomas finished un-doing his transformation of T'Challa, returning him to his original sphere of reference in postcolonial Africa. A year and a half later, in September 1973, the hero began his run in Don McGregor's *Jungle Action, with a yearlong story* set wholly in Wakanda.

It's possible that this reversal of course, from Harlem back to Africa, was imposed on Thomas from above. *Daredevil* #69 ended with both heroes pledging to continue their pursuit of the Thunderbolts in hope of finding out the group's secretive leader, a task precluded by T'Challa's return to Africa. What's more, even as that story pointedly shut down the Panther's connections with the Black Panther Party, it reaffirmed T'Challa's vocation as a schoolteacher, going so far as to give him a civilian identity, "Luke Charles"—a name which to my knowledge was never used again. To this, one might add the evidence of the *Avengers* #87 ending, which practically begged readers to write in to save the Black Panther from retiring to Wakanda. If any readers did so, Stan Lee didn't publish their letters. Just two letters appear on the topic, neither of them much concerned about the Panther's departure: Nelson Fox liked the expanded origin story but demanded equal treatment for Pietro and the Scarlet Witch, while Jim Canepa praised the realism of a king having little time for adventuring.

Yet if Lee was the principal mover in the decision to return T'Challa to Africa, if the hero's revival in *Jungle Tales* could only take place after Thomas took over as Editor-in-Chief, nonetheless it's hard to avoid the impression that, by the end of his stint writing the Black Panther, Roy Thomas was out of patience with the Black Panther Party and their many sympathizers. What started optimistically with a story on police violence ended sardonically with the Hulk destroying the residence of his wealthy supporters. It's all well and good to sympathize with the Hulk from a distance, as a fictional character, but it's quite another thing to invite him into your home. Early in his run, Thomas hoped to find accommodation with black radicals by reaching out in the name of reason, but in his final stories we encounter them as bullies, as "vermin," and, finally, as a brooding menace.

Notes

1. I base this account on Christopher Priest's online memoir, *Adventures in the Funnybook Game*. Priest lists Keith Pollard, Ron Wilson, and Billy Graham as possible contenders for the first black artist at Marvel, and claims that he himself was the company's first black editor (and, later, its first black writer). Working from this list, I obtained dates from the Grand Comics Database (comics.org): Priest's first credits were in 1978, Pollard's in 1974, Wilson's in 1973, and Graham's in 1969—though Graham didn't start work at Marvel until 1972, when he drew the cover for the third issue of *Luke Cage: Hero for Hire*.

2. The arc spanned from *ToS* #97–99 to *Captain America* #100. The new title opened with issue #100 rather than #1, continuing the numbering from *Tales of Suspense*.

3. As documented by articles in the *Chicago Tribune* ("Negroes") and the *New York Times* (T. Johnson).

4. For two examples, see the *LA Times*' editorial, "'Why Me,' Wails Draft Bait Clay" or Art Buchwald's satirical column proposing that Ali be airlifted into enemy territory "to bore the Vietcong to death."

Works Cited

Albensi, Anthony. Untitled Fan Letter. *The Avengers* 78, Jul. 1970.
Bernstein, Jamie. "The Time My Parents 'Took a Knee' for the Black Panthers." *HuffPost*, 18 Oct. 2017.

Bingham, Howard, and Max Wallace. *Muhammad Ali's Greatest Fight: Cassius Clay vs. the United States of America*. M. Evans & Co., 2012.
"The Black Panthers." *Firing Line*. Interview with Eldridge Cleaver, hosted by William F. Buckley. KQED, San Francisco, 13 Nov. 1968. Hoover Institution Library & Archives, Stanford U.
"Black Power Idea Long in Planning." *New York Times*, 5 Aug. 1966, 1. ProQuest Historical Newspapers.
"Black Power Prophet: Stokely Carmichael." *New York Times*, 5 Aug. 1966, 10. ProQuest Historical Newspapers.
Brown, Christopher, Brandon McCasland, Mandy Paris and Sachi Sekimoto. "Walking Through Wakanda: A Critical Multimodal Analysis of Afrofuturism in the Black Panther Comic Book." *Media Across the African Diaspora: Content, Audiences, and Influence*, edited by Omotayo O. Banjo, Routledge, 2018.
Buchwald, Art. "Capitol Punishment…: Project X (Malcolm)." *Washington Post*, 24 Feb. 1966. ProQuest Historical Newspapers.
Canepa, Jim. Untitled Fan Letter. *The Avengers* 92, Sep. 1971.
"Capitol Is Invaded: State Police Halt Armed Negro Band." *Sacramento Bee*, 2 May 1967. Article text republished online at www.sacbee.com/news/local/history/article148667224.html, though without the original headline.
Carson, Clayborne. *In Struggle: SNCC and the Black Awakening of the 1960s*. Harvard University Press, 1995.
Clay, Henry B. Untitled Fan Letter. *Fantastic Four* 56, Nov. 1966.
"Clay Plans to Apologize in Chicago for Remarks About Draft Classification." *New York Times*, 22 Feb. 1966, 17. ProQuest Historical Newspapers.
Curtis, Charlotte. "Black Panther Philosophy Is Debated at the Bernsteins." *New York Times*, 15 Jan. 1970, 48. ProQuest Historical Newspapers.
Cushing, Lincoln. "The Women Behind the Black Panther Party Logo." *Design Observer*, Feb. 1, 2018.
Eskenazi, Gerald. "Tickets for Bout Moving Slowly." *New York Times*, 29 Mar. 1966, 47. ProQuest Historical Newspapers.
"Excerpts from Paper on Which the 'Black Power' Philosophy is Based." *New York Times*, 5 Aug. 1966, 10. ProQuest Historical Newspapers.
Fox, Nelson. Untitled Fan Letter. *The Avengers* 91, Aug. 1971.
Greene, Ken. Untitled Fan Letter. *Fantastic Four* 55, Oct. 1966.
Hayden, Eric. Untitled Fan Letter. *The Avengers* 77, Jun. 1970.
Holm, Michael. *America in the World: Ideology and U.S. Foreign Policy, 1944–1950*. 2013. Boston University, Ph.D. dissertation.
Hoover Archivist. Item Description. "The Black Panthers." *Firing Line*. KQED, San Francisco, 13 Nov. 1968. Hoover Institution Library & Archives, Stanford University.
Howe, Sean. *Marvel Comics: The Untold Story*. HarperCollins, 2013.
Hutto, Cecil. Untitled Fan Letter. *The Avengers* 78, Jul. 1970.
In the Heat of the Night. Directed by Norman Jewison from a script by Stirling Silliphant, United Artists, 1967.
Isaacson, Lawrence. Untitled Fan Letter. *The Avengers* 54, Jul. 1968.
Jefferson, David. "The Black Panther: An Archetype, Not a Stereotype." *The Collected Jack Kirby Collector: Celebrating the Life and Career of the King*, vol 1. Two Morrows Publishing, 2004, 215–216. Originally published in *The Jack Kirby Collector* #9 (Feb. 1996).
Johnson, Linda Lee. Untitled Fan Letter. *Fantastic Four* 57, Dec. 1966.
Johnson, Thomas A. "Black Panthers Picket a School." *New York Times*, Sep. 13, 1966, 38. ProQuest Historical Newspapers.
Jones, Philip Mallory. Untitled Fan Letter. *The Avengers* 79, Aug. 1970.
_____. "About." *Philip Malory Jones*. www.philipmaloryjones.com. 2018. Accessed May 15, 2019.
Kuhne, Michael. Untitled Fan Letter. *The Avengers* 77, Jun. 1970.
Lee, Stan. Response to Henry Clay. *Fantastic Four* 56. Nov. 1966.
_____. Response to Kieth Pollard. *The Avengers* 72. Jan. 1970.
_____. Response to Esau Simmons. *The Avengers* 73. Feb. 1970.

_____. Response to Anthony Albensi. *The Avengers 78*. Jul. 1970.
_____. Editorial frame for Philip Mallory Jones' letter. *The Avengers 79*. Aug. 1970.
_____. "Stan Lee's Amazing Marvel Interview." Ed. Roy Thomas. *Alter Ego* #104 (Aug. 2011). Transcription of a 2005 interview.
Lee, Stan, and Gene Colan. "The Coming of … the Falcon!" *Captain America* #117 (Sep. 1969).
Lee, Stan, and Jack Kirby. "This Monster Unmasked!" *Captain America* #100 (Apr. 1968).
_____. "A Skrull Walks Among Us!" *Fantastic Four* #18 (Sep. 1963).
_____. "The Mysterious Molecule Man!" *Fantastic Four* #20 (Nov. 1963).
_____. "The Black Panther!" *Fantastic Four* #52 (Jul. 1966).
_____. "The Way It Began…!" *Fantastic Four* #53 (Aug. 1966).
_____. "Klaw: The Murderous Master of Sound!" *Fantastic Four* #56 (Nov. 1966).
_____. "Divide—and Conquer!" *Fantastic Four Annual* #5 (Nov. 1967).
_____. "And So It Begins—!" *Tales of Suspense* #97 (Jan. 1968).
_____. "The Claws of the Panther!" *Tales of Suspense* #98 (Feb. 1968).
_____. "The Man Who Lived Twice!" *Tales of Suspense* #99 (Mar. 1968).
Life Editorial Staff. "The Hopeful Launching of a Proud and Free Nigeria." *Life*, 26 Sep. 1960, 54–74.
Los Angeles Times Editorial Staff. "'Why Me?' Wails Draft Bait Clay" *Los Angeles Times*, 18 Feb. 1966, B1. ProQuest Historical Newspapers.
"Negroes Will Police Police in Detroit," *Chicago Tribune*, Oct. 29, 1966, 11. ProQuest Historical Newspapers.
New York Times Editorial Staff. "False Note on Black Panthers." *New York Times*, 16 Jan. 1970, 38. ProQuest Historical Newspapers.
Podair, Jerald. *The Strike that Changed New York: Blacks, Whites, and the Ocean Hill-Brownsville Crisis*. Yale University Press, 2002.
Priest, Christopher. "Adventures in the Funnybook Game, Chapter Three: The Last Time Priest Discussed Race in Comics." (May 2002). www.digitalpriest.com/legacy/comics/chips.html.
Puckett, Dave. Untitled Fan Letter. *The Avengers* 77, Jun. 1970.
Roberts, Gene. "2 Rights Groups Promote All-Negro Slates for Local Elections in the South." *New York Times*, 23 Jan. 1966, 73. ProQuest Historical Newspapers.
_____. "The Story of Snick: From Freedom High to Black Power." *New York Times*, 25 Sep. 1966, 242–249. ProQuest Historical Newspapers.
Simmons, Esau. Untitled Fan Letter. *The Avengers* 73, Feb. 1970.
Stern, Sol. "The Call of the Black Panthers." *New York Times*, Aug. 6, 1967, 186–191. ProQuest Historical Newspapers.
Thomas, Roy. "Death Calls for the Arch-Heroes!" *The Avengers* #52 (May 1968).
_____. "…And Deliver Us from—the Masters of Evil!" *The Avengers* #54 (Jul. 1968).
_____. "Behold … the Vision!" *The Avengers* #57 (Oct. 1968).
_____. "Even an Android Can Cry." *The Avengers* #58 (Nov. 1968).
_____. "The Name Is … Yellowjacket!" *The Avengers* #59 (Dec. 1968).
_____. "The Sting of the Serpent" *The Avengers* #73 (Feb. 1970).
_____. "Pursue the Panther!" *The Avengers* #74 (Mar. 1970).
_____. "Heroes for Hire!" *The Avengers* #77 (Jun. 1970).
_____. "The Man-Ape Always Strikes Twice!" *The Avengers* #78 (Jul. 1970).
_____. "The Coming of Red Wolf!" *The Avengers* #80 (Sep. 1970).
_____. Untitled response to Philip Mallory Jones' letter. *The Avengers* #80 (Sep. 1970).
_____. "Look Homeward, Avenger!" *The Avengers* #87 (Apr. 1971).
_____. "Night of the Panther!" *Daredevil* #52 (May 1969).
_____. "A Life on the Line." *Daredevil* #69 (Oct. 1970).
_____. "Three Stood Together!" *Fantastic Four* #102 (Feb. 1972).
_____. "They Shoot Hulks, Don't They?" *The Incredible Hulk* #142 (Aug. 1971).
Turner, Wallace. "A Gun Is Power, Black Panther Says." *New York Times*, May 21, 1967, 66. ProQuest Historical Newspapers.
Wolfe, Tom. "Radical Chic: That Party at Lenny's." *New York*, Jun. 8, 1970. Republished online at nymag.com/news/features/46170.

Wakanda Forever! (Except for That One Time...)

The Black Panther Party, Apartheid and the Brief Identity Crisis of the Black LEOPARD?!?

Christopher Maverick

If your first exposure to superheroes was the year 2018, you might be excused for assuming that Marvel Comics' the Black Panther was anything other than a top-tier character. You would probably be amazed to learn that there was a time when he was not even considered a B-List property. While his debut film earned the highest box office for a solo lead character in a Marvel Cinematic Universe film to date, the concept was originally considered economically unviable and production was delayed for over a decade while the studio focused on films starring White protagonists. However, since its release, it has been lauded as a victory for African American representation in film (Wallace). Its African American writers, director and predominantly black cast are pointed to as proof that a film need not be white in order to achieve mainstream four quadrant success.[1] The Black Panther's "Wakanda Forever" salute and hand gesture used throughout the movie quickly entered the pop cultural lexicon as a sort of spiritual successor to the classic "Black Power" raised fist. The character is now idolized and immediately recognizable as the signifier of Black pride that he was always meant to be.

Always, except for that one time in 1972 when for a single very confusing issue, with little explanation, the Black Panther disavowed his own name and began calling himself "the Black Leopard." This was done to distance Black Panther from African American politics, while at the same time paradoxically taking a strong stance against systemic racism and oppression both in the United States and abroad. Almost immediately afterwards, the character reclaimed his identity, again with minimal rationalization. This brief period in T'Challa's history not only highlights the racial tensions and fears that America faced throughout the late 1960s and early '70s, but also the anxieties that white comic creators of the time felt when attempting to address these complex social issues.

Although the Black Panther character is often assumed to be related to the political party of the same name, his first appearance actually predates the founding of the most prominent incarnation of the Black Panther Party by several months. T'Challa was created by the legendary comics team of Stan Lee and Jack Kirby in *Fantastic Four* #52, cover dated July 1966, specifically to address the lack of ethnic representation and diversity in superhero comics of the day. While their intention may have been to take a progressive stance in the burgeoning civil rights movement, they also desired to remain apolitical from a corporate perspective. Lee has claimed that he was unaware of any political connotations of the name at the time and it was simply a "a strange coincidence" (Free and Lee 38). That said, by the end of the 1960s, the words "Black Panther Party" had achieved enough notoriety in the public zeitgeist that public association of the Marvel Comics character with the political movement would have to be expected. In fact, actor Wesley Snipes, who was for some time attached to star as the character in a film adaptation, cites the misidentification of the name as a connection to the controversial political party as one of the primary reasons that initial attempts to launch the film failed (Parker and Couch). The confusion is understandable for reasons beyond the name and the fact that both came to prominence at nearly the same time.

The first group to be unofficially called the Black Panthers was more properly known as the Lowndes County Freedom Organization (LCFO), an Alabama-based political activism group. The LCFO was founded in March 1965 as a political party with the express purpose of registering African Americans to vote and ultimately achieve elected representation within the then all-white government of Lowndes County, which at the time boasted an eighty percent black population. While the LCFO ultimately failed to elect a black candidate at that time, as the United States' first political party devoted solely to the advancement of African Americans, they directly inspired the formation of similar groups in other cities.

The LCFO and many of the other local groups became known colloquially known as "Black Panthers" after the LCFO's panther logo. LCFO founder John Hulette recalls that the panther logo was chosen because it was "a vicious animal ... that never bothers anything, but when you start pushing him, it moves backwards ... into his corner, and then he comes out to destroy everything that's before him" (qtd. in Austin location 639). Hulette argued that this was symbolic of the way the blacks of Lowndes County had been mistreated and their intention to fight back. While the group did not specifically advocate violence, they were not averse to it, with Hulette noting that they were "out to take power legally, but if stopped by the government from doing it legally, we're going to take it the way that everyone else took it including the way the Americans took it in the American Revolution" (qtd. in Austin location 639). The LCFO's choice of the panther symbol seems particularly prescient towards this stance. It signified both a willingness to engage in violence if pushed and a declaration of ferocity when that violence occurs.

While the LCFO was influential within the African American community of the 1960s, particularly in the South, it is conceivable that Stan Lee, a Jewish man living and working in New York City, might have been unaware of the details of their movement and certainly of their nickname when he and Kirby created their first African superhero character less than a year later. If he had heard the term in passing, it seems unlikely that he would have consciously chosen it for a character in his company's flagship publication, *Fantastic Four*. Instead, this is more likely an example of parallel thinking. Like Hulette, Lee would have seen the panther as not only an indigenous creature of Africa and therefore a strong signifier of blackness, but also as a powerful predator capable of defending his people and ideology, the very character traits that defined T'Challa from his earliest appearances.

Huey P. Newton and Bobby Seale founded the Black Panther Party for Self-Defense (BPP) in Oakland, California, in October 1966, several months after the first appearance of the comic book character. Although they were also likely unaware at the time of the coincidental naming of the comic character, they were certainly inspired by the LCFO and took their name directly in reference to the LCFO panther symbol and the growing association of the name "Black Panthers" with Black Power. Unlike Hulette, Newton and Seale didn't see violence as a last resort so much as an inevitability. Events like the February 1965 assassination of Malcolm X and the August 1965 Watts Riots in Los Angeles had convinced them that the Black community needed to be able to defend itself from deadly attacks. Thus, their version of the Black Panther Party not only focused on advancing the political stance, but also preparing the community so that, like the panther of their symbol, when "backed into a corner" they could "strike out" (qtd. in Austin location 1043). To the BPP, this meant proactively arming and training the black populace. Where the LCFO's public mission was to work within the system, so long as the system was working, the BPP considered the system to have already failed. They felt that salvation for the black community could only come if it took matters into its own hands. Where the LCFO was preparing for a possible revolution, to the BPP, the revolution had already begun.

Though the "self-defense" portion of the name called immediate attention to itself, the BPP's platform was in actuality quite diverse. In addition to their support of political candidates and continuing the voter registration drives started by the LCFO, they also organized petition drives, promoted racial awareness, provided healthcare services including testing for sickle cell anemia, as well as provided education and schooling opportunities for children and other community outreach and service programs. However, they gained the most notoriety for their anti-establishment reputation. Newton, whose official title within the BPP was Minister of Defense, was openly mistrustful of law-enforcement. Not only did he advocate arming the black community, he organized the BPP to patrol the streets as watchdogs against police brutality. They did so while carrying shotguns and clad in berets and black leather, which gave them a distinct revolutionary appearance.

This paramilitary styling of black men—already considered dangerous by white America's inherent racial biases—overshadowed any good that the group was doing in the public eye. In October 1968, Newton was detained in a traffic stop by the Oakland Police Department. An altercation occurred while he was in custody that left Officer John Frey dead and Officer Herbert Heanes and Newton both with gunshot wounds. Though no weapon was ever found on Newton, he was convicted of voluntary manslaughter and shooting Frey with the officer's own gun. Though the conviction was later overturned on appeal, the controversy would follow Newton for the rest of his life. Similar altercations would befall other members of the BPP over the following years as their watchdog activities brought them into conflict with law enforcement officials. In 1969, Director of the FBI J. Edgar Hoover declared that "the Black Panther Party without question, represents the greatest threat to internal security of the country" (qtd. in Austin location 344). Regardless of the validity of the allegations that the BPP faced, it was clear that public trepidation surrounding the group was high by the early 1970s.

It is thus unsurprising that Marvel Comics would consider distancing themselves from association with the name and they officially did so in *Fantastic Four* #119, cover dated February 1972. The story, written by Roy Thomas and drawn by John Buscema, with Lee now serving as editor, saw Ben Grimm and Johnny Storm, two members of the titular team, team up with T'Challa who leaps into battle now calling himself "the Black Leopard" (13). When later questioned about the name change, T'Challa explains, "I contemplate a return to **your** country, Ben Grimm, where the latter term has—**political** connotations. I neither confirm **nor** condone those who have taken up the name—but **T'Challa** is a law unto **himself**. Hence the **new** name—a **minor** point, at best, since the panther **is** a leopard" (14).[2] The explanation seems simple enough, and likely reflects the real-life thinking that Thomas, a white writer, had for making the name change. However, closer inspection of the dialogue Thomas uses to announce the change, as well as details of the narrative that frame it, reveal not only the apprehension of white America towards the real-life BPP, but also the neoliberal anxiety of reconciling the decidedly progressive and pro-social stories that Thomas and Marvel Comics were trying to create with selling those stories to that same apprehensive and predominantly white audience.

Nonetheless, regardless of how altruistically T'Challa's rationalization was intended, it appears to sacrifice the agency of his pre-established character. Within his fictional history, the mantle of the Black Panther is the title given to the king of the tribes of Wakanda. As sovereign, the Black Panther is bound to protect and defend his country, both as political ruler and as a champion against physical threats. Previous comics explain that the mantle has been passed on for generations through hundreds if not thousands of years. It is his birthright, inherited from his father and grandfather before him. It therefore signifies not only his office but also his cultural heritage and his familial line. His rationalization therefore appears incongruous. In choosing to abandon the mantle, he is, in effect, abandoning his family name. While the decision to renounce an ancestral claim for a hero characterized almost entirely by his heritage for personal reasons could be seen as a powerful one, Thomas attempts to downplay its significance in this narrative. Indeed, the text bolds the word "minor" as if to underscore that the Panther name, and therefore T'Challa's heritage, is largely irrelevant to him.

Furthermore, T'Challa emphasizes that he has made this decision because he is considering returning to "**your** country ... where the term has **political** connotations" referring to the Caucasian Grimm and Storm's homeland of the United States. This implies that he is renouncing his birthright not because he is personally offended by the racial politics, but instead because he is worried about the white perception that he is associated with the BPP *on the chance* that he elects to journey to the United States, a decision that he has not yet made. Here, Thomas inadvertently portrays T'Challa as privileging foreign white comfort over his own politics and those of the nation he rules. This America-centrism undermines the character. Moreover, the stance that T'Challa is neither condemning nor condoning the politics of the BPP seems particularly out of place given that the rest of that particular comic is an allegorical treatise against apartheid.

The racial tensions and systemic oppression that the LCFO and the BPP stood against were not localized to America. In fact, it was amplified a thousandfold in the country of South Africa. Beginning in 1948, the South African government implemented a system of laws and policies known as apartheid[3] that enforced racial segregation and discrimination and privileged the minority white population in the overwhelmingly majority black country (DeSilver). Laws of apartheid included racial registration, prohibition of interracial marriage and miscegenation, restrictions on black property ownership, restriction and eventual prohibition of non-whites holding political office, and ultimately the effective disenfranchisement of non-white voters.

Apartheid was opposed by the African National Congress (ANC), South Africa's predominantly black political party. The ANC was primarily devoted to non-violent protests as a means of bringing awareness and calling for increased rights for the black populace. On March 21, 1960, one such protest rally tuned violent as a protest in Sharpeville, Transvaal, saw police open fire on protesters they were unable to disperse. This resulted in the deaths of 69 people and injury of 180 others. Though the Sharpeville massacre was denounced by the many other countries, with the United Nations officially condemning the South African police and government with Resolution 134 on April 1, 1960, the South African government responded by banning the legal existence of the ANC. In response a year later, Nelson Mandela, president of the ANC's Transvaal province branch, and a prominent organizer within the organization, founded the Umkhonto we Sizwe[4] (MK), an armed spin-off of the ANC devoted to ending apartheid through whatever means necessary, issuing a manifesto that stated:

> The time comes in the life of any nation when there remain only two choices—submit or fight. That time has now come to South Africa. We shall not submit, and we have no choice but to hit back by all means in our power in defense of our people, our future, and our freedom.

Naturally, the South African government classified the MK as a terrorist organization, a move backed by the United States. An arrest warrant was issued for Mandela and in 1962 he was imprisoned. During his trial he gave a speech declaring his devotion to the cause of racial equality stating "I have fought against white domination, and I have fought against black domination. I have cherished the ideal of a democratic and free society in which all persons will live together in harmony and with equal opportunities. It is an ideal which I hope to live for and to see realized. But if it needs be, it is an ideal for which I am prepared to die" (qtd. in Simpson location 2567). In 1964 he was convicted and sentenced to life imprisonment for conspiring to overthrow the government. From prison Mandela was seen as a political prisoner and became an icon for civil rights and racial equality across the world.[5] In effect, the plight of Mandela, the ANC and the MK illustrates exactly the contemporary racial fears that led Newton to found the BPP in the first place.

While *Fantastic Four* #119 never mentions the word "apartheid" or the country of South Africa by name, it presents a clear allegory for the state of racial affairs in that country during the early 1970s. The story begins with the eponymous heroes receiving a video call from Taku, T'Challa's Chief

Advisor. Taku explains that several days ago two thieves stole a piece of Wakanda's advanced technology called the Vibrotron. The invention effectively serves as a McGuffin in this story, but Taku notes that it is dangerous enough that if it fell into the wrong hands, it would threaten the safety of the world. The Wakandans discovered that the thieves had fled Wakanda to the neighboring Republic of Rudyarda. T'Challa pursued the criminals and had not been heard from in two days. Like Wakanda, Rudyarda is fictional, though it is a clear analogue for South Africa as Taku explains that it is "one of the last remaining strongholds of **white supremacy** upon our continent" (6).[6] Ben Grimm, the member of the Fantastic Four also known as the Thing, admits that he had previously read about Rudyarda, but forgotten. Taku retorts "you can **afford** to forget it. My people **cannot**" (6),[7] calling attention to the racial privilege that Ben, and by extension the presumed white American reader, has to ignore racial injustice. Ben, along with Johnny Storm, also known as the Human Torch, then agrees to depart for Rudyarda to search for and rescue T'Challa.

Once in Rudyarda, Ben and Johnny are struck by the blatant discrimination and segregation. A cab driver initially refuses to give them a ride because he mistakes Ben's mutated orange hide for the brown skin of a black African. They are shocked to see signs labeled "Europeans" and "Coloreds" denoting separate entrances to buildings.[8] After following a series of leads, they find T'Challa who has been arrested for being a black man walking the streets of Rudyarda without registration papers. Storm uses his flame powers to melt through T'Challa's cell and help him escape. As the three battle guards, it is at this point that T'Challa first announces himself as the Black Leopard and explains to Ben and Johnny his reasoning behind his name change and how he came to be jailed for being without papers. He notes that he was unable to "convince the authorities that my hidden **costume** made me anything more than the member of some secret **terrorist sect**" (15).[9] In the diegesis of the comic, Rudyarda is the neighboring country to Wakanda. T'Challa should be quite recognizable to law enforcement officials. They should be very much aware of his position as head of state and his Black Panther uniform would be public knowledge. Thomas's emphasis here connecting the uniform to terrorism in the minds of the authorities recalls the connection of Mandela to the MK in the real South Africa. This interlude where T'Challa explains his plight to Ben and Johnny, while breaking the action of the main narrative, serves to underscore the story's function as racial awareness allegory to the reader.

While Thomas's narrative clearly takes a progressive stance towards 1970s racial dynamics, it is not without problematic racial stances. Aside from T'Challa's aforementioned privileging of white comfort above his familial heritages and national pride, much of the story is predicated on Ben and

Johnny's white experience in coming to understand the racial injustices that T'Challa and people who look like him face, rather than T'Challa's racial challenges directly. The Fantastic Four are the very definition of white saviors here. In one troubling scene, Ben and Johnny locate one of the two thieves, Nathan Kumalo, in Rudyarda before they find T'Challa. Kumalo's partner, the white Jeth Robards, double-crossed him once they entered Rudyarda and absconded with the Vibrotron. Since Kumalo, like T'Challa, is a black man without papers, he is forced to stay confined to an apartment for fear of similarly being arrested. Once Ben and Johnny have questioned Kumalo and he wonders if he is going to be arrested sent to prison, Johnny simply responds "you're already **in** one, Kumalo—or hadn't you **noticed?**" (11)[10] and walks away, implying that the racial injustice that Kumalo will undoubtedly face is appropriate because he is a criminal. For Johnny, it seems, liberty must be preserved only for the most moral of black men. While he is devoted to rescuing T'Challa, his friend and a hero, he is not concerned with affording due process to a man Johnny has already prejudged as guilty. Thus, the story implies, blackness is only deserving of equality when it agrees to work within the pre-established boundaries of white society. Perhaps knowing this lends even more motivation for T'Challa to subjugate his heritage in favor of white comfort.

Once Johnny and Ben free T'Challa, the three team up to track down Robards and destroy the Vibrotron to ensure that it never falls into the wrong hands. As they are congratulating each other on a successful mission, Ben once again notices the separate entrances to a building for "Coloreds" and "Europeans" and decides that the very concept has infuriated him enough. He decides to take a stance against racism and oppression and uses his superhuman strength to destroy the wall and both doors, stating that there's "**some things you just gotta get out of your system!**" (21)[11] emphasizing the final word as if to call attention to the fact that he is not only assuaging his own conscience but striking out against the systemic racism of apartheid state in general. He understands that the gesture is symbolic and will not simply end the racist regime in and of itself, telling T'Challa "I feel a little bit **better** about every thin' now. Not **much** though" (21).[12]

This exchange shows important growth for Ben. In the beginning of the story, when Taku first mentions Rudyarda's government codified white supremacy, Ben admits that he had read about the country but forgotten (6). Now, after seeing the horrors of racism with his own eyes he is moved to action. When T'Challa struggles to find the words to thank him, Ben continues "I didn't do that for **you**.... I did it ... for **me**" (21).[13] Much of the Ben Grimm's struggle throughout the history of the *Fantastic Four* comic's publication has surrounded his position as Other. His mutated rocky orange skin immediately separates him from humanity and he thinks of himself as a monster. However, Thomas reminds us that despite how Ben looks, he is still a white man and enjoys the racial privilege that goes with it. The cab driver that initially mistook Ben for black immediately apologizes upon realizing who he is (9); however, when a Rudyardan police officer thanking Ben and Johnny for their assistance realizes that T'Challa has assisted them in the destruction of the Vibrotron and therefore saved the world, the officer's first inclination is still to point out that T'Challa is technically breaking the law by being in the wrong part of town after curfew (21). Ben understands that if he can be a human being, deserving dignity, despite his skin of orange rock, then T'Challa should be no less because of his brown pigmented flesh. It is this hypocrisy that ultimately spurs Ben to action and the destruction of the separate but equal entrances. His act of defiance is literally to break down a racial barrier.

However, in a sense Ben's position as white savior normalizes some subtle aspects of whiteness while challenging the more blatant aspects of superiority. Since most of the racial injustice is seen through Ben's eyes, there is something of an implication that he can only recognize the mistreatment of minorities because he is himself ostracized due to his monstrous appearance. Johnny, while certainly not condoning the racial prejudices, is never as put-off by them. During the aforementioned cab driver scene, Johnny even makes the joke that Ben's attempts to hail a taxi in Rudyarda are as difficult as "a **black man** trying to [hail a cab] to **Harlem**" (9).[14] While Thomas seems to intend this line to point out injustice of racial profiling, because the line is uttered by the white hero who has no problem passing in society despite his mutation, it appears insensitive in comparison to Ben whose monstrous appearance precludes him being able to do the same, as well as the surrounding native Africans who will never be afforded the luxury of privilege. Furthermore, while this perhaps correctly points to the reason that systemic racism might have been invisible to the white reader, it also equates the simple reality of being black with Ben Grimm's monstrous mutation. However, given the ways in which the BPP and the MK were viewed by the typical white reader of the 1970s, this may have been the only way or normalizing them to the reader. If the militant black man is seen as a monster, then perhaps the only way to illustrate his humanity is in reference to the humanity implicit in a literal monster like the Thing.

Thomas closes his story by trying to bring some understanding of the evils of state sponsored racial injustice to his presumed white readers. While Ben, Johnny and T'Challa realize that the problem of racism is not over, taking this small step towards progress seems to be enough for them. After his act of defiance, Ben addresses his companions, "**c'mon** you two let's get **outta** here" (21).[15] The story ends with Johnny, Ben and T'Challa walking away from the police officers, and stepping directly on the remnants of the

"Colored" and "European" signs, trampling signifiers of racism beneath their feet, as the policemen stare after them with, as the narrator notes, their "mouths slack and their minds a-gape and perhaps they understand just a little" (21). This is a direct entreaty to the readers to consider their privilege and the lack that others may have. At least that is the case for this single issue. Ben's actuations of defiance may have been one step towards raising racial awareness, but he and Johnny, as white men, are in fact able to "get outta here." As they walk over the broken and discarded signs and out of frame, they are able to walk away from the problem. In their next issue they have already returned to the United States to face a cosmic menace with no mention of the T'Challa, Rudyarda, their adventure, or any lessons they have learned.

For T'Challa, the solution is not that easy. He cannot escape his blackness by walking out of frame any more than he can by discarding his name. Perhaps this is why the change did not stand beyond this single issue. He is as tied to the plight of blackness as Newton or Mandela, and no change in name can escape that. Thomas next writes the character a mere three months later in *Avengers* #99 and the following month in #100. Apparently, as per T'Challa's original comment about considering a return to the United States, he has followed through; however, in both cases Thomas avoids using a codename entirely and refers to the character only as T'Challa, even though he appears in his superhero costume. Finally in *Avengers* #105, cover dated November of 1972, now written by Steve Englehart but edited by Thomas, T'Challa is once again featured by the name Black Panther.[16] When Ironman and Hawkeye question him about this decision, T'Challa again coaches it in terms of politics, saying "I did not want my **personal** goals and tribal **heritage** confused with **political** plans made by **others**. But in the final **analysis**, I have decided that made as much **sense** as altering the **Scarlet Witch's** name because **witches** are generally thought of as **ugly**. I am not a **stereotype**. I am **myself**. And I am the **Black Panther!**" (6).[17] Once again, the bold words Englehart chooses seem quite deliberate. Here he is finally able to reestablish T'Challa's priorities and agency, placing his personal heritage and identity above political aspirations and stereotypes of others. In doing so Englehart makes a conscious step to establish T'Challa as an icon of blackness, proclaiming his power to his white audience regardless of—and in fact in spite of—the contemporary connotations of the Black Panther moniker. It is perhaps unfortunate that he does so at the expense of Wanda Maximoff, the Scarlet Witch—objectifying her as a woman and disparaging the Wiccan religion—in effect having T'Challa stereotype her in the same manner he is attempting to resist. If nothing else, this shows that the 1970s had as far to go with gender equality and religious tolerance as they did with racial politics. But that may be a question for a volume focusing on another character. Here,

74   The Ages of the Black Panther

at least for that moment, the Black Panther took a clear step onto the path of racial progressiveness and black pride. Wakanda Forever … except for that one time.

Notes

1. Hollywood often designates films based on their assumed appeal to various demographics. Most commonly this is split along two axes, gender and age. A film that is expected to appeal to male and female viewers whether they are over or under the age of twenty-five is said to be a "four quadrant film."
2. Emphasis in original.
3. Literally translated as "separateness" from Afrikaans.
4. Literally translated as "Spear of the Nation" from Xhosa.
5. Mandela was ultimately released from prison in 1990 and became the first post–Apartheid president of South Africa in 1994.
6. Emphasis in original.
7. Emphasis in original.
8. This detail is actually anachronistic towards the actual South Africa of the time which, unlike the United States, did not use the word "Colored" as a synonym for "black" but instead considered the two to be separate group with latter referring to the Negro race and the former, or rather "Coloured" with the European "U" spelling, being used to distinguish multiracial individuals. Under the apartheid system, both groups were heavily discriminated against.
9. Emphasis in original.
10. Emphasis in original.
11. Emphasis in original.
12. Emphasis in original.
13. Emphasis in original.
14. Emphasis in original.
15. Emphasis in original.
16. T'Challa appears in only one other Marvel Comic during this time period. *Daredevil* #92 written by Gerry Conway, T'Challa's only appearance in 1972 not written or edited by Roy Thomas, features a brief cameo by the character where he inexplicably refers to himself as the Black Panther in the final panel (21). It should be noted that this is a curious choice as the central focus of this narrative is Matt Murdock's attempts to protect his own dual identity as Daredevil, an endeavor in which he enlists T'Challa to aid him. T'Challa seems to understand the importance of the Daredevil identity to Matt, and is happy to assist, but makes no mention of the Black Leopard identity at all.
17. Emphasis in original.

Works Cited

Austin, Curtis J. *Up Against the Wall: Violence in the Making and Unmaking of the Black Panther Party*. University of Arkansas Press, 2008.
Conway, Gerry, and Gene Colan. "On the Eve of the Talon!" *Daredevil*, vol. 1, no. 92, Oct. 1972.
Coogler, Ryan, director. *Black Panther*. Marvel Studios, 2018.
DeSilver, Drew. "Chart of the Week: How South Africa Changed, and Didn't, Over Mandela's Lifetime." *Pew Research Center*, Pew Research Center, 7 Feb. 2014, www.pewresearch.org/fact-tank/2013/12/06/chart-of-the-week-how-south-africa-changed-and-didnt-over-mandelas-lifetime/.
Englehart, Steve, and John Buscema. "In the Beginning Was … the World Within!" *Avengers*, vol. 1, no. 105, Nov. 1972.
Free, Jenna Land, and Stan Lee. "Stan Lee's Amazing Marvel Interview!: Two Extraordinary 2005 Audio Sessions with the Man Who Spearheaded Marvel Comics." *Alter Ego*, no. 104, 4 Aug. 2011.

Goldberg, David Theo. *The Threat of Race: Reflections on Racial Neoliberalism*. Crane Library at the University of British Columbia, 2011.
Lee, Stan, and Jack Kirby. "The Black Panther!" *Fantastic Four*, vol. 1, no. 52, July 1966.
Manifesto of Umkhonto We Sizwe. Umkhonto We Sizwe, 1961.
Parker, Ryan, and Aaron Couch. "Wesley Snipes Reveals Untold Story Behind His 'Black Panther' Film." *The Hollywood Reporter*, 30 Jan. 2018, www.hollywoodreporter.com/heat-vision/black-panther-wesley-snipes-reveals-untold-story-behind-90s-film-1078868.
Simpson, Thula. *Umkhonto We Sizwe: The ANC's Armed Struggle*. Penguin Books, 2016.
Thomas, Roy, and Barry Smith. "They First Make Mad!" *Avengers*, vol. 1, no. 99, May 1972.
_____. "Whatever Gods There Be!" *Avengers*, vol. 1, no. 100, June 1972.
Thomas, Roy, and John Buscema. "Three Stood Together!" *Fantastic Four*, vol. 1, no. 119, Feb. 1972.
"Umkhonto We Sizwe." *The African National Congress: South Africa's National Liberation Movement*, African National Congress, 2011, www.web.archive.org/web/20150220033111/http://anc.org.za/themes.php?t=Umkhonto%2Bwe%2BSizwe.
Wallace, Carvell. "Why 'Black Panther' Is a Defining Moment for Black America." *The New York Times*, 12 Feb. 2018, www.nytimes.com/2018/02/12/magazine/why-black-panther-is-a-defining-moment-for-black-america.html.

Wakanda Speaks

Animals and Animacy in "Panther's Rage"

José Alaniz

In "There Are Serpents Lurking in Paradise," chapter nine of the "Panther's Rage" storyline (*Jungle Action* #14, March 1975), King T'Challa/Black Panther and the forest-dweller Mokadi stumble upon a sorry sight: an oil slick choking a river deep in Wakanda's remote Serpent Valley. As the two gaze from overhanging tree branches, a textbox proclaims, "The scent of *oil* is overpowering, spreading black, leprous fingers. The river *struggles* to continue its *ageless flow*—/The struggle has been *lost!*" (Sedlmeier 186).[1]

They soon discover the black ooze's source: the villain N'Jadaka/Killmonger and his crew created the slick to immobilize and capture dinosaurs, which they will weaponize in a bid to seize the Wakandan throne. A splash page shows the primeval giants struggling against the crude-contaminated waters as men in boats cast nets over them. The leader of the operation looks on, grinning: "*Killmonger* is in good spirits. The day has gone *well*" (Sedlmeier 187).

Writer Don McGregor and artist Billy Graham here pause in their sprawling, multi-year epic to comment on an extractive, domineering mindset towards nature, one heedless of consequences. The narrative, however, does heed—and to a remarkable degree: over the course of six panels, in the midst of other human-centered business, we zoom in on a tiny bird (resembling a grebe) stuck in the sludge. One of Killmonger's henchmen, himself pushed into the muck by his master, tries to save the trapped creature ("frail figures *merged* in ... *tragedies*"), only to be censured by the villain: "Tayete, if we lost time saving each *helpless stray* on our road to *greatness*—/we would never *reach* our destination" (Sedlmeier 188).

As strongman and lackeys stride off into the distance, we maintain focus on the foreground and its feathered, sinking, doomed victim: "The graceful wings flutter. Weak bird-trilling seems to ask what has happened to the gift of *flight./*...[I]ts plaintive death-cries are *lost* in the *vastness of events./As usual!*" (Sedlmeier 188). A few pages later, at the climax of a battle between the Panther and a Tyrannosaurus Rex, we once again, over three thick-bordered panels, zero in on the oil-encrusted bird in its last moments, as its eye closes forever. "A few *crucial* elements of the scene are missed," the captions say. "For some, night does *not* arrive. As usual" (Sedlmeier 197). The page makes for a startling contrast in scale: the towering T-Rex collapses from a *coup de grâce*-by-boulder in the two largest panels, while in the smallest, the bird suffocates silently, unnoticed, unmourned.

Animals of all sizes suffer violent deaths throughout "Panther's Rage." But as punctuated by that echoing *"as usual!,"* McGregor and Graham insist that there are no "insignificant" casualties in the unending war between man and nature. To underscore that point, they seize on an image which by 1975 would have struck many U.S. readers as depressingly familiar.

Santa Barbara

On January 28, 1969, a Union Oil offshore well six miles off the coast of Santa Barbara, California, catastrophically malfunctioned. Despite attempts to cap it, the well blew, spilling between 22,000 and 220,000 gallons of oil into the ocean each day for the next eleven days (Spezio: xvi–xvii), creating a slick 35 miles long along the coast and killing thousands of birds, fish and sea mammals. At the time it was the third-largest oil spill in the country's history (Nash 22).

Citing a study by the Santa Barbara–based General Research Corporation, A.E. Keir Nash and his co-authors noted in 1972 that:

> By February 3, six days after the blowout, oil had spread over 251 square miles of the [Santa Barbara] Channel. Eighty-six square miles were covered with heavy, dark oil, the remainder by a lighter film. By February 5, Santa Barbara County beaches were blanketed with a layer of crude oil which was several inches thick in most places. Its odor was noticeable several miles inland; 660 square miles of the Channel were covered—160 square miles by the heavy, dark oil [Nash et al.: 22].

By the end of April 1969, more than three million gallons (about 70,000 barrels) had spilled, a black stain stretching from Santa Barbara to the nearby Channel Islands, as far away as Pismo Beach (90 miles north) and Malibu Beach (65 miles south) (Nash et al.: 22). "The thing I remember most about it was the noise of the waves breaking on the beach ended," author Robert Sollen told the *LA Times*. "The water was heavy and lubricated with oil. There was a total silence" (Grad).

In the end, according to geographers K.C. Clarke and Jeffrey J. Hemphill:

Eight hundred square miles of ocean were impacted, and 35 miles of coastline were coated with oil up to six inches thick. The oil muted the sound of the waves on the beach and the odor of petroleum was inescapable. The ecological impact was catastrophic.

Rescuers counted 3,600 dead ocean feeding seabirds and a large number of poisoned seals and dolphins were removed from the shoreline. The spilled oil killed innumerable fish and intertidal invertebrates, devastated kelp forests and displaced many populations of endangered birds [159].

Dead and suffering animals dominated media coverage of the Santa Barbara spill, spurring public demands for government action to safeguard the environment from similar disasters. Much of the imagery featured oil-smothered birds. On February 6, 1969, *The Los Angeles Times* led with "Drifting Oil Smears Beaches for 12 Miles" in screaming bold, with a photograph of a blackened cormorant and caption reporting that the animal was "beyond saving" (Spezio 137).[2] As historian Kathryn Morse notes:

> *The Los Angeles Times, the Washington Post, the Boston Globe,* and *Time* ran photographs of the rig, the slick, the makeshift oil booms, the beaches, and volunteers and workers bathing oily grebes (diving birds that spend almost all of their time in water). *Newsweek* included a dying cormorant (a coastal seabird), along with workers raking up oil-absorbent straw. *Life* published images of two grebes, one dead, one being bathed. Reports and images emphasized a sense of tragic, heartbreaking helplessness. Volunteers watched, the *Los Angeles Times* reported, as cormorants "tried vainly to clean one another off with their beaks," and then died from ingested oil. Fleeing well-intentioned rescuers, birds headed into the surf. "Falling into the black liquid," the report read, "they lay in the ooze, crying weakly." In June *Life* covered the spill's effects with photographs from San Miguel Island off the coast. Pictures included an oil-drenched seal pup stranded in slippery rocks. The island, the reporter wrote, provided "the black vision of the dead world which may come" [129–130].

In a McLuhanesque twist, technical advances in home entertainment may also have played a role in viewer emotional engagement with the tragedy. Historian Teresa Sabol Spezio argues, "With the spread of color television technology, many Americans experienced an environmental catastrophe in color for the first time. The contrast between the blue water, white sand beaches, and multicolored plumage of birds and the oil that now covered them shocked the viewing public" (131).

Workers spreading straw along the slick to soak it up, bulldozers scraping the top layers of beaches, contaminated sand being trucked away, and heroic volunteers desperately scrubbing oil off animals became familiar fare on TV screens and newspapers for the duration of the disaster[3] (setting the mold for reportage of such events in the future). The immediacy of the coverage and something more ineffable, maintains historian J. Brooks Flippen, broke through a late-60s public consciousness in ways previous natural catastrophes had not: "The disaster was, in fact, no greater than several oil tanker spills the world had suffered[4] but, with the scenic beauty of the Californian coast as a backdrop, it still made for great television. Birds covered with sticky oil struggled for life; dead seals floated ashore; enraged Santa Barbara housewives cried for the cameras" (25).[5]

Whatever it was, Santa Barbara had a galvanizing effect on a U.S. environmentalist movement[6] that had remained relatively quiet since the eruption following Rachel Carson's 1962 publication of *Silent Spring;* "It shocked Americans, placing environmental protection on the front burner in a way it never had been before, turning a concerned public into an activist one" (Flippen: 25). Investigations into the disaster first and foremost demonstrated that (1) the cozy relationship between the federal government and the oil industry had led to and exacerbated the disaster[7] and (2) there existed no federal policy on preventing and containing such spills.[8] President Richard Nixon, inaugurated just eight days before the well blew, faced heightened pressure to lead proactively on the environment—which, to put it mildly, had not formed one the central pillars of the Republican's successful campaign.[9]

To further encourage the administration, Senator Henry "Scoop" Jackson (D–WA) introduced the framework for the National Environmental Policy Act (NEPA) on February 18, 1969, less than a month after the spill (Spezio144). It passed the Senate with a unanimous voice vote in July; then it passed the House with a vote of 372 to 15 in September. The president signed it into law on January 1, 1970, at his residence in San Clemente, California, along the Pacific coast about 160 miles from Santa Barbara itself (Spezio 152–153). Among other things, the act mandated public input and environmental review for all federally-funded projects and led to the creation of the Environmental Protection Agency (EPA) later that year.

Activists built on this groundswell, further pressuring the young administration to take seriously the safeguarding of the environment. More than 20 million people in the U.S. (or one in ten of the population) took part in the first Earth Day on April 22, 1970 (Rinde); the conservative but pragmatic Nixon made the environment a centerpiece of his first State of the Union address, and in his first term signed several other landmark pieces of environmentalist legislation, including the Endangered Species Conservation Act (1969); the Clean Air Act (1970); the Water Quality Improvement Act (1970), which made oil companies fully liable for cleanup of spills; and what became known as the Clean Water Act (1972). In his second term he signed the Endangered Species Act (1973). In the words of Russel Train, a former Republican judge who had helped create the World Wildlife Fund and who as head of the Task Force on Natural Resources and Environment had urged Nixon to lead on the issue: "Serious students of the environmental movement agree that the Santa Barbara oil spill was the single incident that crystallized the amorphous concern for the environment into an international movement" (Spezio 143).

McGregor and Graham, by invoking in their dinosaur-hunting scene the birds smothered to death at Santa Barbara—those who perish "as usual" to maintain our modern lifestyle—were tying superheroic "jungle action" to real-world headlines of the ecologically-conscious early 1970s. In fact, as argued in this essay, "Panther's Rage," fulfills an environmentalist vision of animals, land and resources only implied in the character's origin.

"Man-Made Jungle"

"Wakanda! It is a nation of *paradoxes*," writes McGregor. "Technology existing with primitive traditions ... and *not always* coexisting peacefully" (Sedlmeier 97). A hidden African nation harboring the only known stores of a fantastic metal, vibranium, which fuels its astoundingly advanced society, not only nodded to the decolonization movements then ongoing in the real-world Africa; it also reflected Marvel's (specifically artist/co-creator Jack Kirby's) "growing interest in the collision of ancient civilizations and futuristic technologies" (Howe 86). Such innovations also broke with sordid and long-standing representational practices directed at non-white races in comics. In the words of Cathy Thomas, "Wakanda's techno-organic jungle disrupts past depictions of African primitivism and Black natives who, for instance, supported Tarzan. The jungle is reclaimed as a site of Black self-reliance, self-sufficiency, and self-determination" (79).

Thomas here refers specifically to Wakanda's most outré environmental feature, the "man-made jungle," which debuted along with T'Challa/Black Panther, the first black superhero, in *Fantastic Four* #52 (July 1966). Writer Stan Lee and Kirby heighten the drama of the "jungle's" first appearance through suspense: as the eponymous quartet (plus Wyatt Wingfoot) speed over lushly overgrown terrain at the king's invitation, Reed Richards/Mr. Fantastic proclaims, "The jungle looks so *primitive*—so undeveloped! Are you *sure* we have reached *Wakanda* territory?" The king's emissary responds, in part, "[Y]ou would do well to remember ... in this land, things are not always as they *seem!*" (Sedlmeier 12). The foliage parts, and the ship suddenly enters a bizarre techno-space which defies understanding, an instance of what Charles Hatfield calls Kirby's "technological sublime."[10] Utterly enthralled, the guests can only strive at words to describe the spectacle:

> RICHARDS: It's truly a *jungle*—but like nothing ever spawned by nature! It's a *man-made* jungle!
> EMISSARY: Indeed you are *correct!* The entire topography and flora are electronically-controlled *mechanical apparatus!* The very *branches* about us are composed of

delicately constructed *wires*—while the *flowers* which abound here are highly complex buttons and dials! Even the *boulders* can be heard to hum with the steady pulse of *computer dynamos!* [Sedlmeier 13].

Our first glimpse of the mechanical "jungle" highlights—extraordinarily so— what Adilifu Namu calls "a high-tech African Shangri-La where African tradition and advanced scientific technology are fused together to create a wonderland of futuristic weapons and flying machines" (43). But this panel also presents a readerly conundrum: none of the emissary's descriptions match what we see. No "branches," "flowers" or "boulders" appear; rather, crystalline shapes, contained explosions and psychedelic machine-tubes, of a sort that would not feel out of place in the alien Galactus' mother ship, confront our senses.

How to account for such an oddly drastic disjunct between the dialogue and image, as if Lee and Kirby were depicting two different spaces independently of each other? Perhaps owing to the so-called Marvel Method, whereby scripter and artist worked largely independently,[11] art here conflicts mightily with text; Kirby's imagery is much weirder, even opaque, reflecting the "psychic unstitching, the mind-bending excess" of the 1960s, as Hatfield puts it (154). (This rendering in fact anticipates Kirby's late baroque style of *The Eternals* and *2001: A Space Odyssey* from ten years later.)

The most obvious explanation, it seems to me, stems from the fundamental paradox implied by the oxymoron "man-made jungle."[12] Its unnerving hybridity—nature as human construction—evokes a melding of objects which the modern mind defines as opposites; to imagine it requires an imaginative feat akin to Romantic Negative Capability.[13] In short, Thomas' chimaeric, overdetermined "techno-organic" has no predetermined visual correlate, hence Lee and Kirby's disparate results.[14]

Future Marvel creators and artists, too, often seemed uncertain of how to approach the concept. They would portray T'Challa's creation in very different and inconsistent ways, underscoring its instability, unrepresentability and sublimity. John Buscema essentially takes a pass; his depiction of Wakanda's "man-made jungle" in *Avengers* #62 (March 1969) simply duplicates (2) Kirby's original from *Fantastic Four* #52. In another version, from *Fantastic Four* #311 (February 1988), the concept is broadened; it presents as a typical jungle setting, from whose foliage spring up communication and surveillance devices, as well as weapons—a different sort of nature/tech blend (19, 22).[15] More recently, Ta-Nehisi Coates and Brian Stelfreeze, in their 2016 story arc, "A Nation Under Our Feet," portray the "man-made jungle" as T'Challa's scientific lab/botanical garden.[16]

Over decades of Black Panther continuity, Wakanda would shift identities and aspects many times. In their celebrated mid–1970s storyline, McGregor and Graham turned their vision to the land itself, and away from the "man-made jungle," which served as mere metonym for a vast African nation of multiple and contradictory ideas—as multiple and contradictory as our feelings over nature itself.

"Panther's Rage": Wakanda as Ecosystem of Meanings

In the groundbreaking, 13-issue "Panther's Rage" (*Jungle Action* #s 6–18, 1973–1975),[17] McGregor along with artists Rich Buckler, Graham and others, brought a new maturity and sophistication to King T'Challa/Black Panther. In the storyline, hailed by fans and critics as a proto-graphic novel unfolding bi-monthly over two years, T'Challa battles revolutionary upstart Killmonger and his cadre of mutated henchmen, at the same time dealing with doubts and divisions within his own court. Taking place entirely within the borders of the fictional kingdom, remarkable for its almost exclusively black cast, McGregor et al.'s epic imparts on Wakanda and its people a degree of detail and topographic variety unbroached by creators Lee and Kirby, whose vision had bordered on that of the colonialist "jungle hero."[18] As comics scholar Rebecca Wanzo puts it, "Panther's Rage" proved "the first major step in decolonizing the character. The story arc introduced long-form epic storytelling to Marvel comics and is considered by many to be the story that allowed T'Challa to develop as a character and Wakanda as a place" (Wanzo).

Indeed, "Panther's Rage" for the first time explored the country's quite varied geography, which manifests as afrofuturist paradise, open savannahs, prehistoric wilderness, fetid swamp, snowy waste, future shock battlefield and commanding waterfall, among other settings. The storyline even includes detailed maps in its back pages, the better to keep track of such locales as "Killmonger's village (N'Zhadaha)," "Panther Island" and the "Woods of Solitude."[19]

As noted, the role of the "man-made jungle" in "Panther's Rage" is largely reduced to an "underground computerized complex" and weapons manufacturing center infiltrated by Killmonger's "death regiments." Graham's depiction skews to the minimalist and bare, with a few flourishes and shapes all that remains of Kirby's techno-sprawl (Sedlmeier 127).

Instead, "Panther's Rage" shifts much of the action to the outdoors, far from Wakanda's urban capital, to rural settings where McGregor and Graham trouble the line between African "authenticity" (through a Western gaze) and sci-fi adventure. We see a good example when T'Challa and his comrades attack Killmonger's village, whose thatched huts and crude paling fences resemble the "Tarzan"-era works which Thomas decries.[20] But in combat, "*hydraulic systems* strip away the *façade* of primitivism," as the villain Lord

Karnaj puts it; the thatched huts reveal a metallic structure beneath, out of which scramble troops with laser rifles (134).

The storyline makes animals and the country's natural splendors (and perils) much more the focus, particularly when T'Challa tracks Killmonger's movements through various environments for several chapters. Here Wakanda itself becomes a central, animate, agential character which the increasingly beset, exhausted and injured T'Challa must traverse and appease. His is also an inner journey, a vision quest. As the critics Tucker Stone and David Brothers write: "the Panther moves deeper into Wakanda's hinterlands, discovering truths about his country that he either didn't believe in, or was completely unaware of in the first place." In sum, "Panther's Rage" puts Wakandan geography at center stage—doubly so; during his grueling journey back to civilization, its changing landscapes mirror the protagonist's growing desperation and will to triumph. To a degree not seen before in superhero comics, the natural setting entails the character.[21]

Of the many examples one could cite, these especially resonate with me as both supplying genre thrills *and* doing the figurative labor of landscape-as-mirror: a long footbridge extending into the fog-filled distance over a dizzying chasm, towards the Land of the Chilling Mist as T'Challa embarks on his journey (Sedlmeier 148); a two-page spread of T'Challa warding off a pack of wolves in the snowy wastes (Sedlmeier 158–159); a pain-induced reminiscence of T'Chaka, the hero's father, on a "golden afternoo[n]" by the water (Sedlmeier 206); an idyllic interlude with his U.S. lover Monica Lynne, in twinned silhouettes against a sunset suffused with pink, orange and lavender before the big final battle (Sedlmeier 222); and the storyline's most iconic image, T'Challa tossed down the waterfall where he first knows defeat at the hands of Killmonger (Sedlmeier 59, 63–65) and where he must confront him again at saga's end (Sedlmeier 252–257).

Our discussion of the Wakandan landscape brings us to the Romantics, whose legacy, as historian William Cronon contends, "means that wilderness is more a state of mind than a fact of nature," and further, that "the state of mind that today most defines wilderness is *wonder*" (88, emphasis in original). Such wonder, according to W.K. Wimsatt, stems from a metaphysics "of an animate, plastic Nature, not transcending but immanent in and breathing through all things," adding, "to discount for the moment such differences as may relate to Wordsworth's naturalism, Coleridge's theology, Shelley's Platonism, or Blake's visions: we may observe that the common feat of the romantic nature poets was *to read meanings into the landscape*" (83, my emphasis). Nature in this understanding is both a subjective "state of mind" that read meanings into things as well as an independent force which moves the beholder-poet; as Geoffrey H. Hartman describes it: "not an 'object' but a presence and a power; a motion and spirit; not something to be worshiped and consumed, but always a guide leading beyond itself" (290).

Let us not forget, though, that contemporary understandings of landscape (both our personal witnessing of it and as genre painting) owe much not only to the Romantic poets but to the history of Western imperialism. W.J.T. Mitchell, in fact, calls landscape "something like the dreamwork of imperialism," disclosing both "utopian fantasies of the perfected imperial prospect and fractured images of unresolved ambivalence and unsuppressed resistance" (10).[22] He too acknowledges that "[l]andscape is a medium not only for expressing value but also for expressing meaning … most radically for communication between the Human and the non–Human" (15)—in the sense that it constantly mediates between the cultural and the natural.[23]

For Laguna Pueblo author Leslie Marmon Silko, the act of designating a landscape itself betrays modernity's imagined severance from nature[24]:

> [T]he term landscape, as it has entered the English language, is misleading. "A portion of territory the eye can comprehend in a single view" does not correctly describe the relationship between the human being and his or her surroundings. This assumes the viewer is somehow outside or separate from the territory he or she surveys. Viewers are as much a part of the landscape as the boulders they stand on. There is no high mesa edge or mountain peak where one can stand and not immediately be a part of all that surrounds [32].

In chapters 12 through 15 of "Panther's Rage," when T'Challa pursues his nemesis across numerous distinct and remote regions of Wakanda, McGregor and Graham depict their hero less as Mitchell's imperialist master of all he surveys and more in Silko's terms—as part of the natural environment with which he nonetheless must contend on equal footing. Gracefully stalking in jungles, trundling through barren snowscapes, scaling mountains, the Panther (whose superhero identity already blurs the human/animal boundary) "fits in" with these rustic settings in ways a more "futuristic" hero such as Iron Man would not.

The authors enhance this "naturalistic" effect in two ways: through the often extreme violence of T'Challa's battles with animals (see below), and the severe traces this violence leaves. For in "Panther's Rage," the hero's costume does not stay in one piece for long; it often deteriorates to tatters within a few panels after the start of a melee. As the costume tears, the Panther's dark skin beneath routinely suffers deep gashes and blunt force trauma, muscles rippling and blood-smeared.[25] We see two particularly gruesome examples at the conclusion of the battle with the White Gorilla (Sedlmeier 177) and the "collage of wounds" which overwhelm the hero during his encounter with the thorn-covered villain Salamander K'ruel (Sedlmeier 204).[26] Stone and Brothers call such episodes "education through suffering." T'Challa in fact appears with costume ripped on more than half the covers of the "Panther's

Rage" storyline, namely *Jungle Action* #6, 9, 10, 12, 13, 14, and 15. Through such visual-verbal devices, T'Challa "blends in" with his irregular surroundings rather than standing apart from them, as when he tracks the villain Sombre through the dense jungle of Serpent Valley (Sedlmeier 180) and when he surfs the back of a flying pterodactyl, his remaining scraps of costume flapping in the wind, mirroring the dinosaur's wings (Sedlmeier 215).

And yet nothing conveys the savagery of McGregor/Graham's vision of life and death in the wild like Black Panther's gory, flesh-ripping, blood-spewing struggles against animals—an incomplete list of which includes dinosaurs, wolves, a crocodile, Venomm's snakes and Killmonger's jaguar Preyy. While long a staple of the "jungle action" genre, Stone and Brothers argue these forays into graphic ultraviolence allowed the authors to dodge the Comics Code's strictures against "lyrical journeys into flayed skin," which would otherwise have applied were the combatants exclusively human.[27]

Whatever their motivation, these episodes—especially those resulting in animal death—function as tests for T'Challa's resilience in his mission, as well as reminders of the victims felled by Killmonger's revolution (whether a bird drowned in oil or a gorilla-god impaled in battle). Yet these descriptions only begin to account for the many variegated meanings and associations which non-human animals bear or invoke in this narrative. Let us examine three instances of animal encounter—two of them violent—in "Panther's Rage."

On the opening page of chapter four, "But Now the Spears Are Broken" (*Jungle Action* #9, May 1974), the young boy Kantu is charged by a raging black rhinoceros (Sedlmeier 97). The Panther immediately leaps into action, straddling the 3,000-pound beast, whose unexplained aggression[28] leads T'Challa to drastic measures. Over five panels, the lithe hero swings from a branch, once more grabs hold of the rushing animal (which had shaken him off before) and exerts his superhuman strength on its neck. Artist Gil Kane draws the Panther and rhino exceeding the bounds of the panel borders in the largest, central frame, as they seem to erupt out of the page towards the reader. Color plays an important role as well: mostly yellow backgrounds heighten the excitement, the in-the-moment stakes, while the Panther's black/blue costume offset the veritable wall of grey of the rhino's body. The hero's efforts succeed, killing the pachyderm, and in the final panel a drained T'Challa leans languidly on the animal's corpse.

So we see, at any rate—but a reading of McGregor's characteristically overdetermined textboxes shifts our perception of the event. They proclaim, in part:

> Fingers taut, he takes *hold*. This grip must not weaken else he will fall *beneath* these pounding hooves—/—left *maimed* and *bloody* under their tread. And how, he wonders, would that affect his *kingdom,* held in turmoil as it is by the chaos of Killmon-

ger's *brutal insurrection./Erik Killmonger.* Mustn't forget the Erik!/Yet, Killmonger does fade from mind, replaced by the task at hand ... an *insane* task ...
—inspired by *American* "B" *Western mythos* of Hopalong Cassidy vintage and others, seen on idle Saturday afternoons at *Avengers' Mansion./The Panther bulldogs this 1½-ton monstrosity—/carving it into the mire ... and snapping its vertebrae!* [Sedlmeier 99].[29]

McGregor's free indirect speech, no less than his stream of consciousness, alter the significance of the titanic tussle between hero and beast. T'Challa's anxieties over the ongoing insurgency in his kingdom; his reluctance to demonize his enemy; even memories of his time in the United States, where he watched Western hero Hop-along Cassidy,[30] all figure into this critical do-or-die moment. The scene demonstrates the crucial role played by text-image interaction in comics, how the medium's multimodal "double track" can enliven and deepen even the most formulaic fare. But it also shows how the rhino acts as more than mere unthinking antagonist; rather, the animal body—despite or even because of its eminent threat—sparks thoughts and associations in T'Challa that would not have occurred otherwise. The charging rhino in its final moments thus delivers both superficial genre thrills and a real-time trace of T'Challa's mind in motion.[31]

An even grander scope of animal signification asserts itself in Chapter 8, "The God Killer" (*Jungle Action* #13, Jan. 1975), as T'Challa navigates the snow-bound Land of the Chilling Mist on the trail of the villain Sombre. In these wastes, the scientifically-minded king confronts nothing less than the source of one of Wakanda's religions.[32] McGregor and Graham construct the setting so as to highlight its metaphysical dimensions: the Panther stalks his prey across the white wastes beneath a multicolored, aurora borealis-like effect in the sky. The textbox reads, "It is a night when a man can *reach* and believe he can *touch* the stars—/—that he is *part* of the cosmological scheme of things!/A night when a man could believe he is an *integral part* of the universe./Not *omnipotent*. Not *superior*./Just *unique* and unto himself" (Sedlmeier 170).

The description, recalling Silko's lack of division between subject and landscape, blurs the human/non-human realms and prepares the ground for the *"staggering"* (*ibid.*) sight that comes next. T'Challa climbs a precipice, to an overlook. From there, the astounded Panther glimpses a plain strewn with bones, in which a troop of mammoth, agitated White Gorillas howl at Sombre's promise of a ritualistic sacrifice (Sedlmeier 171). Snaggle-toothed, red-eyed, long-clawed, standing at least 12 feet tall, they only somewhat resemble their ordinary namesakes, and inspire fearful worship: "They are overpowering. *Ancient specimens* to some forgotten era when early Wakandan legends were at their *birth*" (Sedlmeier 172).

The White Gorillas are *sublime;* they dissolve borders between self and other no less than does the "magical" northern landscape. As one engages T'Challa in battle, with its towering bulk of furred muscle and fearsome fangs, the terrifying monster seems to exact worship. McGregor's very descriptors are Biblical: "He is *staggered* by its *immensity!* This is no god or love or charity. This is a *vengeful god*, rising full and malevolent—*demanding its tribute!*" (Sedlmeier172).

Which only makes the outcome of their clash seem all the more tragic— albeit, by the logic of the superhero "jungle action" narrative, inevitable. Yet something more than the fulfillment of generic expectations is going on in the White Gorilla's downfall; T'Challa here kills more than an animal, and something other than a god. The scene literalizes a process akin to that which cultural historian Steve Baker sees as vital to "free" the animal from human preconceptions of it as "pure" emblem of the real:

> The visual stereotyping of the animal necessarily focuses on its body, and my concerns over notions of "how animals should be seen" are that they seek to fix the image of that body in an image of nature, taking both to be an unproblematic reflection of reality. It is therefore the image of the animal body, I suggest, which needs *to be taken out of nature and rendered unstable as a sign.*
>
> Only when the animal body is taken "out" of this myth of nature does it become clearer what culture has invested in the animal. Once the body is regarded as abstract, conceptual, arbitrary, unstable, and not as the site of the fixed "real," it is more easily recognized as a prime symbolic site: the very site of identity [223].

We may liken what Baker describes as the animal's imprisonment in the "natural" (that which for many "transcends" signification) to the White Gorilla's casting in the role of god. Once T'Challa—after much physical struggle and bodily injury—manages to grievously wound the giant, he declares, "My *legends* have been given the vulnerability of flesh, Sombre—and have *lost* their grandiose mythology!" (Sedlmeier 176). Ultimately, the Panther coaxes his foe over the precipice, where it plummets to a grisly death, gored through the chest by a sharp animal bone. (The beast-god's body is literally decentered; upside-down, skewered through the heart, its feet protrude from the middle frame into the top tier, as if "fallen" from there.) In the final panel, T'Challa lies battered and spent on the icy ground. McGregor's pronouncement on this resolution captures the immensity of the act: "The death of this god is stark and barren—and as *ugly* as most violent, senseless death. The Panther is consumed by a sense of his own *mortality*./He has killed a *myth* ... and his life is *lessened* by the act. He has *lost* part of his past without anything to replace it in the future" (Sedlmeier 177).

The Wakandan scientist-king's face-off with the mythic white deity ends as most such "jungle action" set-pieces do, with the beast's violent demise. But the episode—vouchsafed, again, with T'Challa's blood—also allegorizes the modern disenchantment of the animal, its diminution since the

Enlightenment to mere sentiment or meat.[33] It is a dethronement, a desublimation comparable to deicide. Or more precisely, semiocide.[34]

The final animal encounter in "Panther's Rage" which I will examine would seem to reinstate non-human life to the realm, if not of divinity, then certainly of "unknowable" Otherness—an emblem of the Real (and thus a different aspect of the sublime). In the tenth chapter, "Thorns in the Flesh, Thorns in the Mind," (*Jungle Action* #15, May 1975), a profusely bleeding T'Challa finds himself strapped to a pair of trees in the swampy Serpent Valley, prisoner of K'ruel. His gruesome injuries, which include thorn punctures all over his body, induce a degree of pain that "makes *articulate* speech impossible" (Sedlmeier 203). In this tormented daze, he sinks into a warm memory of whiling away a golden afternoon with his father, alluded to earlier.[35]

But T'Challa's reverie is soon "obliterate[d]"—a newt is scrambling down his body, lapping at his blood. A page of five red-bordered, descending horizontal panels against a hyper-frame of the Panther's gloved hand (riddled with thorns) show the green and yellow scaled creature clinging to a finger, then progressing down his forearm, bicep, shoulder and face. "[B]lood and saliva, both life essences, drip from its ridged mouth," the caption notes (in an echo of the Tyrannosaurus Rex which the hero defeated earlier), while its large yellow eye stares off-panel against the hyper-frame's solid black background (Sedlmeier 207).

This seems, to say the least, an odd development in the middle of "Panther's Rage," a fast-paced epic of grand emotions and life-or-death thrills and chills. The stakes—as well as T'Challa's fearful reaction—seem all out of proportion; is Wakanda's throne now threatened by a tiny pond dweller? McGregor's text, meanwhile, comes off as both evasive and weirdly nature-documentary pedantic: "the newt is *lungless,* and breathes through small capillaries in its lung lining"; "It seems to be *testing* the sticky red liquid to see if it is to its *liking*" (*ibid.*). The scene fashions a mood of suspended "otherworldliness," an effect heightened by the strangeness of the situation; the hero's repulsion and befuddlement ("What in hell is it *waiting for?* He almost asks the question aloud"); and the episode's interstitial position between much grander events of the narrative.[36] As the drooling petty demon stares directly into the cross-eyed T'Challa's face, then crawls on his forehead, the final caption reads: "The *ordeal* lasts forever! Its meaning, if it has any, is lost with the other senseless acts. In its *own context, like most of the negative aspects of life, the action is natural. To the reasoning mind, it is supremely alien and uncomprehendable*" (*ibid.*).

This text appears as yellow set off against black, accentuating the ordeal's "alienness," which McGregor relates both to the natural and to the "negative aspects of life." Negative in that nature stands in binary opposition to the "reasoning" human mind—dubious as that sounds. In short, we are presented here with nature as absolute Other. As with the "unaccountable" rhino charge before, the animal acts as an animal, motivated by its own inscrutable impulses, free of man's interference. The newt thus appears in its "wholeness"—simply as newt. Such an image brings up an important consideration put forth by naturalist and author Aldo Leopold: "We can be ethical only in relation to something we can see, feel, understand, love or otherwise have faith in" (214). The newt, due to T'Challa's extreme and helpless circumstances, has made it onto his radar for a true contemplation, as an equal. (And an amphibian, with its particular sensitivity to environmental changes, would seem a good representative for or extension of nature itself.)

But another problem rears up: the newt as Other renders it conceptually inert. As ecocritic Mimei Ito warns: "Essentialization of 'otherness' in images leads to a mode of animal representation in which otherness in the animal identity tends to be essentialized, just as the word *animal* essentializes the idea of animals in general" (127, emphasis in original). To avoid such visual essentialism of the animal other, "which is the very presupposition that ecology wants to problematize" (132), Ito argues we should "abandon the very idea of otherness itself in order not to essentialize the visual and the natural" (133).

I argue that the multimodal representational strategies of comics offer significant advantages for accomplishing precisely that (resistance to essentialism), with the newt in "Panther's Rage" a particularly good example. For one thing, in Graham's rendering the critter resembles more a baby alligator; the visual-verbal discrepancy subverts the straightforward meaning of the signifier "newt." Secondly, the text presupposes, infers but does not access the newt's inner world—"*it is supremely alien and uncomprehendable.*" We see only its actions, not its subjective life. (Thought balloons would have made for a very different story!) At the same time, a reader takes McGregor's quasi-scientific assertions and philosophical musings into account in consuming the art, making once more for a doubly-valent, unfinalizable aesthetic experience. Comics always operates this way, destabilizing clear-cut meanings (even of "otherness") through text-image tension.

Thus, more often than not, from gorilla gods to rhinos to newts, animals in "Panther's Rage" occur, in the words of political theorist Jane Bennett, not as objects but as "vivid entities not entirely reducible to the contexts in which (human) subjects set them, never entirely exhausted by their semiotics" (5).

Conclusion: Wakanda Speaks

> Posthumanism possesses a deeply utopian bent. Its practitioners sometimes proceed as if the breeching of ontological

> categories were in itself affirmative or transcendent. Yet violence is omnipresent, part of the world's fabric, the provenance of plants, animals and materiality itself. Storied matter possesses many genres, including horror...
> —Jeffrey Jerome Cohen (36).

In their influential and innovative storyline, McGregor et al. portray Wakanda's wilderness as both threatening and threatened. Dead animals appear over and over: a strangled rhino, an impaled gorilla, a decapitated tyrannosaurus rex, a humble bird trapped in an oil slick. Such imagery, as I have argued, tapped into a dawning collective angst over the death of nature in the decade before the term Anthropocene (denoting the age of human-caused mass extinctions, global pollution and climate change) first started emerging in U.S. public discourses as a means to frame the enormity of the problem. Such comics works of the 1970s Marvel/DC Bronze Age typified an era in which the superhero genre sought a new political relevance, often exploring progressive themes such as the ecological crisis.[37] Events like the 1969 Santa Barbara oil spill *spoke*—they showed that in the post-industrial age a reckoning with environmental apocalypse was coming due. The time was short to stop what Ta-Nehisi Coates calls the "Dream" of whiteness from "plunder[ing] not just the bodies of humans but the body of the Earth itself" (150), from putting a "noose around the neck of the earth" (151).

There is a moment in "Panther's Rage" when Wakanda itself speaks, in human language. Just before the oil pollution scene whose discussion began this essay, T'Challa meets, interacts with and misapprehends the mysterious jungle inhabitant Mokadi. Bald, short of stature, with a perpetual grin on his face, Mokadi risks associations with minstrelsy figures such as Stepin Fetchit (Lincoln Theodore Monroe Andrew Perry). But his dialogue reveals a cutting intelligence and wisdom of a different order:

> BLACK PANTHER: Are you even aware there is a land *beyond* the mist that *hovers* over this valley?
> MOKADI: And if I *was,* what would I see?
> BP: A *beautiful* land./*Sunsets* and *dawns.* Exquisite gardens and superbly crafted palaces and homes and *shrines.*
> M: And what do they *stand* for? *More* than these trees? *More* than this river ... which once ran free and clear and now chokes on the *miseries* you and this Killmonger have brought *with* you [Sedlmeier186].

This scene, as much of an odd narrative digression as the newt episode, provides a crucial perspective to T'Challa's journey. What exactly is he fighting for? What ultimate values does he uphold? Is human scale too shallow a container for the things that truly matter? Mokadi supplies answers to none of these questions; as unexpectedly as he appears out of the Serpent Valley's jungle mist, he soon vanishes again. The Panther is left to wonder (on the same page that shows the oil-slicked bird's demise): "Was he ever really there?" The text then reads: "He has heard the word mokadi before. To the *Bomitaba tribe* in the *Likuala region* of Africa the terms means.../spirit./...[38] Who were you, Mokadi? A thought mirror or sage pygmi?" (Sedlmeier 197, some ellipses mine). In short, Mokadi is the "spirit" of Serpent Valley, a personification of the wild; like the newt (only much more human-looking), he acts as an emanation of the natural world itself. And like the newt, he is there to show T'Challa his place.[39]

The role of Mokadi in of all places a bloody superhero adventure serial resonates with recent interdisciplinary research into so-called Animacy and/or Vibrant Matter Theory, from scholars working in Posthuman Anthropology (Eduardo Kohn, Helen Kopnina), Political Theory (Jane Bennett), Queer Theory, Critical Animal Studies (Mel Chen) and Ecocriticism. This approach to life/non-life relations sees all matter as "storied," or as Serpil Oppermann and Serenella Iovino put it, "a material mesh of meanings, properties, and processes, in which human and nonhuman players are interlocked in networks that produce undeniable signifying forces" (quoted in Cohen: 25). Jeffrey Jerome Cohen elaborates: "Forming a biosemiotic web through which forests become sites of shared cognition, plants and animals possess an animacy that can alter human perspectives and disrupt the equation of being with being human" (28).

In her book *Vibrant Matter: A Political Ecology of Things,* Bennett emphasizes the "negative power or recalcitrance of things" (1), both living (trees, animals) and not (stones, bottle caps).[40] To orient attention to the nontheistic "agentic capacity" (9) of things, she claims, means *"to experience* the relationship between persons and other materialities more horizontally," so as "to take a step toward a more ecological sensibility" (10, emphasis in original).[41]

As seen from these samplings, much of this work centers on an ethics of care for human and non-human life, itself stemming from a post-industrial vision of profound interdependence:

> The world is also "enchanted." Thanks to this living semiotic dynamic, meaning (i.e., means-ends relations, significance, "aboutness," telos) is a constitutive feature of the world and not just something we humans impose on it. Appreciating life and thought in this manner changes our understanding of what selves are and how they emerge, dissolve, and also merge into new kinds of we as they interact with the other beings that make the tropical forest their home in that complex web of relations that I call an "ecology of selves" [Kohn 16].

To sum up, animacy conceptualizes the ways matter *affects* across the life/non-life divide, troubling it. In her study of the discourses surrounding the April 2010 Deepwater Horizon oil spill in the Gulf of Mexico (at

210,000,000 gallons [4.9 million barrels], a slick several orders of magnitude larger than its 1969 predecessor), Mel Chen notes:

> At bottom, the overbearing use of *dead* and *killed* functioned as an admission that a toxic spill was a *lifely* thing: lifely, perhaps, beyond its proper bounds. The well itself was alive, and not only because something had flowed out of it with such vivid animation. It was a threat to life in the Gulf, as well as to a *way* of life. This occlusion of life over marginal life speaks, as I see it, to the inadequacy of lifely notions as a framework for governance, medicine, and vernacular affect and makes room for a concept like animacy, which encodes forces without being beholden to the failing categories of life and nonlife [227, emphasis in original].

This is what I mean when I say the Santa Barbara disaster *spoke,* and popular fictions like "Panther's Rage" picked up its call. The violence, devastation and death toll of the Anthropocene quite literally *speaks volumes,* prompts a response. For as Bennett cautions, "in a knotted world of vibrant matter, to harm one section of the web may very well be to harm oneself" (13). Yet as Cohen mentions in this conclusion's epigraph, mass death holds sway in our era, on a planetary scale, to an almost banal degree. It can serve as only partial consolation, the fact that the natural world is, after all, red in tooth and claw—a fact McGregor and Graham have plenty of generic license to wallow in—which dry-eyed environmentalists such as Paul Shepard have long insisted we remember:

> The traditional insistence upon the overwhelmingly tragic and unequivocal nature of death ignores the adaptive role of early death in most animal populations. It presumes that the landscape is a collection of *things.* In this view the dissolution of body and personality are always tragic and disruptive, and do not contribute to the perfection of an intelligible world. But death, as transformation in a larger system, is an essential aspect of elegant patterns which are orderly as well as beautiful: without death growth could not occur, energy could not flow beyond plants, nutrient substances would be trapped forever. Without death the pond, the forest, the prairie, the city could not exist. The extremely complicated structure of living communities has yet to be fully explored, but constitutes a field pattern. Plants and animals participate in them without question in an attitude of acceptance which in human terms would be called faith [207, emphasis in original].[42]

Cold comfort when gazing upon a grebe drowned in oil, and in any case an age of mass extinctions goes beyond a "field pattern" in any normal sense.

In the paragraphs left me, I want to discuss how animacy functions—what ethics of interdependence it fosters—in Black Panther continuity. Let us begin with the derivation of the word "Wakanda." According to an 1894 Bureau of American Ethnology report, among the U.S. Plains Indian peoples it was a word for Great Spirit: "The ancestors of the Omaha and Ponka believed that there was a Supreme Being, whom they called Wakanda. They did not know where He was, nor did they undertake to say how He existed.... Wakanda means 'the mysterious'..." (quoted in Manseau).

Whether conceived as such or not,[43] then, the very name Wakanda betokens a far-reaching, agential actor, with or without an anthropomorphic "spokesperson" such as Mokadi. Wakanda hides from the world; Wakanda cultivates the Panther and White Gorilla cults; Wakanda, uniquely on Earth, grows the heart-shaped herb that gives its kings and queens their supernatural powers.[44] Wakanda speaks.

No more forcefully, perhaps, than through vibranium—the ultimate "vibrant matter." Vibranium: which moves nations, drives economies, masses armies and hi-tech holograms in its defense, lures neo-colonialists like Ulysses Klaw to kill T'Chaka, setting in motion the entire arc of the series protagonist himself. For critic Teju Cole, the substance overflows the banks of its own diegesis: "What is 'vibranium'? Too simple to think of it as a metal, and tie it to resource curses. Could it be something less palpable, could it be a stand-in for blackness itself, blackness as an embodied riposte to anti-blackness, a quintessence of mystery, resilience, self-containedness, and irreducibility?" Picking up that thread, Reynaldo Anderson reminds how sooner or later the ethical mission of afrofuturism redounds to the human: "Black speculative work is serious, necessary work. It provides a compass so we—black people—can forecast and do what is needed to take care of ourselves, our communities, and our environments" (140).[45]

In chapter three of "A Nation Under Our Feet," the Griot informs Shuri in the Djalia (the plane of ancient memory) that "Wakanda was great before it had things, and its secrets are older than any vaunted metal" (Coates and Stelfreeze: n.p.). Its greatness, as in Silko's vision of the Hopi landscape, owes to its conversation in all senses: of story, of place, of life: "Nothing is overlooked or taken for granted. Each ant, each lizard, each lark is imbued with great value simply because the creature is there, simply because the creature is alive in a place where any life at all is precious" (42).

Precious indeed, what could survive—come to terms with—the Land of Chilling Mist, the dank depths of Serpent Valley, the vertiginous heights of Warrior Falls.

In "Panther's Rage," Wakanda the land, no less than the nation, found its voice.

Notes

1. Unless otherwise noted, all comics emphases and ellipses in original.
2. According to A.E. Keir Nash et al.: "Within five days after the Santa Barbara spill, tidal pools and beaches were covered with sheets of oil. Hundreds of birds became covered with the sticky mess and began to die unpleasant deaths. Almost immediately, three treatment centers were set up by the local residents to care for oil-soaked birds. During the first month after the spill 1,575 birds were brought in for treatment. Initial estimates were that 80 percent of these birds died, and that the total number of birds killed, those treated and untreated, was as high as 8,000" (25). Later estimates brought the total of dead birds down to below 4,000, with survival rates for those treated below 11 percent. We will never know the exact

death toll, since "Countless birds that died were unaccounted for because many responders and residents discarded them without bringing them to the centers" (Spezio 138).

3. Popular books continued to fan public interest in the years after the event, including Lee Dye's *Blowout at Platform A: The Crisis That Awakened a Nation* (1971); Robert Easton's *Black Tide: The Santa Barbara Oil Spill and Its Consequences* (1972); and Carol and John Steinhart's *Blowout: A Case Study of the Santa Barbara Oil Spill* (1972).

4. The British supertanker *Torrey Canyon* had spilled much more, up to 36 million gallons, off the coast of the UK in 1967 (Nash 25).

5. Such coverage also made those with a perceived lack of sensitivity on the environment stand out all the more. [President of Union Oil Fred] Hartley struck the wrong chord with the public when he expressed in a 1969 congressional hearing that he was "always tremendously impressed at the publicity that death of birds receives versus the loss of people in our country in this day and age" (Spezio 136–137).

6. Along with other high profile environmental debacles like Ohio's thoroughly polluted Cuyohoga River infamously catching fire on June 22, 1969.

7. For more on the federal leases negotiated by the previous Johnson administration with the oil industry and the initial ham-handed response to the spill, see Spezio chapter 5.

8. In Spezio's words: "The lack of federal leadership in pollution control and prevention would be the defining lesson of the spill" (140).

9. By the time he took office, the new president had built a reputation on foreign policy expertise and political ruthlessness. As Rinde put it: "In retrospect Nixon is hardly thought of as a nature lover. Reviewing his crucial role in the establishment of the nation's environmental-protection apparatus induces not admiration but cognitive dissonance."

10. Through the technological sublime, Hatfield argues, Kirby combined the "retrograde ... gosh-wow effusiveness and social naïveté of the seminal SF pulps" with his own "graphic mythopoesis" and will to worldbuilding (Hatfield 153). For more on Kirby's technological sublime, see Hatfield 2012, chapter 4.

11. On the Marvel Method, see Hatfield 2012, 90–95 and Howe, 50.

12. The term built in part on such pop culture precursors marking the harsh realities of city life as the noir heist film *The Asphalt Jungle* (d. John Huston, 1950); the inner-city drama *Blackboard Jungle* (d. Richard Brooks, 1955); and *The Concrete Jungle* (a.k.a. *The Criminal,* directed by Joseph Losey, 1960). Bob Marley released his urban alienation song *Concrete Jungle* in 1973.

13. On Negative Capability, John Keats' quality of "being in uncertainties, Mysteries, doubts, without any irritable reaching after fact and reason" (quoted in Bate 331), see Bate.

14. Other critics see reflected in the "man-made jungle's" instability the ideological contradictions of T'Challa himself. Martin Lund, reading these stories through their original Cold War framework, argues that "Wakanda's progress is limited to a hi-tech 'man-made jungle,' created by Black Panther 'just for a lark,' and to a partial modernization of the tribal warriors' arsenal. Moreover, as the site where Black Panther chooses to attack the FF, the techno-jungle is not only an irresponsible use of technology, but one that signifies African development as a potential threat to the West."

15. This iteration anticipates the 1990s restaurant/retail chain Rainforest Café, with its animatronic animals, talking banyan trees, hanging vines and a sky of fiber-optic stars, along with jungle noises and "a simulated thunder and lightning storm that sweeps through the restaurant every 18 minutes" (Heimlich). See also Price on the Nature Company stores. Both profit-driven ventures exemplify a middle-class urban engagement with nature in late capitalism.

16. It first appears in chapter 3 (n.p.).

17. Up until issue 5, which reprints "The Monarch and the Man-Ape" from *Avengers* #62, *Jungle Action* was an embarrassing anachronism, "devoted to reprints of white imperialist fantasies from the 1950s" (Howe 132).

18. McGregor (b. 1945) had worked primarily as a proofreader and editor for Marvel starting in 1972. When offered the *Jungle Action* gig, the writer had as his only stipulation that he had to set the Black Panther stories in Africa. The second tier title had minimal editorial input and oversight, which contributed to its creators' experimental ethos (Howe 132).

McGregor came to earn a reputation for "gravitas," "extreme wordiness" and purple prose (Howe 133).

19. See *Jungle Action* #6 (Sedlmeier 60). Howe claims that McGregor intended these paratextual materials to fill out the back of the book so that they wouldn't be taken up by old jungle comics reprints (133), though this issue of *Jungle Action* features a back-up story, "Double Danger," starring Lorna the Jungle Girl, which originally appeared in *Lorna the Jungle Girl* No. 13 (May, 1955).

20. Killmonger's cronies Tayete and Kazibe sit on the ground and eat matoke, mashed and steamed bananas (Sedlmeier 133). Other "ordinary" Wakandans come off as stereotypically uneducated and superstitious, like the xenophobic village woman Karota (Sedlmeier 173).

21. Kirby's own *Kamandi: The Last Boy on Earth* comes close; see Hatfield 2017.

22. In a key passage, Mitchell writes, "Landscape *painting* is best understood ... not as the uniquely central medium that gives us access to ways of seeing landscape, but as a representation of something that is already a representation in its own right.... Landscape is already artifice in the moment of its beholding, long before it becomes the subject of pictorial representation" (14, emphasis in original). Art historian Simon Schama too reminds that the Germanic root *landschaft*, from which the English word is derived, originally meant a unit of human occupation (10).

23. Such mediation has important potential for ethics. As historian William Cronon puts it: "The autonomy of nonhuman nature seems to me an indispensable corrective to human arrogance. Any way of looking at nature that helps us remember—as wilderness tends to do—that the interests of people are not necessarily identical to those of every other creature or of the earth itself is likely to foster *responsible* behavior" (87, emphasis in original).

24. On Leonardo's *La Gioconda* (aka Mona Lisa, ca. 1510) as the first modern portrait subject "estranged from the landscape," see Van den Berg, 60. See also Mimei Ito's discussion of imagery in J.B. Callicott's apprehension of landscape as an "articulate unity" (130).

25. As critic Tom Speelman put it, "he gets put through hell. Death by waterfall, extreme heat and cold, wolf attack, and being bashed into a rock by leopards are just some of the traumas Panther endures. And he doesn't get away cleanly. His costume gets torn to shreds, he's battered and torn and bloody. At some points, he can't even speak because of how exhausted he is."

26. Throughout his career, McGregor has displayed a fetish for loving descriptions of bloody torture and violence, as when T'Challa contends with the T-Rex: "His blood flows again.... The panther's torn costume has become a dark cloth sponge that absorbs the *warmth* of his blood.... Saliva, the consistency of *membranous tissue*, falls upon his chest ... mixing with the red fluid that *rushes* from *new* wounds" (Sedlmeier 194, my ellipses). McGregor famously subjected T'Challa to crucifixion on a burning cross in a later storyline featuring the Ku Klux Klan *(Jungle Action* #s 20 and 21 [March and May, 1976]). In that storyline, an older white woman opens a gash on his forehead with a can of cat food. The textbox says, "The scar will be *slight*, hardly noticeable, but he will *carry* it for the *rest* of his life" (Sedlmeier 302).

27. In their words: "There's limitations on how far the comic could've gone with the violence—I couldn't begin to specify what they are, but it was 1973 and we know that there were lines McGregor wouldn't have tried to cross—but if you examine the language and results of the battles that do occur, it's obvious how much more graphic all of the Panther's fights are against these non-human opponents."

28. McGregor describes the rhinoceros as "unaccountably infuriated," with "no conscious thought process here, only blind unreasoning *fury*" (Sedlmeier 98). But wouldn't mere territoriality account for its behavior?

29. McGregor's much-mocked writing often comes off as verbose and over the top— even by 1970s superhero comics standards. In the words of Stone and Brothers: "he plays it like some bastard version of Shakespeare, predating the soap-dripping mouth of Chris Claremont's Phoenix love poems completely, choosing instead to channel Robert E. Howard's barbarian violence through a Jack Kirby view of the world." Yet in many cases, his text is not merely restating what the art already shows, opening up productive avenues for visual-verbal tension and complexity, as seen here.

30. William Boyd played Hopalong Cassidy in dozens of western films in the 1930s and 1940s. For Lund, episodes like this typify T'Challa's Cold War ideological allegiance to the West: "Black Panther is made to embrace and express values and tastes thought to be central to the culture and society of the United States and thus become 'American.'" In a self-reflective moment courtesy of McGregor, when the Panther references Hitchcock's MacGuffin, he reprimands himself: "Must all of his reference points be so foreign to his native land?" (Sedlmeier 139).

31. The rhinoceros scene has taken on iconic status in Black Panther continuity, generating homages in *Black Panther* Vol. 2 (1988), *Black Panther* Vol. 3 (1998); *Black Panther* Vol. 4 (2005) and in the 2018 Ryan Coogler film adaptation.

32. As McGregor's text informs us, two major religions developed in Wakanda, one based on the Panther cult and the other on "*the awe-inspiring White Gorillas!*" (171). "The Monarch and the Man-Ape" in *Avengers* #62 (1969), featuring the gorilla-worshipping villain M'Baku, had earlier established this piece of continuity.

33. As argued by, among others, Jean Baudrillard: "Whatever it may be, animals have always had, until our era, a divine or sacrificial nobility that all mythologies recount.... The trajectory animals have followed, from divine sacrifice to dog cemeteries with atmospheric music, from sacred defiance to ecological sentimentality, speaks loudly enough of the vulgarization of the status of man himself—it once again describes an unexpected reciprocity between the two" (134).

34. The term, coined by Estonian semiotician Ivar Puura, denotes "a situation in which signs and stories that are significant for someone are destroyed because of someone else's malevolence or carelessness, thereby stealing a part of the former's identity" (quoted in Maran 147). Ecocritics and environmentalists have applied the concept to conditions in the Anthropocene; see Wheeler.

35. Pieces of the thick frame "bleed" into the next borderless panel, showing T'Chaka and his son enjoying themselves on a body of water. These black fragments, appear viscous in the water, subtly recalling the oil slick in Serpent Valley—a marker of the present "contaminating" a precious memory.

36. The bizarre blend of bathos and wonder recalls Emily Dickinson's "I Heard a Buzz Fly When I Died" ("With Blue—uncertain—stumbling buzz—between the light—and me") (before 1887).

37. For more on the "relevance movement" in U.S. superhero comics, see Wright, chapter 8.

38. Guirand confirms these details, adding that a neighboring tribe of the Bomitaba, the Kakar, had a "'man-panther' or fetish-doctor. He is especially consulted to detect the committer of a crime or misdemeanor" (482).

39. Irreverently, Mokadi also recalls John Keats' "Ode to Autumn" (1819), in which a manifestation of the season "watches the last oozings hours by hours" (Perkins 1271).

40. She relates vibrant matter to Henry David Thoreau's attitude to Wildness: "not-quite-human force that addled and altered human and other bodies. It named an irreducibly strange dimension of matter, an *out-side*" (2–3, emphasis in original).

41. Note how Bennett to some extent reinscribes Aldo Leopold's "land ethic," which "changes the role of *Homo sapiens* from conqueror of the land community to plain member and citizen of it. It implies respect for his fellow-members, and also respect for the community as such" (204).

42. See also Leopold's comments on extirpating wolves (130–132).

43. Doubts remains about whether creators Lee and Kirby knew about this connection. Kirby's granddaughter, Jilian Kirby, tweeted in March, 2018: "My grandfather, Jack Kirby, self taught [sic], well versed in religion and philosophy, researching his Western comics in the 50's & 60's, predating Black Panther, no doubt would have encountered and understood the significance of Wakanda" (quoted in Manseau). A to me more relevant and direct source for the word "Wakanda" comes from *The Man-Eater*, a 1915 novel by *Tarzan* creator Edgar Rice Burroughs. (Kirby was an avid reader of scifi and adventure tales.) In it, a native tribe in Belgian Congo, the Wakandas, murder some white hunters and missionaries.

44. See Thomas/Sal Buscema and Hudlin/Lashley.

45. Once more, this language overlaps with that of Leopold: "In short, a land ethic changes the role of *Homo sapiens* from conqueror of the land community to plain member and citizen of it. It implies respect for his fellow-members, and also respect for the community as such" (204).

Works Cited

Barber, Tiffany. "25 Years of Afrofuturism and Black Speculative Thought: Roundtable with Tiffany E. Barber, Reynaldo Anderson, Mark Dery, and Sheree Renée Thomas." *Topia: Canadian Journal of Cultural Studies*. Vol. 39 (2018): 136–142.

Bate, Walter Jackson. "Negative Capability." *Romanticism and Consciousness: Essays in Criticism*. Ed. Harold Bloom. New York: W.W. Norton, 1970: 326–343.

Baudrillard, Jean. *Simulacra and Simulation*. Ann Arbor: University of Michigan Press, 1994.

Bennett, Jane. *Vibrant Matter: A Political Ecology of Things*. Durham: Duke University Press, 2010.

Chen, Mel Y. *Animacies: Biopolitics, Racial Mattering, and Queer Affect*. Durham: Duke University Press, 2012.

Clarke, K.C., and Jeffrey J. Hemphill. "The Santa Barbara Oil Spill, A Retrospective." *Yearbook of the Association of Pacific Coast Geographers*. Vol. 64 (2002): 157–162.

Coates, Ta-Nehisi. *Between the World and Me*. New York: Spiegel & Grau, 2015.

Coates, Ta-Nehisi, and Stelfreeze, Brian. *Black Panther: A Nation Under Our Feet*. New York: Marvel, 2017.

Cohen, Jeffrey Jerome. "Posthuman Environs." *Environmental Humanities: Voices from the Anthropocene*. Ed. Serpil Oppermann and Serenella Iovino. New York: Rowman & Littlefield International, 2017: 25–44.

Cole, Teju. "On the Blackness of the Panther." *Medium* (March 6, 2018). https://medium.com/s/story/on-the-blackness-of-the-panther-f76d771b0e80.

Cronon, William. "The Trouble with Wilderness; or, Getting Back to the Wrong Nature." *Uncommon Ground: Rethinking the Human Place in Nature*. Ed. Cronon. New York: W.W. Norton, 1996: 69–90.

Englehart, Steve, and Keith Pollard. "I Want to Die!" *Fantastic Four*. Vol. 1, No. 311 (February 1988): 1–22.

Flippen, J. Brooks. *Nixon and the Environment*. Albuquerque: University of New Mexico Press, 2012.

Grad, Shelby. "The Environmental Disaster That Changed California—And Started the Movement Against Offshore Oil Drilling." *The Los Angeles Times* (April 28, 2017). https://www.latimes.com/local/lanow/la-me-santa-barbara-spill-20170428-htmlstory.html.

Guirand, Félix. *New Larousse Encyclopedia of Mythology*. New York: Prometheus, 1968.

Hartman, Geoffrey H. "The Romance of Nature and the Negative Way." *Romanticism and Consciousness: Essays in Criticism*. Ed. Harold Bloom. New York: W.W. Norton, 1970: 280–305.

Hatfield, Charles. "Kirby's Post-Apocalyptic Child." *Hand of Fire: The Comics Art of Jack Kirby* (January 28, 2017). https://handoffire.wordpress.com/2017/01/28/kirbys-post-apocalyptic-child/.

_____. *Hand of Fire: The Comics Art of Jack Kirby*. Jackson: University Press of Mississippi, 2012.

Heimlich, Cheryl Kane. "Rainforest Café Becoming the 'Disney World' of Eateries." *South Florida Business Journal*. Vol. 17, No.3 (November 15, 1996): 1. http://link.galegroup.com/apps/doc/A19064311/ITOF?u=wash_main&sid=ITOF&xid=0214d055.

Howe, Sean. *Marvel Comics: The Untold Story*. New York: Harper, 2012.

Hudlin, Reginald, and Lashley, Ken. *Black Panther: Shuri—Deadliest of the Species*. New York: Marvel, 2018.

Ito, Mimei. "Seeing Animals, Speaking of Nature: Visual Culture and the Question of the Animal." *Theory, Culture & Society*. Vol. 25, No. 4 (2008): 119–37.

Leopold, Aldo. *A Sand County Almanac and Sketches Here and There*. New York: Oxford University Press, 1987.

Lund, Martin. "'Introducing the Sensational Black Panther!' *Fantastic Four* #52–53, the Cold War, and Marvel's Imagined Africa." *The Comics Grid: Journal of Comics Scholarship.* No. 6 (May 23, 2016). https://www.comicsgrid.com/articles/10.16995/cg.80/.
Manseau, Peter. "The Surprising Religious Backstory of 'Black Panther's' Wakanda." *Washington Post* (March 7, 2018). https://www.washingtonpost.com/news/acts-of-faith/wp/2018/03/07/the-surprising-religious-backstory-of-black-panthers-wakanda/?noredirect=on&utm_term=.91d290c8582d.
Maran, Timo. "Enchantment of the Past and Semiocide. Remembering Ivar Puura." *Sign Systems Studies.* Vol. 41, No. 1 (2013): 146–149.
Mitchell, W.J.T. "Imperial Landscape." *Landscape and Power.* Ed. Mitchell. Chicago: University of Chicago Press, 1994: 5–34.
Morse, Kathryn. "There Will Be Birds: Images of Oil Disasters in the Nineteenth and Twentieth Centuries." *Journal of American History.* Vol. 99, No. 1 (2012): 124–34.
Nama, Adilifu. *Super Black: American Pop Culture and Black Superheroes.* Austin: University of Texas, 2011.
Nash, A.E. Keir et al. *Oil Pollution and the Public Interest: A Study of the Santa Barbara Oil Spill.* Institute of Governmental Studies, Berkeley: University of California Press, 1972.
Perkins, David, ed. *English Romantic Writers.* New York: Harcourt Brace,1995.
Price, Jennifer. "Looking for Nature at the Mall: A Field Guide to the Nature Company." *Uncommon Ground: Rethinking the Human Place in Nature.* Ed. Cronon. New York: W.W. Norton, 1996: 186–203.
Rinde, Meir. "Richard Nixon and the Rise of American Environmentalism." *Distillations* (June 2, 2017). https://www.sciencehistory.org/distillations/richard-nixon-and-the-rise-of-american-environmentalism.
Schama, Simon. *Landscape and Memory.* New York: A.A. Knopf, 1995.
Sedlmeier, Cory, ed. *Black Panther Epic Collection: Panther's Rage.* New York: Marvel, 2016.
Shepard, Paul. *Man in the Landscape: A Historic View of the Esthetics of Nature.* College Station: Texas A&M University Press, 1991.
Silko, Leslie Marmon. "Landscape, History and the Pueblo Imagination." *At Home on the Earth: Becoming Native to Our Place: A Multicultural Anthology.* Ed. David Landis Barnhill. Berkeley: University of California Press, 1999: 30–42.
Speelman, Tom. "How Black Panther Pioneered Modern Comics with 'Panther's Rage.'" *Comics Alliance* (May 16, 2016). https://comicsalliance.com/black-panther-panthers-rage-don-mcgregor/.
Spezio, Teresa Sabol. *Slick Policy: Environmental and Science Policy in the Aftermath of the Santa Barbara Oil Spill.* Pittsburgh: University of Pittsburgh, 2018.
Stone, Tucker, and Brothers, David. "Fear of a Black Panther." *The Comics Journal* (February 16, 2018). http://www.tcj.com/fear-of-a-black-panther/.
Thomas, Cathy. "'Black' Comics as Cultural Archive of Black Life in America." *Feminist Media Histories.* Vol. 4, Number 3 (2018): 49–95.
Thomas, Roy, and Buscema, John. "The Monarch and the Man-Ape!" *Avengers* Vol. 1, No. 62 (March 1969): 1–18.
Thomas, Roy, and Buscema, Sal. "Look Homeward, Avenger!" *Avengers.* Vol. 1, No 87 (April 1971): 1–20.
Van den Berg, J.H. "The Subject and His Landscape." *Romanticism and Consciousness: Essays in Criticism.* Ed. Harold Bloom. New York: W.W. Norton, 1970: 57–65.
Wanzo, Rebecca. "And All Our Past Decades Have Seen Revolutions: The Decolonization of Black Panther." *The Black Scholar* (February 19, 2018). https://www.theblackscholar.org/past-decades-seen-revolutions-long-decolonization-black-panther-rebecca-wanzo/.
Wheeler, Wendy. "Ecologies of Meaning and Loss." *The Dark Mountain Project* (August 25, 2017). https://dark-mountain.net/in-other-tongues-ecologies-of-meaning-and-loss/.
Wimsatt, W.K. "The Structure of Romantic Nature Imagery." *Romanticism and Consciousness: Essays in Criticism.* Ed. Harold Bloom. New York: W.W. Norton, 1970: 77–88.
Wright, Bradford W. *Comic Book Nation: The Transformation of Youth Culture in America.* Baltimore: Johns Hopkins University Press, 2001.

Fighting the Long War Against the Klan

The Black Panther as a Symbol of Self-Defense and Social Justice

BURTON P. BUCHANAN, IVON ALCIME *and* CARLOS D. MORRISON

One of the earliest solo appearances of Marvel Comic's Black Panther was in the comic book *Jungle Action featuring the Black Panther* in 1973. During this time, writer Don McGregor and a handful of artists used the *Jungle Action* series to create what would be among "the earliest self-contained multi-part comic book story lines, with a beginning and an end" (Beard) that all started with *Jungle Action* #6 titled the "Panther's Rage." *Jungle Action* #6 is significant in Marvel history because it includes "virtually an all-black cast of characters" (Beard), a notable outlier for the comic books produced up to that point in time.

One of the more interesting story arcs in the *Jungle Action* series focuses on the Black Panther returning to the United States, specifically Georgia, from his native homeland of Wakanda with his girlfriend, Monica Lynne. Black Panther then fights both the Ku Klux Klan and a cult called the Dragon Circle. The following is a rhetorical analysis of the KKK story arc that ran from *Jungle Action* #19–22. The analysis will rely on two concepts as critical tools of analysis: metonymy and empowerment/disempowerment. Brummett posits that "public issues must be reduced or *metonymized* into the signs, artifacts, and texts of popular culture" in order for the public or reader to "make sense" of the issues (119). Moreover, the analysis will show that (1) fighting the KKK and racism has taken a variety approaches in the South and in Georgia in particular, (2) the KKK story arc suggests that fighting the Klan in 1970s Georgia required a *self-defense* approach and (3) the Black Panther, whether in real life or comic form, is an empowering symbol of self-defense and protest fighter.

The Theory—Semiotics

Semiotics is the study of signs. More specifically, it is the way signs generate meaning via language, symbols, or text. Some of the early scholars associated with the study of semiotics include Ferdinand de Saussure, Roland Barthes, Charles Sanders Peirce, and Umberto Eco. A central tenet of semiotic theory is that "all texts convey meaning through signs or *signifiers* that refer to objects, concepts, or events called *signifieds*. These signifiers interact with one another in meaningful and sophisticated but not obvious relationships, or *sign systems* which make up the 'language,' or 'code' or the text" (Larson 94). For example, the blowing of pages off a calendar signifies the passing of time. Or the blue and red lightsaber in a *Star Wars* movie signifies the "good" Jedi Knight and the "evil" Sith Lord. Larson further posits that "the semiotician approaches any communication event as if it were a 'text' to be 'read' by the receiver/analyst" (Larson 95). Thus, the intent in this analysis is to examine the *Black Panther's* KKK story arc in an effort to determine its meaning in the context of 1970s American culture, racism, etc.

One of the critical concepts that will assist in the "reading" of the *Black Panther* KKK story arc as text is metonymy. In *A Grammar of Motives*, Rhetorician/Philosopher Kenneth Burke views "*metonymy* and *reduction* as substitutes for each other. […] The basic 'strategy' in metonymy is this: to convey some incorporeal or intangible state in terms of the corporeal or tangible. e.g., to speak of 'the heart' rather than the 'emotions'" (Burke 506). In *Rhetoric in Popular Culture*, Rhetorical scholar Barry Brummett also views metonymy within the context of reduction and further suggests that "metonymy occurs when something complex is reduced to a more manageable sign of that complex thing, as when the complexities of British government are reduced into the public figures of the Prime Minister, or of the reigning monarch" (Brummett 230).

Both Burke's and Brummett's thinking about metonymy serve to guide the analysis. Given that public issues, i.e., racism, discrimination, poverty and crime of the 1970s were extremely complex, those public issues can be metonymized or reduced in order to be more easily addressed. In addition to using metonymy as a critical tool, the concepts of empowerment/disempowerment are used in this analysis. To empower is to give power or authority to someone to do something. Here an analysis will be provided of who is empowered or disempowered in the KKK story arc as a result of the way in which issues of race and politics are metonymized "by the meanings that might be assigned to or generated by the text" (Brummett 120).

"Sleepy Southern Georgia Town" as Symbol of Klan Activity in 1970s Georgia

One of the first issues that the Black Panther KKK story arc metonymizes is Klan activity in Georgia in the 1970s. The history of the region as well as the specific cultural context of the 1970s made this a particularly powerful moment in time for such a story to be told. The post–World War II period saw a time of rapid economic growth and expansion. The United States attained the highest standard of living on the globe. The burgeoning American middle class had moved to suburbia which was, by and large, a white person's experience. Segregated American armed forces had won World War II and brought the opportunity for such prosperity in the post-war period. Still, in the 1950s and 1960s, segregation was the rule whether unwritten or as written law.

The struggle for racial equality in America began to bear fruit with the 1964 passage of the Civil Rights Act. With vehement opposition among Southern political leaders during the period, the act ended segregation in public places and placed a ban on employment discrimination on the basis of race, color, religion, sex, or national origin. Subsequent legislation also addressed racial discrimination with respect to housing. The American cultural landscape began a slow trek of more inclusion of African Americans and other minority groups. Clear changes were taking place with respect to popular culture, mass media, politics, and sports.

Change was on the horizon and visible in areas such as fashion. In the mid–1970s Beverly Johnson became the first black woman to appear on the cover of *Vogue*. During this same period, the careers of fellow black models Grace Jones and Iman reached historic heights. African American women were beginning to be seen in the major runways and magazines of the period (The History of Black Models).

Television, the predominant mass medium during the mid–1970s had created a cultural shift of sorts with respect to programming. Although not large in numbers, or completely positive in portrayals and cultural reflection, producers did begin to portray African American characters in regularly scheduled programming. Roles were starting to be less background characters but portrayals were lacking when it came to showing characters in a more truthful, accurate and meaningful manner. Several television shows such as *Good Times, What's Happening, Sanford and Son, That's My Mama,* and *The Jeffersons* all received high ratings from the American viewing public.

With respect to American cinema, the 1970s saw the rise of the black exploitation or "Blaxploitation" film sub-genre. The genre was fraught with wildly stereotypical imagery of blacks in urban settings, with colorful clothes, almost absurd violence and rampant sex scenes set against soulful musical scores. Despite its controversial elements, the genre did begin to depict the world of the 1970s where African Americans were gaining social, political and economic power. Black nationalism themes can be seen throughout much of the genre. Also seen is the clash of the white power establishment and the newly empowered, charismatic male and female black protagonists shown in the films (Morris).

Politics in America in the mid–1970s was undergoing change, including the election of African Americas to Congress as well as elections of African Americans to mayoral posts in several major American cities. In 1972, Barbara Jordan was elected to the United States Congress as representative for the eighteenth district from the state of Texas. She was the first African American woman to be elected to Congress and among the first black representatives since the 19th century. Jordan served as a committee member for the House Judiciary Committee as well as the Committee on Government Operations. During her tenure on the Judiciary Committee, she gained national attention during the tumultuous Watergate hearings.

In 1972 Andrew Young was elected to the United States Congress, serving as the representative from Georgia's fifth district. He became the first African American representative in Congress from the Deep South since Reconstruction. He originated legislation that founded a U.S. Institute for Peace. Young also negotiated federal funding for Atlanta's public transportation system, the Metropolitan Atlanta Rapid Transit Authority or MARTA, the Atlanta Highway System, and the establishment of a new International airport for the city of Atlanta. Young would later be appointed as United States Ambassador to the United Nations by President Jimmy Carter, and serve as the mayor of Atlanta. Additionally, a little over a decade following the enactment of the 1964 Civil Rights Act, Atlanta, Detroit, and Los Angeles elected their first African American mayors.

American sport exemplifies yet another area of the culture where improvements were made with respect to opportunities for African Americans. African Americans had broken through the color barrier in baseball some decades earlier but still were prevented from actively participating in other scholastic and professional sports. Some personalities did make their mark on American sports. In this decade, Wayne Embry became the first African American general manager in all of professional sports. Embry was appointed to the position of general manager of the Milwaukee Bucks in 1972, and held that post until 1979 (Spears). In 1975, Frank Robinson debuted as the manager for the Major League Baseball team the Cleveland Indians. Robinson had been hired as a player but was offered the position of player/manager later that year on October 3 (Walker and Ginsburg). Also, in 1975 golfer Lee Elder became the first African American to play in the Masters, golf's most prestigious tournament. Elder qualified for play by winning the Monsanto Open in 1974 (Wickham).

> In addition, Henry "Hank" Aaron hit is 715th home run during this period and Muhammad Ali caused quite a stir worldwide as he prepared for the "Thrilla in Manila." The world champion boxer faced off against Joe Frazier in the Philippines at the world heavy weight boxing championship. And in the word of professional tennis, the sport was celebrating the career of Arthur Ashe. Ashe was American professional tennis player who won three Grand Slam titles. He was also the first black player selected to the U.S. Davis Cup team and the only black man ever to wind the singles match at Wimbledon, the Australian Open and the U.S. Open. He squared off in 1975 against opponent Jimmy Connors, who was heavily favored to take the match. Through quiet strength and determination, Ashe proved that courage and thought are important in tennis ("Ashe Upsets Connors in Wimbledon Final").
> The period represented a time of great hope for social, political and economic change for African Americans. Following decades of oppression, segregation and deprivation, the American cultural landscape was beginning to change and a more representative culture had begun to emerge. African Americans were emerging in all aspects of culture and taking their place among the best.

In reaction, the Ku Klux Klan experienced a rebirth throughout the South and in Georgia in particular. In *The Way It Was in the South: The Black Experience in Georgia*, Donald L. Grant posits that "Georgia has long been linked with the Ku Klux Klan in the popular mind.... Since Reconstruction, the Klan has risen up more than once in an attempt to thwart black political and economic gains" (Grant 556). Segregationists and Klansman such as David Duke and J.B. Stoner were very active in 1970s Georgia. Louisiana's David Duke put a modern and updated face on the Klan. Duke seemed to embody this late 20th century concept of the angry white man who has lost power and fears for the future of his race (Bridges 1). Duke had been raised in a middle class home by parents who exhibited a great deal of family dysfunction. By the time Duke had reached middle school age, he had become quite interested in white supremacy (Bridges 9). In 1971, Duke had taken his senior year off from Louisiana State University to work on the organization of his supremacist group the National Party (Bridges 2). David Duke's ultimate rise to power and influence was representative of the modern Klan and other supremacist viewpoints of this period of the mid 1970s. Such attitudes shared by Duke and others of his ilk promulgated further the formation and rise of this last iteration of the Ku Klux Klan in America. David Duke founded the Knights of the Ku Klux Klan in 1975 in an effort to recast the Klan in a more "favorable light." Duke rebranded the Klan as being a defender of the white man's political and economic rights much like the NAACP was a champion for the rights of blacks.

While Duke sought to move the Klan away from its historical past of what Dr. Martin Luther King called "hooded perpetrators of violence" and burning crosses, J.B Stoner embraced the old practices of the Klan. Stoner preached a rhetoric of hate towards Blacks and Jews throughout Georgia, his home state, and the South. Moreover J.B. Stoner was allegedly connected to several bombings including the Sixteenth Street Baptist Church bombing and the Bethel Baptist Church bombing in Birmingham, Alabama, in the 1960s.

Beginning in the late-1960s, many working class Southerners and others sympathetic to their concerns felt a palpable loss of their perceived social, political and economic power due to the changes brought by the civil rights movement and passage of the 1964 Civil Rights Act (Ellis). They looked to organizations like the Klan to attempt to recoup the power that they felt they had lost. The Ku Klux Klan in this period saw a resurgence. While the original formation of the Klan was by upper class white men, this more recent rebirth of the organization was predominantly made up of lower and middle class white men. (Cunningham 127). Along the Southern United States, chapters of the secret organization began to spring forward from earlier roots.

The mid–1970s was a period of transition. With the Civil Rights Act striking a blow to a culture steeped in institutional racism, America was changing and African Americans were beginning to be more an integral part of the cultural landscape in social and political contexts. African Americans began to make a showing, in American society and in particular, in entertainment, politics and sports during the decade.

It is in this social setting that *Jungle Action* #19 (Jan. 1976) begins the story of T'Challa's fight with the Ku Klux Klan. Black Panther visits his friend Monica Lynne in her home state of Georgia, as she deals with the death of her sister. In 1976, the Civil Rights Act passed during the Johnson administration has been in effect for roughly a dozen years. America has begun a cultural change where people of color began to gain more social economic and personal power. Prior to the Act's passage, in many states, racial segregation was the law and a common social feature of many southern states. Employment discrimination was rampant and the overwhelming majority of African Americans had little power to combat such blatant discrimination. Blacks were overtly disenfranchised, had their economic capabilities seriously curtailed and were not able to share public accommodations, facilities, and educational institutions enjoyed by whites.

It is logical for a superhero such as T'Challa to face head on, the Ku Klux Klan in America in the 1970s. Moreover, it stands to reason that his fight against the Klan would take place in a Southern state. The fight against the Klan also represents a pure struggle of good over evil, a fight where the powers of morality and decency prevail over the despicable.

Jungle Action #19–21

In the early scenes in the Jungle Action story arc, the reader finds that T'Challa is in the state of Georgia, visiting his girlfriend Monica Lynne. The reader also finds that Monica is in Georgia to mourn the death of her sister Angela. In the opening imagery, Monica is lost in thought in the cemetery while a mass of dark strangers draws near to her location. Her solitude is interrupted by a gathering of hooded men. They are intercepted by T'Challa before Monica is harmed. They also meet Kevin Trublood a reporter from the Georgia Sun, an idealistic journalist. Trublood offers an idea that he knows who killed Angela.

Monica's sister Angela discovered that there was Klan activity in not only the real estate firm for which she was working but also in the town's political structure. Angela's official cause of death was ruled a suicide by gunshot to the head, but Trublood is convinced it was murder and suspects the Klan. Angela came across documentation of a land manipulation deal while at her job and relayed it to Trublood to investigate. Trublood seeks to investigate the story due to both feelings he had for Angela and due to his self-proclaimed idealism. He knows that his country is not perfect. Even with the issues of the war in Vietnam, civil rights issues and Watergate, Trublood has not lost his idealism. Besides, he has his eye on his dream of one day winning a Pulitzer prize.

T'Challa later confronts the Klan at a clandestine meeting complete with burning cross. The hooded members overpower him and begin a physical battle with T'Challa complete with guns and ropes. He is tied to a cross. T'Challa's physical strength allows him to use the cross as a ram to ward off the Klansmen.

Within the *Jungle Action featuring the Black Panther* KKK story arc, the disruption of black equality and political gains by the Klan is metonymized in the comic book text via one overarching entity: *The Soul Strangler*. In the story, "Death Riders on the Horizon," (Jungle Action 22) Jessica Lynne, Monica Lynne's mother tells a story of Caleb, her grandfather's cousin confronting and fighting the Klan during the Reconstruction period after the Civil War. In Jessica Lynne retelling of the story, Caleb, an ex-enslaved African, and his family are confronted by the Klan. The Klan, led by the Soul Strangler, sought to thwart any attempt by Caleb to obtain political and economic rights by way of the Freedman's Bureau, which was a federal agency created by the Department of War to assistant the ex-enslaved African with food, clothing, and shelter. The Soul Strangler tells Caleb, who is afraid and timid, the following: "**Beware** nigra … for we are watching you even when you **cannot see us!** If we see you near the Freedman's Bureau or the Loyal Leagues, **WE WILL RETURN!**" (Jungle Action 22, 10). Caleb is silent with fear as he attempts to stand his ground. He is trampled by the "ghostly stallion" ridden by Soul Strangler as the Klan ride off. By the end of the story arc, Caleb is lynched by the Klan.

However, Monica reimagines the telling of the story a bit differently in the text. In Monica's version, Caleb is not afraid, timid nor does he die in her narrative. Caleb has the look on his face of confidence and self-determination as he confronts the Klan and the Soul Strangler. When Soul Strangler says "**Beware** nigra … for we are watching you even when you **cannot see us!** If we see you near the Freedman's Bureau or the Loyal Leagues, **WE WILL RETURN!**" (Jungle Action 22, 10), Caleb says, "If you **do**…. Might be **you'll regret it!**" (Jungle Action No. 22 11). And in a tree overlooking both Caleb and the Soul Strangler lurks the *Black Panther*. Soon the panther leaps down from the tree and strikes the Soul Strangler knocking him from his horse while saying, "You **claim** you have **ridden** from the flames of hell. That seems a fitting place for such beings as you. Ride **back** to it …while you **still** have the **chance**. And you will **ride**…. **Along!**" (Jungle Action 22, 11). By the end of the story arc, Caleb and the *Black Panther* walk away in victory after defeating the Klan.

Caleb and Jessica as "Old Guard" Response to Racism and Discrimination

Both Jessica and Monica Lynne's recollections of Caleb's confrontation with the Klan during the Reconstruction Period explains two types of approaches to dealing with the Klan: *Civil Rights/non-violence resistance* and *Black* Nationalism/self-defense. The second dynamic that emerges from the text is that Jessica and Monica's narrative further suggest, via the writers of the comic text, which strategy is the *more favorable* approach to be understood and managed by the reader.

Both Caleb and Jessica are a representation of a segment of the black community, i.e., the "old guard," activists that grew up in the shadows of Jim Crow laws, segregation and racial violence against blacks. These blacks, or Negroes as they considered themselves at the time, were there when *Plessy vs Ferguson* became the law of the land making public facilities "separate but equal" for Negroes. They were there during the "Red Summer of 1919" when Negroes were lynched and their homes burned to the ground by white lynch mobs throughout the South and Midwest. The "Calebs and Jessicas" of the Negro community were considered second class citizens and viewed by the white power structure at the time to be inferior. This was Negro life in America for much of the 20th century. And when *Brown vs. Board of Education of Topeka, Kansas* became the law of the land in 1954, the "Calebs and Jessicas" rejoiced because now "separate but equal" was ruled unconstitutional by the Supreme Court.

Yet, "white terror" had taken its toll on the Negro. The same fear, trepidation and ignorance experienced by Caleb when he was confronted by the Soul Strangler was the same fear, trepidation and ignorance that the Negro experienced and internalized in response to racial violence in 20th century America. *Brown vs. Board* more than anything revealed the psychological effects of racism and discrimination on the "Calebs and Jessicas." Dr. Martin L. King, Jr., and the civil rights movement of the 1950s and 1960s were instrumental in helping the "Calebs and Jessicas" do three important things: (1) gain their civil rights, i.e., voting, public accommodations, etc., (2) embrace non-violent resistance as a strategy for dealing with white racism and discrimination and (3) begin to break the psychological barriers of inferiority. These three attributes, particularly, the use of non-violent/passive resistance as a strategic approach to dealing with racism and the Klan, would carry over into the black community of the 1970s, particularly in the South.

The 1970s witnessed black Americans fighting the white power structure by still using the civil rights strategies and tactics, i.e., marches, sit-ins, etc., of the 1960s. Organizations such as the NAACP, PUSH and the Jesse Jackson's *Rainbow Coalition* lead the way by fighting racism in the "suites" of white corporate America. The "Calebs and the Jessicas" were also fighting in the courtrooms too just as they did during the 1960s. And while successful, young black activists like "Monica" in the text were getting restless and wanted their "rights" now. Moreover, they felt that a different response was needed with the resurrection of the Klan under David Duke.

Monica and the Black Panther as "New Guard" Response to Racism and the Klan

While Caleb and Jessica Lynne were a representation of the "old guard" activists that embraced the strategy of passive resistance/non-violent direction action, Monica and the *Black Panther* were a representation of the "new guard" black activist that came to fruition during the civil rights struggle of the 1960s and early 1970s. These black activists were often young black college students who wanted their voices to be heard and who wanted a complete overhaul of the white establishment. While non-violent direction action was the strategy of the "old guard," the "new guard's" preferred strategy, as suggested earlier, was *Black Nationalism/self-defense*.

Jungle Action featuring the Black Panther #21 has a story titled "Blood and Sacrifices!" where Monica, while visiting her sister's grave, is attacked by members of the Dragon Circle, a local cult, seeking to make a "blood sacrifice" as part of an initiation-rite into the organization. However, before members of the cult can drive their knives into Monica's back, Monica and the Black Panther attacks the cult members in self-defense.

It is safe to say that Monica and the Black Panther are the embodiment of the enslaved Africans, who during the antebellum period, fought back against their oppressor. Enslaved Africans such as Nat Turner, Denmark Vesey, David Walker and Gabriel Prosser were black insurrectionists who led slave revolts valiantly against the cruel slave master and his whip. Their first act of resistance was an act of self-defense. The "Monicas" and the "Black Panthers" were the black abolitionists of the day such as Prince Hall, Richard Allen, Henry Highland Garnet, and Frederick Douglass, who unlike Nat Turner, relied on the power of the spoken word to agitate against the Southern slave system.

By the end of the Civil War and Reconstruction, the "Monicas" and the "Black Panthers" were present in the voices of dissent that rose up against the Ku Klux Klan, The Camelias, and other secret orders that sought to disenfranchise the Negro. Having gained some "rights" under Reconstruction (which were later taken away), the "Monicas" and the "Black Panthers" would continue to provide a response to white violence and white supremacy well into the turn of the 20th century. Every black man or woman that fought back in self-defense of white violence was a "Monica" or a *"Black Panther."*

In the midst of the Great Debate between Booker T. Washington, founder of Tuskegee University, and W.E.B. Dubois over the "proper" education for the Negro, there was the representation of "Monica" and the *"Black Panther"* in the Garvey Movement, founded by Marcus Mosiah Garvey. Like the Wakandans of Black Panther's homeland, the Garveyites, who were members of the United Negro Improvement Association (U.N.I.A.), placed an emphasis on (1) Pan-Africanism (African people everywhere coming together to fight white oppression), (2) race pride, (3) black self-determination and black unity, (4) black self-defense against white racism through Black Nationalism. Throughout the 1920 and 1930s, the movement would flourish and lay the foundation for the Black Power movement of the 1960s and 1970s. The "Monicas" and the "Black Panthers" are manifested in the black power movement of the 1960s and the *Black Panther* movement of the 1970s. The black power movement, as articulated by Stokely Carmichael, placed and emphasis on blacks obtaining their political and economic rights much like the Garveyites did in the 1920s. Moreover, the black power movement, composed mainly of young black Americans, embraced the strategy of self-defense.

In the 1970s, the strategy of self-defense would carry over to the Black Panther Party under the leadership of activist Bobby Seale and Huey Newton in Oakland, California, in 1966. Members of the Black Panther party would often arm themselves with guns in self-defense during rallies in the black community for fear of retaliation from the white police. The Black Panther Party for Self-Defense had chapters all over the country including the South. In places like Georgia, the Black Panther party along with various civil rights groups provided an alternative yet important response to J.B. Stoner and David Duke.

Empowering the Monica and Black Panther Position

One is able to discern that of two options—Jessica/Caleb (civil rights/passive resistance) and Monica/Black Panther (Black Nationalism/self-defense)—Marvel writer Don McGregor pushes the reader toward the Monica/Black Panther course of action. If the political and economic interest of Black Georgians is to be wrestled away from white supremacists such as David Duke and J.B. Stoner, it will be done by young African Americans like Monica. These Black Panther issues are grounded in race-pride, self-determination, black unity, and a strong desire to end white oppression and not in the approach of the "old guard" per se of the civil rights era. McGregor uses the contrasting dialogue about Caleb to address the "generational divide" that exists in the African American community. In 2015, this divide in the black community came to a hilt during the 50th anniversary of the Bloody Sunday march in Selma, Alabama, when veteran civil rights heads clashed with the Ferguson, Missouri, protesters during President Obama's speech at the foot of the Edmund Pettus Bridge. In the *Montgomery Advertiser* Duane Rankin characterized the two groups this way: "On the one side, you have young people who have traveled 600 miles to speak their mind.... They are angry and hurting that Michael Brown died by police bullets and vented to the 10th power.... On the other side, there are folks who came from a time and part of the country that went about creating change in a different manner. Led by the late Rev. Martin Luther King Jr., those down here in the South were all about making a difference too but doing it in a nonviolent way" (Rankin 10A).

In addition to the issue of the "generational divide," McGregor further suggests that present day Soul Stranglers such as J.B. Stoner and David Duke must be dealt with via the strategy of self-defense. Marvel artist Bill Graham's Black Panther is a symbol of black pride, strength and self-determination in the face of white violence. Throughout the story arc, the Black Panther strikes only when struck or others are attacked.

Conclusion

The KKK story arc that unfolded in Marvel's *Jungle Action featuring the Black Panther* in 1976 was a very important storyline for the *Black Panther* comic. Not only was the book entertaining to comic fans, but it was socially conscious in its attempt to manage some of the public issues of the day. The story arc metonymizes some very important racial dynamics facing 1970s Georgia through the character Soul Strangler.

Soul Strangler is a symbolic representation of real-world racists who head organizations meant to ensure a racist status quo. Such figures include J.B. Stoner, who sought to use the intimidation tactics of the old Ku Klux Klan to thwart the social equality and political gains made by blacks, and David Duke, the man responsible for re-inventing the Klan via the Knights of the Ku Klux Klan in the 1970s. And what is the best strategy for dealing with and containing both J.B. Stoner and David Duke in 1970s Georgia?

The public issue of civil rights/non-violence resistance is metonymized in the Caleb and Jessica Lynne (Old Guard) characters in the comic text. And the public issue of *Black* Nationalism/self-defense is metonymized in the Monica and the Black Panther (New Guard) characters in the text. While both civil rights and black nationalism have played a major role in black America's quest for freedom, justice and equality, the authors take the position that writer Don McGregor favors the black nationalism/self-defense strategy for containing the real life Soul Stranglers.

There are at least three reasons for the position on Black Nationalism/self-defense being the preferred reading McGregor wants his audience to take: (1) The Monica and the Black Panther narrative is *empowering*. In Monica's retelling, Caleb is fierce, determined and strong in his conviction to face and defeat the Soul Strangler and the Klan members. With the help of the Black Panther, he bests the Ku Klux Klan and lives to tell the tale; (2) Black Panther, throughout the story arc, is also empowered in the text in and of himself. From fighting and defeating the Dragon Circle and the Klan to insightful conversations with both Monica and her parents, the Black Panther is strong and determined in defending that which is right and just. He uses force only as a self-defense tactic to defend those he loves (Monica and Mr. and Mrs. Lynne), the defenseless (Kevin Trublood) or himself; and finally (3) The Caleb and Jessica narrative is disempowering. In Jessica's story, Caleb is weak, timid and scared in his confrontation with the Klan. Moreover, Caleb is lynched by the Klan at the end of Jessica's retelling of the events.

Jungle Action featuring the Black Panther is still an important book historically in the Marvel comic universe. The story arc is a good example of art imitating life in its attempt to address issues of racism, bigotry, and hate. Moreover, the strength of the *Black Panther* character is in its representational power as a positive image for people of color and of Africa. This image flies in stark contrast to historically stereotypical images of the black male in popular culture as lazy, indolent, and bestial or of Africa as being backwards and "Third World." In the article "Super Powered: *Black Panther* Marks a Major Milestone for Culture," writer Jamil Smith says, "Black Panther was an expression of Afrofuturism-an ethos that fuses African mythologies, technology and science fiction and serves to rebuke conventional depictions of (or, worse, efforts to bring about) a future bereft of black people" (Smith). In the end, the KKK story arc presents a rhetoric of resistance to the negative portrayals of people of color, whether in comic book form or in real life.

Works Cited

Beard, James. "Path of the Black Panther: A Retrospective, pt. 1." Marvel.com. www.marvel.com/news/comic/22621/path_of_the_black_panther_a_retrospective_pt_2. Accessed 21 November 2018.
Bridges, Tyler. *The Rise of David Duke*. Oxford: University of Mississippi Press, 1995.
Brummet, Barry. *Rhetoric in Popular Culture*. Sage Publishing, 2015.
Burke, Kenneth. *A Grammar of Motives*. Berkeley: University of California Press, 1969.
"A Champion for Atlanta: Maynard Jackson, A Memorial Section." Atlanta Constitution, 29 June 2003.
Cunningham, David. *Klansville, USA: The Rise and Fall of the Civil Rights-Era Ku Klux Klan*. New York: Oxford University Press, 2013.
Ellis, C.P. "Why I Quit the Klan" from *American Dreams: Lost and Found* by Studs Terkel. Dialogic.blogspot.com. http://dialogic.blogspot.com/2013/01/why-i-quit-klan-an-interview-with-c-p.html. Accessed 15 October 2018.
Grant, Donald L. *The Way It Was in the South: The Black Experience in Georgia*. Athens: University of Georgia Press, 1993.
"The History of Black Models." Essence.com. https://www.essence.com/fashion-week/history-black-models/#299579. Accessed 18 October 2018.
Larson, Charles U. *Persuasion: Reception and Responsibility*. Wadsworth/Cengage, 2013.
"Mayor of Detroit and Political Symbol for Blacks Is Dead." *New York Times*, 30 Nov. 1997. https://www.nytimes.com/1997/11/30/us/coleman-a-young-79-mayor-of-detroit-and-political-symbol-for-blacks-is-dead.html. Accessed 19 September 2018.
McGregor, Don. "Jungle Action Featuring: The Black Panther # 19." *Jungle Action Featuring the Black Panther: Sacrifice of Blood*, no. 19, Marvel, Jan. 1976.
_____. "Jungle Action Featuring: The Black Panther # 20." *Jungle Action Featuring the Black Panther: Slaughter in the Streets!*, no. 20, Marvel, Mar. 1976.
_____. "Jungle Action Featuring: The Black Panther # 21." *Jungle Action Featuring the Black Panther: Cross of Fire … Cross of Death!*, no. 21, Marvel, May 1976.
_____. "Jungle Action Featuring: The Black Panther # 22." *Jungle Action Featuring the Black Panther: Doom Is the Death Rider!*, no. 22, Marvel, Jul. 1976.
Merl, Jean, and Bill Boyarsky. "Mayor Who Reshaped L.A. Dies." Latimes.com, 30 Sep. 1998, https://www.latimes.com/local/obituaries/archives/la-me-tom-bradley-19980930-story.html. Accessed 21November 2018.
Morris, Gary. "Blaxploitation: A Sketch," Brightlightsfilm.com, Bright Lights Film Journal, 1 Mar. 1997. https://brightlightsfilm.com/wp-content/cache/all/blaxploitation-a-sketch/#.XGCX_M9Kh0t. Accessed 11 October 2018.
Rankin, Duane. "This Time, the Gap Is Generational: Attitudes Both Past, Present Collide During Obama's Speech." *Montgomery Advertiser*, 8 March 2015, pp. 1A, 10A.
Roney, M. "Alabama's Black Belt Helped Form the Black Panther Party." *Montgomery Advertiser*, 1 Feb. 2016. https://www.usatodaycom/story/news/nation-now/2016/02/01/lowndes-county-black-panther-party-alabama/78943998/ Accessed November 18, 2018.

Smith, Jamil. "The Revolutionary Power of Black Panther: Marvel's New Movie Marks a Major Milestone." *Time,* vol. 191, no. 6, Feb. 2018, p. 43.

Spears, Marc J. "Wayne Embry: Raptor's Anthem Stance Similar to Selma-to-Montgomery March." Theundefeated.com, 4 Oct. 2016. https://theundefeated.com/features/wayne-embry-raptors-anthem-stance-similar-to-selma-to-montgomery-march/. Accessed 9 October 2018.

Tignor, Steve. "Ashe Upsets Connors in Wimbledon Final." Tennis.com, 30 Apr. 2015. http://www.tennis.com/pro-game/2015/04/1975-ashe-upsets-connors-wimbledon-final/54777/. Accessed 9 October 2018.

Walker, Ben, and David Ginsburg. "Frank Robinson, baseball's fearsome trailblazer, dies at 83." *Seattletimes.com/nation*, 7 Feb. 2019. https://www.seattletimes.com/nation-world/nation/hall-of-famer-pioneering-manager-frank-robinson-dies-at-83/. Accessed 7 February 2019.

Wickham, DeWayne. "Lee Elder Mastered Golf and Life," *USA Today*, 13 Apr. 2015. https://www.usatoday.com/story/opinion/2015/04/13/lee-elder-masters-wickham-column/25674263/. Accessed 19 October 2018.

The Shadow of Apartheid
Analyzing Peter Gillis' Run in the 1980s

FERNANDO GABRIEL PAGNONI BERNS

South Africa's practice of apartheid—government enforced procedures and social/cultural practices that sought to segregate whites and blacks—was and still is an open wound in the fabric of Western history. The U.S was not indifferent to the new climate dominating the 1980s regarding Africa. Within a "constructive engagement" with South Africa, an anti-apartheid sentiment raised resistance efforts against the deeply racist politics of apartheid taking place in South Africa since 1948 that would not end until the first half of the 1990s. During this era, popular culture creators would not be indifferent to the anti-racist struggles.

Predating prominent black superheroes such as DC Comics' Green Lantern John Stewart and Black Lightning—who debuted in 1971 and 1977—and Marvel Comics' Luke Cage and Storm—who first appeared in 1972 and 1975—Black Panther was the most likely character among prominent American comic book heroes to engage with the issues of the African apartheid and its politics of segregation. Further, as an African superhero residing mostly in Africa rather than United States (unlike the majority of the DC and Marvel superheroes), Black Panther was situated closer to the conflict than heroes housed in New York or fictional American cities. It was just a matter of time before T'Challa clashed against the reality of racial segregation.

In the latter half of the 1980s, Marvel comics published the *Black Panther* limited series written by Peter B. Gillis (whose previous work included stories for First Comics and Marvel's Captain America) and penciled by Denys Cowan. This limited series, currently known as Volume 2 of *Black Panther*, was published by Marvel in 1988 but written in 1983, a time when "Phoenix-like, anti-apartheid black organizations" were "rising up again" (Dubow 206), putting racial segregation into the spotlight.

In just four issues, this overlooked limited series addressed social and cultural anxieties of the era. These include the struggle to put the apartheid to an end thanks to efforts sustained both in Africa, where Apartheid was taking place, and in America, where the comic books were published, as well as the uneasy navigation between non-violent diplomacy and more active approaches through armed insurrection. Whereas some foreign forces regarded the apartheid regime as illegal, others considered this form of government an internal affair to be resolved exclusively by people in South Africa. As Chris Landsberg argues, the world was divided in relation to South Africa; while the Western powers "were not completely co-operative" (29) in their rhetoric, internal economic interests were protected.

Interestingly, T'Challa's behavior follows this division sustained by the world, as the hero struggles to reconcile diplomacy as a means to prevent further bloodshed with calls for armed action. Gillis eschews the oversimplified superheroic approach to illustrate the complex situation shaping South Africa, where any sanction or rebellious struggle negatively affected ordinary people's livelihoods. This essay will trace all the connections between the adventures of T'Challa within the borders of fictional Wakanda and real concerns of the time, finding them inextricably linked. Like the limited series itself, reality offered no simple solutions. Metaphorically constructed upon the basis of an international conflict taking place between two fictitious countries, this second volume narrating the adventures of the Black Panther engages with all-too-real horrors taking place in South Africa.

The Politics of the Apartheid

As recalled by Saul Dubow, the "stunning victory" of the Herenigde Nasionale Party was entirely unanticipated and took everyone, including Nationalist leader D.F. Malan, by surprise (Dubow 1). In 1948, the white supremacist National Party—composed by Boers, the representatives of the white Afrikaner minority in South Africa—was elected to power, making apartheid the official policy beginning that year. Over the next decades the National Party divided the lives of black and white South Africans by means of parliamentary legislation and politics of segregation which amounted to explicit, legalized racism. It instituted policies of racial difference that furthered existing prejudicial policies: "legislation prior to 1948 had already limited the land Africans could purchase and restricted them to certain types of labor, but apartheid was about consolidating this position and separating the population groups comprehensively" (Thomson 13). It was not just about racism, but the enthroning of *legal* racial discrimination as a way of life.

The apartheid was a policy where "pure" white people were superior to "colored" people. One of the aims of the National Party sought was "to ensure the safety of the white race and of Christian civilization" (Guelke 3) and separateness was argued to be necessary to ensure such a state of "safety." Alex Thomson mentions some of the new discriminatory policies formulated with the goal of keeping whites and blacks aggressively separated: marriage between individuals of different races became illegal in 1949; people were segregated into tightly bounded geographical zones (1950); black people were required to carry passes for free mobilization (1952); the education system was segregated (1953); and State security's main task was that of ensuring and policing this separation between black and white people. In brief, engaging with racial difference was turned into a major crime (Thomson 13). Supposedly, the ideology shaping apartheid was giving black South Africans "self-determination, and a right to develop their own culture. In reality, however, apartheid merely amounted to exploitation, hardship, and human rights abuses on a massive scale" (Thomson 14). The result was a geographical and economic distribution where whites possessed the mediums and tools to advance economically, politically, and socially while the South Africans of color faced unemployment, high numbers of infant mortality, and geographical locations that strongly resembled concentration camps. Many historians and scholars even drew an analogy between apartheid and Nazism, as the elements of racism "and grand design lent obvious verisimilitude to such a comparison" (Guelke 32).

As apartheid reached global visibility it became a matter of transnational controversy. As stated by Ali Mazrui, the United States mostly turned a blind eye to the racist policies in South Africa (25) through the years. This attitude was in part sustained on the basis of an anticommunist ethos. In 1950, South African leaders approved the Suppression of Communism Act. This Act's "immediate political effect was to drive the Communist Party underground" (Dubow 37). This attitude pleased the government of the United States, which "refused to accept that South Africa represented a threat to international security. Cold War rivalries persuaded leading western countries of the necessity to retain South Africa as a regional bulwark against Communism" (Dubow 50).

Further, the U.S. was still deeply informed by its own racist philosophy. At the same time that the racist National Party was establishing apartheid legislation in Africa, several southern states in the United States still excluded African Americans, "the Ku Klux Klan continued to terrorize the black community, and southern Dixiecrats were determined to keep 'their way of life' just as much as whites were in South Africa" (Thomson 14). In fact, the practices of lynching were still persistent in some parts of U.S right up until the late 1950s (Brooker 171).

Still, an emergence of anti-apartheid and anti-imperialist sentiments took place during the civil rights movement of the 1960s and 1970s. There were, however, differences in how this support was manifested. For some nationalists such as Carlos Cooks, leader of the African Nationalist Pioneer Movement, or Malcolm X, the resistance against the apartheid should be armed. The black liberal perspective on Africa, on the other hand, was represented by leaders such as Martin Luther King, Jr., whose political and ideological basis was nonviolent and integrationist.

The American 1970s were infused with countercultural collectives and ideologies which coincided with the civil rights movement and the development of black consciousness. This "black consciousness" prompted African American youths to begin to explore their African cultural heritage "and to adopt a black/pan-African identity" (Njubi Nesbitt 69). As a consequence, during the 1970s and 1980s, internal resistance to the politics of apartheid became increasingly radical and militant.

American administrations, however, generally supported the racist policies of South African governments. Soon after being elected, President Ronald Reagan spoke about the necessity of continuing the support "of a country that has stood by us in every war we ever fought" (Njubi Nesbitt 114; actually, the Nationalist Party supported the Nazis in World War II). The United States Congress and the American people, however, "had serious concerns" about this relationship (Mazrui 25). Further, by 1980, "anti-apartheid sentiment was widespread in the African-American community and quickly spreading to white students" (Njubi Nesbitt 69). The anti-apartheid sentiment reached a point where companies doing business with South Africa were forced to withdraw.

On March 2, 1980, the National Black Agenda "adopted by more than one thousand leaders representing three hundred organizations" urged the United States to "sever all economic, diplomatic, political and cultural relations with South Africa" (Njubi Nesbitt 111). Thus, "it was not the Reagan administration that imposed sanctions against South Africa but rather the United States Congress, by overriding the president's veto of the sanctions bill" (Mazrui 25). If the U.S government was not really interested in clashing against the overpowering racist ideology shaping South Africa, the concerns of a vast number of citizens obliged America to cooperate in any measures that could put the infamous apartheid to an end. Further, the 1980s were characterized by renewed anti-apartheid sentiments within the borders of South Africa itself. The decade was "a period when unprecedented numbers of South Africans (on the Left and the Right) set themselves against the state, and all parties to the conflict turned to political violence" (Louw 131).

It is within this cultural climate of transnational support, diplomatic struggles and violence through borders, that the second volume of the adventures of African superhero Black Panther would be published. With just brief explicit mentions of the apartheid, the limited series revolves around a series of upheavals in the fictional nation of Azania, a country geographically localized "at the southern tip of Africa" which shares borders with Wakanda. The name "Azania," in fact, has a long history in the South African mind. As Elizabeth Williams explains, "within the context of Pan-Africanism, the name Azania was used in 1958, and proposed as a replacement name for South Africa at the All-African People's Conference in Accra." Further, usage of the name among "revolutionary black radicals in the diaspora became popular in the late 1970s and began to appear in the names of groups such as the Azania People's Organization" as a way to "counter the Europeanisation of South Africa" (283). Azania is also the name of an autonomous region in southern Somalia. Thus, Azania—like the limited series as a whole—navigates between the fictional and the real.

In Marvel's Azania, white people exert oppression and violence upon the black citizenship. This conceptualization of territorial and racial dispute addressed, through a fantastic narrative, the cruel politics of the apartheid in South Africa. In Gillis' limited series, a supernatural monstrous panther has arisen, killing the white oppressors and inspiring revolts of blacks against the armed white minority. Meanwhile, T'Challa feels that the spirit of the panther is departing him since he is failing Wakanda (and Africa) as a proper leader. As a response to his diplomatic passivity, the natives of Wakanda increasingly criticize the "soft" ways of their leader, in part because he is critical rather than supportive of the black, armed revolt in Azania.

Peter Gillis' run hardly can be labeled an "allegory," speaking publicly of something without a clear reference to that "obscured" something. Gillis' run navigates at the edge of speaking obliquely but the reference is, undoubtedly, clear for everyone to see. In fact, the references to the real horrors of the apartheid were so crystal-clear that the comic saw light only years after its creation in 1983. This miniseries was shelved away "for fears that it would alienate readers" (Chambliss 193) until 1988, a year in which conversations between top South Africa government officials and a still jailed Nelson Mandela were beginning (Cottrell 110). The changes in the times between creation and publication, however, did not obscure many aspects of a comic book speaking about racial segregation and the urgency for heroic activity.

Hero for an Accursed Country

The cover of *Black Panther* # 1, depicting a defeated T'Challa, exclaims "Hero no More!" Next to the Black Panther, a group of black people stare straight to the readers, a way to require participatory engagement with the horror of the apartheid. There is no clear indication if either Azania or

Wakanda is the "accursed country" that gives title to the first issue ("Hero for an Accursed Country!"), as both are in deeply problematic times as the story begins.

Connecting the clues scattered through the first two issues, it can be determined that Azania is a nation sharing borders with Wakanda. Unlike Black Panther's home country, however, Azania exists under an apartheid-like status (the word "apartheid" is even briefly mentioned in issue #1). The white minority subjugates the large populations of black people through politics of segregation and violence. These practices are closely linked to traditional structures of imperialism and colonization—which, in turn, have connections with totalitarianism (Guelke xv)—as all them share policies of segregation and stratification. In *Black Panther* #2, an old black man reflects on the futility of any insurrection. "Even with the Black Panther leading us, it is hopeless! They have the guns, the power, the money! It has been this way for a century. Who can change it?" (Gillis). This reference to a long history of subjugation takes readers through a very long history of colonialism and imperialism exerted upon the African landscape.

Issue #1 begins in action, with Black Panther fighting a huge black rhino. T'Challa wins, the jungle judging him "by its own laws." This mention to territoriality ("by its own laws") is not superfluous. The limited series will frequently return to issues of the local and the global. The word apartheid "helped to turn South Africa's domestic policies into an international issue, rendered the country a pariah, and gave it global significance" (Dubow xi); accordingly, both Wakanda and Azania will become the center of attention of the entire world. The history of apartheid navigated between the local and the global, as politics of foreign intervention were thought, practiced and discarded.

Black Panther #1 opens evoking traditional forms of male heroism in the jungles, at least, as depicted in comics. In many popular culture tales set in Africa, the main hero battles the "dangers" of his own country—frequently illustrated in the form of untamed animals such as big snakes, crocodiles or rhinos—rather than white colonizers. This evocation is fraught with issues of national treason: while the African hero battles savage animals, the country is ravaged by white greed and rapacity. Rather than obscured, this issue of national "treason" in favor of the white minority is brought to the light. T'Challa seems to follow traditional depictions of white (super)heroes while Wakanda and Azania (and, by extension, Africa) need racially charged forms of justice.

As the white cops prepare an electro shock machine to prolong the torture, an unseen beast attacks and kills the torturers. As the story progresses, the creature will be revealed as a monstrous black panther which, unlike T'Challa, does not wear a costume: the creature is a God figure, the cat-spirit that gave T'Challa his powers. This monster has come to replace T'Challa as the real hero of the nation, as the T'Challa seems more invested in globalized/transnational forms of engagement with justice.

The fact that T'Challa was attacked by black panthers leads unmistakably to a conclusion that the spirit of the panther has deserted him. With this fear in mind, T'Challa attends diplomatic meetings with the ambassadors of Somalia and China. There is an apartheid taking place in Azania and nobody, not even Black Panther, seems to give a thought on this. This way, T'Challa has been fully "Americanized," as he follows Reagan's position towards South Africa: complicity.

During the diplomatic meeting, the news about brutal killings taking place in Azania reaches Wakanda. A beast described as a "giant killing cat" has been attacking members of the white minority ruling Azania and it is believed the Black Panther could be deemed responsible for this brutality. Of course, T'Challa is completely innocent, but the news takes him into the spotlight. For some, the Black Panther has turned his back to the problems of Africa. His diplomacy is (mis)understood as passivity and complicity with the white elites. For others, in turn, he is believed to be secretly invading Azania and killing those deemed responsible for the apartheid. T'Challa is accused of doing both too little and too much.

In *Black Panther* #2, Magnus Moorbecx, a general in Azania, claims that the attacks are backed by communism. According to him, "The Black Panther is leading this communist-backed revolt," so Azania will act accordingly to quench any further spread of communist ideology. This attitude closely follows some of the reasons behind the global support given to the cruel apartheid in South Africa. The menace of communism was one of the "two bogeymen" invoked by the National Party to establish and sustain the politics of apartheid; the other one was that black people could take jobs from the whites (Dubow 8).

Besides this anti-communist sentiment, Azania is depicted as a place dominated by fascism. When the news about the brutal killings reaches the world, a reporter comments "the prime minister's words probably will mean, for most Azanians, more secret detentions without trials" (#1, p. 15). Trials weakly sustained in reasons of treason or resistance were common through the period of the South African apartheid. Soon after the instauration of the politics of segregation, the "parliament hurriedly passed draconian new measures to contain and punish protest. One of these, the Criminal Law Amendment Act (1953), sanctioned whipping and fines as punishment for political dissent, even passive resistance" (Dubow 45). This way, Peter Gillis establishes not only a strong connection between Azania and South Africa in times of racial segregation, but also with the fascist and totalitarian politics of Nazism that the apartheid evoked.

The Black Panther as a hero is strongly associated with America (he helped the Avengers and the Fantastic Four in many previous occasions) and is divided in his loyalties. He must respect his position as an American hero who never directly engages in international politics but, also, act properly as the king of his nation. The people of Wakanda want to take advantage of the state of disorder brought by the murders and rise in revolt, uniting themselves with the rebels of Azania to overthrow the white minority through a military coup. Any foreign military intervention seems to be the exact opposite of the Avengers' ethos; thus, the Black Panther prefers rather to continue his role as a diplomat. T'Challa knows, however, that his people soon will lose any patience with his ways: "I must either support a doomed revolt which will result in the slaughter of millions of my brothers ... or do nothing and be branded as a traitor to my race and to freedom" (Gillis #1, 16).

The idea that any revolt will end in defeat and slaughter was common through the history of the apartheid, even when the white rule was in crisis in mid–1980s. By the early 1970s, black consciousness "dug deeper roots" (Cottrell 105) in South African townships, particularly among university students, who were attracted to the idea of emancipation. Africans proved more determined to participate in political activity than ever, which "culminated in the sharpest spate of violence South Africa had endured in several years" (*ibid.*) as "revolts began in Soweto on June 16, 1976, when the Soweto Students' Representative Council spearheaded a march by 20,000 schoolchildren protesting an edict that Afrikaans be one of the languages employed in black schools" (*ibid.*). Some of the students "offered the clenched-fist 'Black Power' salute" (*ibid.*). Taunted by the students, the police fired into the crowd, killing several. Demonstrations, strikes, and riots "swept across the country during the next 12 months, resulting in as many as 1,000 deaths" (*ibid.*). Revolts, including those inspired by the Civil Rights battles, commonly ended in killings. Slaughter, as feared by Black Panther, was likely the outcome of any revolt. T'Challa's fears resonated heavily in a landscape drenched in violence and blood.

Gillis did not shy away from showcasing a complicated landscape where all political and ideological positions were inscribed within the pages of his run. A few days after the first killings, the governor of an Azanian province and a priest meet to discuss the situation within the country. Representing the Catholic Church—and, by extension, Western thought—the priest argues that the apartheid "aids the cultural integration" of races (issue # 1, p. 17). The Governor, however, is doubtful even when he is part of the white minority leading the apartheid: "We uproot them [the natives] from homes they thought they owned, give them scraps of veldt with no resources and then force them to work in our factories as aliens without rights!" The priest quickly warns the governor not to "bite the hand that feeds you." Gillis carefully creates a landscape where the Manichean dichotomy separating good from bad is turned to grey. Still, both the governor and the priest are brutally killed by the giant spirit-cat some panels later. Later, the killing beast attacks a white family, including their small child.

With this approach, Peter Gillis makes an ethical statement: violence encompasses everyone and devours anything in its path. Violence only engenders more violence. The attack of the family is followed by the white elite sending military troops to shoot with machine guns the poorest neighborhoods as a form of punishment on the blacks. This fictional action closely follows the realities of the South African apartheid. As Milli Lake explains,

> In addition to extraordinary high levels of opportunistic violence against black and colored populations, state-sponsored, extralegal assassinations, as well as targeted lynching by vigilantes, not only persisted with impunity between 1948 and 1991, but were actively supported by South Africa's apartheid government against those perceived to be resisting apartheid rule or demonstrating organized or ad hoc opposition [61].

The indiscriminate killing of innocents escalates in more uprisings and claims for freedom, both in the comic and in the real-life apartheid. Meanwhile, the Black Panther insists in diplomatic solutions, even when his people are showing signs of exasperation.

One of the most outraged citizens is a young black man who insists on voting T'Challa out of his throne; for the young black man, the leader has lost touch with the new times. The anonymous boy, as depicted in issue #1 (page 22), wears clothes strikingly different from those worn by his peers. Rather than a tribal robe, he wears black pants and a black t-shirt, his neck covered with a red handkerchief. Unlike the superhero T'Challa, the young man is a real "black panther," as he visually stands with the Black Panther Party. The Black Panther Party was considered "the greatest threat to American apartheid because it was indigenous in composition, interracial in strategies and tactics, and international in vision" as the group understood black America in the light of anti-imperial struggles around the world, especially in Africa (West x). The Black Panther movement stands, both in America and within the comic book's narrative, for black consciousness. "The choice of 'consciousness' in preference to 'power' was significant—and prudent—since it implied an 'attitude of mind' rather than a direct challenge to the state" (Dubow 160). Black consciousness is what the young man wants to impose. At the doubtful gaze of his fellow citizens, the young man angrily retires leaving behind him his own statement: the passivity of the people of Wakanda is another form of ideological enslavement.

Issue #1 ends with the Black Panther fighting to prove his value as a leader. In an interesting note, the hero does not battle a black rhino or panthers in this occasion, but a white gorilla. Rather than fight the dark-skinned animals of the jungle, T'Challa now fights a white foe. The Black Panther wins the battle, but suspicions of cheating cast a shadow on his triumph and he is dethroned, leaving Wakanda and Azania further vulnerable to the politics of apartheid.

Issue #2 sees the only concession to traditional depictions of superheroes and supervillains. A dethroned Black Panther faces the powers of a group of superpowered vigilantes created within the frontiers of Azania: the "supremacists," a league containing members such as Barricade, Captain Blaze, etc. The most powerful among them is called "The White Avenger" and is depicted prominently in the cover of *Black Panther* #2, furthering the connection between white supremacy in South Africa with Gillis' limited series.

The South African government's commitment to white supremacy was heavily sustained "but the precise form of racial ideology and policy shifted significantly through the years. From the mid-1970s a number of interrelated processes began to force more rapid reform. Soon after P.W. Botha came to power in 1978 he warned whites to 'adapt or die'" (Beinart and Dubow 18). Changes were in the wind. In 1983, year in which the limited series was written, white supremacy was coming slowly to an end, so the inclusion of racist supervillains as a desperate measure to prevent any upturning of hierarchies was in synchrony with the climate of the era.

Through *Black Panther* #2, Gillis portrayed T'Challa trying to resolve the conflict through diplomacy. After defeating the supremacists, however, the government of Azania points a nuclear missile against Wakanda, the country blamed for the killings and the acts of insurrection. If the first two issues advocated for diplomatic solutions to the global problems of the apartheid, Gillis lends towards more active measures in the latter half of his limited series. In *Black Panther* #3, T'Challa decides to leave behind him his liberal ways to embrace a more nationalist approach: "Did you expect me to sit in council and debate ways and means?" (p. 4) he says at one point. The Black Panther surrenders to the will of General Moorbecx as a way to put the massacre of black people to a halt.

To further humiliate him, General Moorbecx obliges T'Challa to pronounce a discourse of surrender at live TV. The Black Panther accepts and everything seems to go the way Moorbecx wants, with T'Challa inviting black people through the world to lay down arms. However, his surrender is just a ruse to get closer to General Moorbecx and the nuclear missiles. T'Challa's discourse shifts slowly from diplomacy to heated proclamations in alignment with the "black consciousness" running through the 1970s and 1980s: "Yes, I tell you to lay down your arms, my brothers, to cease throwing your lives away … but never to stop fighting. You must fight this injustice, this racism, this genocide!" His proclamation ends with: "You must fight these murderers, these blackmailers, these tyrants … even as I do here and now!" Immediately after, he engages in a brutal fight against Moorbecx and his guards.

Still, it is too little too late. *Black Panther* #4 reveals that the monstrous cat brutally killing all the oppressors was, indeed, the spirit of the panther that had originally turned T'Challa into the famous hero Black Panther. Rather than a man in a costume or a supervillain, the monster is, actually, part of the main hero. The cat spirit has decided to act on its own since T'Challa, according to the beast, "did not answer" and "hid" rather than respond with actions to the "weeping" and the "screams" of the black people crushed under "the European's boot" (*Black Panther* #4, 11).

While the spirit of the panther (arguably, an ethically good character as he is integral to the superhero) metaphorically stands with the pro-active discourse of nationalists and the black collectives, Black Panther stands for the liberal approach. The hero wants diplomacy and political solutions rather than increasing the bloodshed through helping revolts "with no chances of success" (*Black Panther* #4, 14). Arguably, both characters represent the two main approaches to the horrors of the apartheid, but neither of them has a real solution to offer. After all, the real apartheid will end almost a decade after the scripts for these issues were originally written.

T'Challa chooses to fight actively for the liberation of his brothers and sisters at the end. It is unclear, however, if Peter Gillis wants readers to stand next to the Black Panther or the spirit cat. The monstrous cat even killed innocent people without a doubt. To a degree, T'Challa adopts the ways of the cat spirit, but without killing. Since the Cat-God and the Black Panther are connected, readers are left in an ambiguous spot about who they have to cheer for.

The limited series ends in further ambiguity. T'Challa's fight with the Cat-God ends in a truce. According to the beast, T'Challa has learned what he must have to learn: presumably, that diplomacy is helpful but just to an extent. Action should accompany any diplomatic venture. The tyranny governing Azania is shown receiving a severe backlash through diplomatic mediations taking place through the globe while T'Challa is occupied fighting the Cat-God. In the last panel, depicting the Black Panther resuming his position as a king, there is no clear indication about the future of Azania and what measure—diplomacy or direct action—will lead down the path to independence. Clearly, Gillis was not that sure himself and preferred to leave the limited series open to interpretation.

In fact, the apartheid in South Africa would come to an end thanks in part to the figure of Nelson Mandela and insurrection. The 1990s witnessed of "a broad campaign of civil disobedience targeting segregation in hospitals, beaches, and public transportation. Violence broke out as general elections occurred in September, the results of which weakened the National Party's electoral majority" (Cottrell 112). Those were times for changes and a weakened National Party decided to free Nelson Mandela, a political prisoner, in 1990. "By late 1991, most of the legal edifice of apartheid, with its racially rooted arbitrary borders, crumbled" (Cottrell 113) under the weight of a history of armed insurrection and Mandela's calls for peace, historic reconstruction, and amnesty.

Not everyone, however, was pleased with the proceedings "and many nonwhites condemned the notion of amnesty for terrible crimes, while whites, led by the National Party, viewed some of the proceedings as amounting to a witch hunt" (Cottrell 118). Thus, Peter Gillis' limited series prefigured, almost a decade before, the uneasy blending of diplomacy, amnesty and direct action that would put the apartheid to an end. In both cases—real life and the second volume of the Black Panther—the solution would bring both peace and open wounds.

Works Cited

Beinart, William, and Saul Dubow. "Introduction: The historiography of segregation and apartheid." *Segregation and Apartheid in Twentieth-Century South Africa*. Ed. William Beinart and Saul Dubow, 1–24. New York: Routledge, 2003. Ebook.
Brooker, Russell. *The American Civil Rights Movement 1865–1950: Black Agency and People of Good Will*. Lanham, MD: Lexington, 2017. Print.
Chambliss, Julian. "An Archetype or a Token? The Challenge of the Black Panther." *Marvel Comics into Film: Essays on Adaptations Since the 1940s*. Ed. Matthew McEniry, Robert Moses Peaslee and Robert G. Weiner. Jefferson, NC: McFarland, 2016, 189–199. Print.
Cottrell, Robert. *South Africa: A State of Apartheid*. Philadelphia: Chelsea House Publishing, 2005. Print.
Dubow, Saul. *Apartheid, 1948–1994*. New York: Oxford University Press, 2014.
Guelke, Adrian. *Rethinking the Rise and Fall of Apartheid: South Africa and World Politics*. New York: Palgrave MacMillan, 2005. Print.
Gillis, Peter (w), Denys Cowan and Sam DeLaRosa (a). "A Cat Can Look at a King" *Black Panther* Vol. 2, # 4 (Oct. 1988). New York: Marvel Comics. Print.
____. "Cry, the Accursed Country!" *Black Panther* Vol. 2, # 1 (July. 1988). New York: Marvel Comics. Print.
____. "For Duty, for Honor, for Country." *Black Panther* Vol. 2, # 2 (Aug. 1988). New York: Marvel Comics. Print.
____. "The Moorbecx Communiqué." *Black Panther* Vol. 2, # 3 (Sept. 1988). New York: Marvel Comics. Print.
Lake, Milli. *Strong NGOs and Weak States. Pursuing Gender Justice in the Democratic Republic of Congo and South Africa*. Cambridge: Cambridge University Press, 2018. Print.
Landsberg, Chris. *The Quiet Diplomacy of Liberation: International Politics and South Africa's Transition*. Johannesburg: Jacana, 2004.
Louw, Eric. *The Rise, Fall, and Legacy of Apartheid*. London: Praeger, 2004. Print.
Mazrui, Ali. *The African Predicament and the American Experience: A Tale of Two Edens*. London: Praeger, 2004. Print.
Njubi Nesbitt, Francis. *Race for Sanctions: African Americans Against Apartheid, 1946–1994*. Bloomington: Indiana University Press, 2004. Print.
Thomson, Alex. *U.S. Foreign Policy Towards Apartheid South Africa, 1948–1994: Conflicts of Interest*. New York: Palgrave MacMillan, 2008. Print.
West, Cornel. "Foreword." *The Black Panther Party: Service to the People Programs*. Ed. David Hilliard, ix–x. The Dr. Huey P. Newton Foundation. Ebook.
Williams, Elizabeth. *The Politics of Race in Britain and South Africa: Black British Solidarity and the Anti-Apartheid Struggle*. London: I.B.Tauris, 2015. Print.

The King of Wakanda and the Emperor of the Useless White Boys
Race and Gender in *Christopher Priest's* Black Panther

JOHN DAROWSKI

> The Black Panther is, inexplicably, one of the most underrated guys on the planet. Maybe it's the kitty suit. Maybe it's the BLACK thing. But in the end, our GLOBAL INTELLIGENCE about this guy always seems to deal aces to HIM—the greatest poker face on the planet.

The above assessment, proffered by T'Challa's friend Everett K. Ross (*Black Panther* Vol. 3 #27 [Feb. 2001]; emphasis in original), serves not only as an indictment of the Black Panther's position within the Marvel Universe but also in the collective consciousness of comic book readers at the turn of the millennium.[1] Before Christopher Priest's acclaimed sixty-issue run on *Black Panther* Vol. 3 (Nov. 1998–Sept. 2003; hereafter cited as *BP*),[2] mostly drawn by Sal Velutto,[3] the titular character's solo adventures had a sporadic publication history, with self-titled series appearing approximately every ten years.[4] Black Panther was rarely featured within Marvel Comics during the boom period of the early 1990s, when almost every character was in some title, and was therefore an unlikely candidate to help stabilize the market during the bust in the latter half of the decade. Yet, as part of the initial launch of the Marvel Knights imprint, the series elevated his status in the Marvel Universe, reestablishing him as one of the smartest and shrewdest heroes, and contributed to a return to traditional superheroics as a reaction to the extremes of the Dark Age (1985–2000) and a precursor to the next.[5]

The turn toward tradition mirrored that of American society, which sought stability after the upheavals of the previous years. The end of the Cold War, marked by the dismantling of the Berlin Wall (Nov. 1989–Nov. 1991) and the dissolution of the Soviet Union (Dec. 1991), precipitated a paradigm shift in global politics and culture. The grand narrative of the Cold War, that the triumph of democracy and capitalism would lead to peace and prosperity, was proven false. The United States was recovering from a recession (July 1990–Mar. 1991) even as it stepped into an increased leadership role in international peacekeeping as part of the United Nations. While the U.S. embraced this role during the Gulf War (Aug. 1990–Feb. 1991), the nation became increasingly unsure of its purpose as it became involved in conflicts it little understood, including: the Somalian Civil War (1991–1995), from which U.N. peacekeeping forces withdrew without a ceasefire; the civil war and genocide in Yugoslavia, also known as the Bosnian War (1992–1995); and the genocide in Rwanda (1994). Without clear goals related to American interests, these peacekeeping missions became viewed as potential quagmires that would drain the country's military resources.

Civil conflicts and the resultant refugee emergencies were replacing apocalyptic anxieties of mutually assured destruction with ones, appropriately for the end of the millennium, more biblical in scope: war, famine, and disease. For many, these fears became embodied in a monolithic perception of the continent of Africa. The strife, coups, and brutal dictatorships in several countries, such as Robert Mugabe in Zimbabwe (Prime Minister 1980–1987; President 1987–2017) and Idi Amin in Uganda (President 1971–1979), were regularly reported on. Humanitarian aid was constantly requested for areas affected by drought and famine, such as Somalia, Ethiopia, and Kenya.[6] And when AIDS was recognized as an epidemic, the cost of treatment made Africans the hardest to reach even though they were the most significantly affected by the disease. From a geopolitical perspective, underlying all these crises was a postmodern colonialist attitude that the African nations could not manage themselves and required constant benevolent supervision through reform-contingent economic aid rather than colonization. And there were signs of change, such as the end of apartheid in 1993 and the 1994 presidential election of Nelson Mandela in South Africa. Yet an Orientalist view continued to contextualize the global political discourse linked to Africa.[7]

Domestically, the United States grappled with social and political divisions made manifest by the conclusion of the Cold War. The dissolution of the communist USSR meant the loss of the stable Other against which the nation had defined itself for over forty years. Without this external force, national identity fragmented into competing ideologies. The collapse of Reagan-era neoliberalism following the stock market crash and recession of 1987 created an open field in which to test new societal values. The attempts to establish a new popular consensus to guide the country into the twenty-first century resulted in a culture war. This period of transition in the early nineties was an opportunity for a plurality of voices to make themselves heard. Those who had been marginalized, whether by race, ethnicity, gender, sexuality, or class, made their plight known through both positive and negative means. Sometimes this was accomplished through violence, such as the 1992 Los Angeles riots following the acquittal of four white police officers for the beating of Rodney King, an African American; sometimes it was through peaceful protest, like the 1995 Million Man March, a grassroots movement to call attention to the urban and minority issues affecting particularly black men.[8] However, the hegemonic power structure (i.e., white, male, and heteronormative) sought to maintain its invisible hold on society, resulting in a retreat towards the supposed stability of traditional values by the end of the decade. Ultimately, the progress made had transformed society and there could be no return to tradition. No consensus was found and American society incrementally withdrew into tribalism as it entered the twenty-first century, highlighted by the contentious 2000 presidential race.

The instability of the culture war was endemic of an American identity crisis. According to Kobena Mercer: "One thing at least is clear—identity only becomes an issue when it is in crisis, when something assumed to be fixed, coherent, and stable is displaced by the experience of doubt and uncertainty" (259). The changing identity politics of the era contributed to a moral panic which was pitched against the bedrock of social order and normalcy, the nuclear family. Anything which disrupted the fundamental assumptions about conformity to ordered hierarchies of power was viewed through the lens of violence and needed to be suppressed. Thus, the rising divorce rate and scandals involving political leaders, notably the 1998 Lewinsky scandal which contributed to President Bill Clinton's impeachment, coupled with growing tolerance towards gay culture, was viewed as an attack on family values. The 1996 Defense of Marriage Act attempted to solidify the importance of the nuclear family by defining marriage as between a man and a woman. However, the gendered division of labor implied in the nuclear family had eroded over the previous two decades as women took on increasing leadership roles in business, politics and the military. In 1994, women were banned from combat roles in the military, the same year that the policy of "Don't Ask Don't Tell" prohibited homosexuals from openly serving. African American culture was becoming increasingly visible, whether through the presence of sports superstars, such as the 1992 U.S. Olympic basketball "Dream Team," movie and television stars, or through the surging popularity of rap and hip-hop music. However, this cultural centrality coexisted with political and economic marginality as African Americans' undereducation and underemployment linked them to urban decay and the drug scare (qtd.

in Chambliss 156). Rap's emphasis on violence and the denigration of women, already viewed as a threat to traditional morals, solidified the perceived link between African American men and crime, a link seemingly substantiated by the O.J. Simpson trial in 1994–95. The 1994 Habitual Offender Laws, better known as the Three Strikes laws, were meant to combat the increase in drug trafficking and possession and has disproportionately affected black men. The paradigm shifts of the nineties were treated by the WASP majority as a zero-sum game: any cultural gains for minorities and the disenfranchised was a loss for those in power, but could be offset through legal means.

The combined pressure of these political, economic, and cultural crises contributed to the fracturing of the American psyche which, in turn, created a paradox of American manhood. Masculinity is a performance of normative behaviors structured in relation to class, race, and so forth. The traditional masculine ideal was built around the image of mutually exclusive roles of protector and provider. A man's virility was visible through his physicality, his skills created economic opportunity and success, and he possessed emotional self-control (Kimmel 297). However, the culture of the nineties meant that men were often denied the legitimate means for achieving the ideal against which they were measured (Brown 170). According to Mercer, this paradox had long affected black men in the United States: "Whereas prevailing definitions of masculinity imply power, control, and authority, these attributes have been historically denied to black men since slavery. [...] This also cancelled out their access to positions and prestige which in gender terms are regarded as the essence of masculinity in patriarchy" (142). Now the contradictions were felt by most.

The goal of the self-made man, that success could be achieved solely through the merits of competition, individual talent, and hard work, had become accessible only to the few, not the many. Reaganomics, built on the theory of a "trickle down" economy, instead consolidated wealth in the upper class while the middle and lower classes stagnated or spiraled downward. The technology boom, brought on by decreased size and increased affordability, accelerated the pace of life and cemented the decades-long shift from blue-collar to white-collar jobs; hard work, defined through labor and physical strength, was no longer synonymous with success. The young men of Generation X were "unable to reproduce the prospects and stability of their own fathers' lives" (qtd. in Pagnoni Berns 81), contributing to their cynicism and angst. But these precarious prospects were also an opportunity to reevaluate and redefine masculinity. Manhood was no longer fixed, coherent, nor singular, as defined by consensus, but fragmented into a multiplicity of postmodern performances.

Since their inception, superheroes have embodied ideals of masculinity. According to Jeffrey A. Brown: "Classical comic book depictions of masculinity are perhaps the quintessential expression of our cultural beliefs about what it means to be a man. [...] One of the most obvious and central focal points for characterizing masculinity has been the male body" (168). Superhero bodies are inscribed with external signifiers of strength, purpose, and virility. Additionally, comic books provide a public forum for society to battle out its sense of masculine (and other) identity through simplified narrative within a shared imagination space. During his tenure on *Black Panther*, Christopher Priest used the lens of superheroes to confront the crisis of masculinity for both black and white men and negotiate postmodern alternative identities.

Marvel Knights

Marvel Knights co-editor Jimmy Palmiotti stated: "We wanted to show Marvel that we could do their characters better. It's an arrogant thing, but it was our goal, to do the best we can and show them how it should be done" (Howe 393). In 1997, the year before Marvel Knights launched, Marvel Comics was just coming out of bankruptcy while the comic book market was experiencing a sharp decline in sales.[9] Marvel considered several business models to stabilize itself, including outsourcing editorial control and refocusing on its classic characters. The Marvel Knights imprint was a hybrid of these two approaches and contributed to the reformation of the superhero following the excesses of the Dark Age.

The Dark Age was marked by the deconstruction of the superhero. Landmark titles such as *Watchmen* (Sept. 1986–Oct. 1987) and *The Dark Knight Returns* (Feb.–June 1986) interrogated the motives, morals, and purposes of superheroes and ushered in a "grim-and-gritty" tone. This reflected the questioning of American values which would continue for the subsequent decade. Matthew J. Costello points out: "Without a common language of progress and virtue, only individualism remained as an American value to be asserted" (228). When the individual can only rely on themselves, then, according to Jonathan Rutherford: "the borderline between legitimate violence employed by the state and male violence that threatens social stability is quickly crossed" (31). Heroes who violently act in their own interest, replacing right with might rather than service to the community, become anti-heroes; such characters as Wolverine, Punisher, and Ghost Rider became very popular in the early nineties. And without the consensus values of progress and virtue, these characters could only emphasize their individualism. This was accomplished visually through the style of extreme hyper-sexualization. Men became hyper-muscular to emphasize their ability to enact violence; women became impossibly proportioned to accentuate their desirability. The apex of this extreme style was Image Comics, a new publisher launched in 1992 by seven superstar artists who wanted creative control and rights over their characters, with their emphasis on external spectacle. The epitome of the era was DC Comics characters like Doomsday and Bane, visually pure muscle, who killed and maimed traditional heroes Superman and Batman in order to pave the way for more experimental concepts.[10]

While these radical departures enjoyed success for a few years, by the end of the nineties their popularity was waning as hard-bodied hypermasculinity became viewed as destructive towards society. Image Comics faced critiques for emphasizing style over substance and backlash for increasingly late delivery of books. The replacement of A-list heroes like Superman and Batman was temporary and the characters soon returned to their classic forms. Randy Duncan and Matthew J. Smith term this a move from the Era of Ambition to the Era of Reiteration: "Doing so has tapped into the mythic qualities of the genre, demonstrating the vitality of heroic mythology for generating stories" (78). The turn from ambition to reiteration can be viewed in microcosm through Marvel Comics' Heroes Reborn (Nov. 1996–Nov. 1997). This was an experiment that killed off second-tier mainstays Captain America, Iron Man, Fantastic Four, and the Avengers and placed them in a separate universe as though they had been created by Jim Lee and Rob Leifeld in 1996. Lee and Leifeld, who had defected from Marvel to found Image, were given editorial control over the titles, which emphasized their particular art style and computerized publishing.[11] The experiment lasted for a year and then those heroes were reintegrated into the Marvel Universe under the banner Heroes Reborn, a brand which emphasized the traditional characterization and mythic qualities of the characters under writers such as Mark Waid and Kurt Busiek, who were known for their traditional approach.

It was this neo-classical style which Marvel Knights wished to imitate. Marvel outsourced editorial control of several at-the-time C-list characters, including Daredevil (whose title was facing cancellation), the Punisher (who had gone from three ongoing titles in 1995 to zero in 1997), Black Panther, and the Inhumans to co-editors Jimmy Palmiotti and future Marvel editor-in-chief Joe Quesada. Given more money, more time, and fewer restrictions,[12] Palmiotti and Quesada were able to establish a creator-driven line that attracted top talent from both inside and outside the comic book industry to show that reinterpreting classic elements of the internal characterization of superheroes over external spectacle would appeal to readers of the late 1990s.[13]

The King in the Cat Suit

Palmiotti and Quesada's choice to pen the new *Black Panther* title was Christopher Priest, the first African American to write for the black hero.[14]

Born James "Jim" Owsley, Priest had a long career as a writer and editor at Marvel and DC Comics and was just coming off a tenure at Milestone Comics (which folded in 1997), a publisher which focused on characters and creators of color. Priest expressed his enthusiasm at Palmiotti and Quesada's invitation as follows: "I was a little horrified when I heard the word 'Black' and 'Panther' come out of Joe's mouth. I mean, Black Panther? Who reads Black Panther? Black Panther?! The guy with no powers? The guy in the back of the Avengers class photo, whose main job was to point and cry out loud 'Look—A BIG SCALY MONSTER! THOR—GO GET HIM!!' That guy?!" ("Chapter 11"; emphasis in original). T'Challa had over time become a "colorless cypher" according to Priest (Smith, "Pt. 1"), falling into the clichéd role of competent but passive ethnic supporting character.[15] Part of this was due to the fact that black characters had been created and written by white writers and artists who, despite their best intentions, fell back on positive and negative stereotypes due to cultural ignorance and creative compromises. Another part was that, in order to not challenge the expectations of the majority white readership, black superheroes were made less powerful than their white counterparts, which served to reinforce the white hero's preeminence (Svitavsky 153, 158). According to Priest: "Whether knowingly or subliminally, Marvel marketing—if not Marvel editorial—sees Panther in a racial context and, thus, a less pure character than Drax the Drestroyer or the Sub-Mariner" (Smith, "Pt. 1"). At a time when many creators were returning characters to a previous status quo, Priest chose to rehabilitate the image of the Black Panther, specifically, and black superheroes, generally.

Priest accomplished this by challenging historical notions about race. Racial stereotypes of black men have perpetually centered on their physicality and sexuality, transcribing cultural fears on hypersexualized black male bodies. In *Black Superheroes, Milestone Comics, and Their Fans* (2001), Jeffrey A. Brown describes this as violating the socially constructed ideals of masculinity and placing the black man "in the symbolic space of being *too hard, too physical, too* bodily" (170; italics in original). For example, the success of African American men in sports was once attributed to them possessing more innate talent than white athletes, such as the urban legend that they had an extra muscle in their legs to allow then to run faster and jump higher. Joseph J. Darowski explains: "Thus, if a white athlete won, it was an example of David and Goliath, whereas if an African American athlete won, it meant he was the benefit of a quirk of nature" (36–37). As a result of this, and following the binary logic of mind/body, civilized/barbaric, culture/nature, the black male has been historically represented as possessing a strong body but a small mind, uncivilized and uncultured (Brown 173). This dehumanizing stereotype marginalizes black men as violent and controlled by irrational impulses in contrast to the white majority.

This subordinate position is often reflected in the naming conventions of black superheroes as their codenames either emphasize their race or highlight their violent potential. In his definition of the superhero, Peter Coogan states that the codename should express biography, character, powers, or origin (30). However, as William L. Svitavsky notes, whiteness is usually invisible while ethnicity is expressed, especially for heroes created in the sixties and seventies. "Batman is not white Batman and Green Arrow is not green; whiteness is assumed but unimportant to the concepts that distinguish these characters. For most black superheroes, ethnicity is central to identity, whether expressed in a codename or kept secret by a costume" (159–160). When ethnicity is not labeled in the codename, it instead frequently carries the threat of violence and the accompanying connotations of savagery. Prominent black Marvel superheroes of the nineties, either featured in their own title or introduced as a new character on a team, include names like War Machine, Blade, Deathlok, and Rage. While violent naming conventions are not exclusive to black characters, especially in the nineties, it carries different connotation when combined with race. Black Panther's name carries double significance; not only is he straightforwardly labeled as "black," "panther" implies bestial barbarism. This atavism is reinforced by his costume, all black with cat ears and claws. Though this depiction of masculinity is countered by the content of T'Challa's character, it cannot be assumed and instead must be demonstrated.

This cultural bias has also created unique dilemmas for black superheroes in regard to their secret identity. Superheroes and their secret identities frequently split masculinity into two extremes: the macho and the wimp. Brown argues: "In general, masculinity is defined by what it is not, namely 'feminine,' and by all its associated traits—hard *not* soft, strong *not* weak, reserved *not* emotional, active *not* passive" (168; italics in original). While the premise of the costumed identity idealizes the strong, active traits, the secret identity allows for the inclusion of effeminate traits of emotionality and vulnerability as part of a whole, authentic self (Brown 175). However, black superheroes can be denied this holism. Brown claims:

> If comics book superheroes represent an acceptable, albeit obviously extreme model of hypermasculinity, and if the black male body is already culturally ascribed as a site of hypermasculinity, then the combination of the two—a black male superhero—runs the risk of being read as an overabundance, a potentially threatening cluster of masculine signifiers [178].

This removes the masculine duality, meaning that black superheroes must be hard, strong, and active in both their public and private lives. Many eschew secret identities altogether; Luke Cage, Deathlok, Blade, and Bishop do not have secret identities and the identities of War Machine and Rage are at best an open secret. For Black Panther, his other role is the king of Wakanda and he must therefore adhere to the confidence and power of a patriarchal ideal of manhood at all times. Black Panther and T'Challa behave the same in public and in private with friends and family; it is only rarely, when he is alone, that he may be allowed a vulnerable "third face" which only himself sees (Fingeroth 101).

Black Panther could have been portrayed as a type of noble savage, much like his mentor, Zuri. Zuri dresses in tribal clothes, carries a ceremonial spear, and is always ready for a fight, whether it be mud wrestling or attacking Thor (*BP* #2 [Dec. 1998], #8 [June 1999]). But that would have merely reinforced the fetishistic exoticism which has stereotyped Africa instead of the Afrofuturist exceptionalism of Wakanda. Zuri serves as a foil for the Black Panther. T'Challa is noble (he is a king) but he is not a savage. *Black Panther* presents an alternative black masculinity the synthesizes external and internal representations of manhood by having the hero adopt a cool pose and emphasize his intelligence over his physical strength.

When the reader is introduced to T'Challa in a double-page spread in issue #1 (Nov. 1998), he is wearing a tailored silk Armani suit and sunglasses (even though it is night), is standing in front of a sleek, stretch Lexus LS400, and is flanked by two women who look like supermodels, the Dora Milaje. His shaved head and goatee speak of the latest grooming styles for African American men. The image of wealth, power, and status is, in a word, cool. The cool pose, as defined by Richard G. Majors, is a construction of masculine signifiers of power, detachment, and style by African American men through non-verbal behaviors including clothing, hairstyle, and stance (qtd. in Brown 171). It adopts certain societal values, frequently imitating the white consumerism of the new man, in order mediate the hegemonic systems which had repressed them (Mercer 137). This adoption of elements of white masculinity may allow the cool pose to transcend race. According to Priest: "Black Panther could not be a 'black' book. [...] I feel the most profound statement I can make about race is to make Panther so cool he transcends the racial divide here in America" ("Chapter 11").

However, the cool pose can also be a mask for black masculinity, hiding the authentic self in order to act in a way acceptable to societal norms (Brown 172). Both the skin-tight Armani and the ceremonial Black Panther costume can be constricting, showing a lack of freedom as T'Challa must adhere to certain standards of behavior (Kate Darowski), such as when he reminds the Dora Milaje that killing is frowned upon in the United States (*BP* #1). Beneath this pose appears several stereotypical tropes of black masculinity. The tailored suit is a hologram covering his Black Panther costume, which reveals a mass of muscle, and his female companions imply his virility. However, these expectations are soon subverted. The women are the Dora Milaje (translated as "adored ones") and are the king's concomitants; coming from rival tribes in Wakanda, they form of détente by showing that the king favors neither the city-dwellers nor the swamp tribesman. T'Challa is not meant to form a relationship with either one and therefore they become a representation of his self-control rather than his sexuality. And his battles are not ones that can be that can be overcome by physical strength alone. Violence is used as part of his intelligence gathering. His heroism requires patience and observation first and power second.

In his study of Milestone Comics, Brown argues that the publisher presented a progressive interpretation of black masculinity:

> ... a central appeal of Milestone comic books is how they are read by many fans as an alternative masculine ideal, a masculine ideal that reverses the most prevalent contemporary superhero model of hypermasculinity by emphasizing brain over brawn, a reversal that is especially powerful and progressive because it is written on the bodies of black men, who have historically been aligned with the unthinking, bestial side of Western culture's nature-versus-civilization dichotomy [12–13].

This is an agenda carried on in *Black Panther*. Part of Priest's interpretation was to bring Black Panther back to the roots of his first appearance in *Fantastic Four* #52 (July 1966), where he single-handedly defeated the Fantastic Four by outsmarting them. The importance of T'Challa's intelligence is reestablished early on by his step-mother, Ramonda: "Your father taught you all that warrior nonsense—but he also taught you how to think" (*BP* #2); and by Zuri: "Victory is not a matter of might—but of mind" (*BP* #3 [Jan. 1999]). It is advice that T'Challa takes to heart as Priest treated the series more as a political thriller than a standard superhero story.

Black Panther's cunning is illustrated early on when he reveals his real reasons for joining the Avengers. In *The Avengers* #52 (May 1968), the reason given is altruistic: "Then let the word go forth.... That today you have gained an ally.... One who has given up a throne, that he may better serve a greater kingdom.... The whole of mankind itself! For, now the Panther is truly an AVENGER!!" However, it is retconned in *Black Panther* #8 to be a matter of Wakandan national security: "And, as for why—given the potential threat these people posed to the kingdom—accepting their invitation afforded me the chance to thoroughly investigate their claims—." It is a stark reminder that T'Challa is a monarch and not a subordinate masculinity. He will use his authority as a head of state to put the concerns and well-being of his nation first.

T'Challa's role as the sovereign leader of a powerful African nation places him in conflict with western hegemony, whether that be the Avengers or the United States. The subordinate position of black masculinity, and by extension Africa, is refuted by Black Panther and Wakanda. The country's advanced technology, such as vibranium-woven suits that protect from bullet impacts or an early form of the iPhone in Kimoyo cards, reveals their intelligence and places the country in a superior position to the rest of the world. And though Wakanda is passive in global politics, it is prepared to be active, including hiding warships in strategic locations such as the Hudson River or near Lemuria (*BP* #11 [Sept. 1999]; # 27). Wakanda becomes a transformative statement on Africa, moving the characterization of the continent from a passive, feminized to a masculine position. Black Panther reflects this through his revisionist variation of black masculinity.

Black Panther's political savvy and intelligence gathering is on full display throughout Priest's run, but particularly in the first year as he reestablishes Panther's position as a powerful figure in the Marvel Universe. While in New York City investigating the murder of the poster child for the Tomorrow Fund, a non-profit community service organization supported by grants from Wakanda (there is some political satire in an African nation giving aid to Brooklyn), T'Challa is ousted from power by a coup by the Rev. Doctor Michael Ibn al-Hajj Achebe. The Tomorrow Fund had become a corrupt front for laundering drug money, which is then used as part of a conspiracy by rogue factions of the U.S. government through the Russian mob and the Latin American terrorist state Volcan Domuyo with cooperation of multinational tech companies. The money funds rebels in Wakanda's neighbor Ghudaza, which creates a refugee crisis that destabilizes the region, allowing for a puppet government run by Achebe to be established, all in order for western powers to gain access to Wakanda's vibranium resources and advanced technology. It is eventually revealed that T'Challa anticipated and planned for the coup, including that his step-mother Ramonda aligned herself with Achebe while secretly feeding information to T'Challa, as it was the course of action that would result in the least number of casualties. Everett K. Ross explains: "Far from being this naïve dupe—lured away from his homeland and taken by surprise—I was beginning to realize the client [T'Challa] was much more like the Puppet Master. Always one step ahead of the bad guys and manipulating things to his advantage" (*BP* #11).

Black Panther's acumen continued to be on display in subsequent adventure. As part of his battle with Erik Killmonger (though, as a pin-up accompanying an early appearance informed readers, "no one calls him Erik") for the leadership of the Panther Clan, T'Challa crashes the world stock market, threatening a global depression (*BP* #18 [May 2000]). Though T'Challa loses his clan leadership, he retains his title as king of Wakanda and is quickly able to stabilize the world economy as Killmonger goes into a coma after ingesting the heart-shaped herb, the source of the Black Panther's power. He brings the world to the brink of World War III due to mutual defense alliances among Wakanda, Lemuria, Atlantis, Latvaria, and Genosha (*BP* #27). He manipulates the stock market so he could stage a hostile takeover of Stark Enterprises with a single phone call. And, in that same issue, contingent to revealing a coup in the United States and Canada by the transcontinental covert alliance XCon, he annexes a small island in Lake Superior between the countries, thereby disrupting an international trade route (*BP* #43 [June 2002]). By emphasizing wisdom, Priest depicted a progressive black masculinity that does not reject previous iterations but rather offers a promising alternative that builds on what came before by combining physicality with intelligence.

This alternative masculinity is challenged by Black Panther's enemies, who consider this new model of manhood weak and ineffective. They trade on the idea that any man who did not conform to the "masculine mystique," the impossible synthesis of stoic yet emotionally supportive, responsible yet carefree, and strong yet vulnerable, is not fully masculine (Kimmel 222). Achebe belittles the hero by calling him "Ukatana," which is Aula for "kitten." Inspired by real-world eccentric dictators,[16] Achebe is physically frail with a giant grin and can therefore only challenge T'Challa intellectually. Hunter, T'Challa's adopted white brother, is the White Wolf, leader of the banished Wakandan secret police Hatut Zerze (Dogs of War). Costumed similar to Black Panther except in all white instead of black, Hunter wants to manipulate T'Challa into becoming a fearsome, Machiavellian king by reinstating kidnappings, assassinations, and the torture of political prisoners. For Hunter, mercy, even his own banishment, is a weakness. Malice (formerly Nakia of the Dora Milaje) wants to release T'Challa of his sexual repression. Only Killmonger, MIT-educated in economy but with a body genetically enhanced for strength, can approach Black Panther as an equal because both embrace the hybrid masculinity of intelligence and strength. It is solely when T'Challa is afflicted with an inoperable brain aneurysm that he encounters a foe his intelligence cannot overcome (*BP* #39 [Feb. 2002]). Through these challengers, Black Panther's new black masculinity passes through a crucible and comes out restructured for a twenty-first century American society.

"I Sold My Soul for a Pair of Pants"

Part of returning Black Panther to the roots of his first appearance was to make him a mysterious and enigmatic figure. Priest viewed Panther as part Batman and part Ra's al Ghul; the reader should never know what he is thinking ("Chapter 11").[17] To facilitate this required another voice to be the narrator and point-of-view character. This may be interpreted as denying a voice to a minority character; despite having plenty to say throughout the series, the reader is never privy to T'Challa's thought process. However, Priest viewed this as making the series accessible to the broadest market of comic book readers. "Comics are traditionally created by white males for white

Emperor of the Useless White Boys (J. Darowski) 137

males. I figured, and believe rightly, that for Black Panther to succeed, it needed a white male at the center, and that white male had to give voice to the audience's misgivings or apprehensions or assumptions about the character and this book." (Smith, "Pt. 2"). Enter government liaison Everett K. Ross, attaché to the Office of the Chief of Protocol.

Created by Priest in *Ka-Zar* Vol. 3 #17 (Sept. 1998), Ross is introduced to readers on the opening page of *Black Panther* #1 sitting atop a toilet in his underwear pointing a gun at a giant rat. In his stream-of consciousness narration, he recounts:

> THE STORY THUS FAR: BUSTER, a rat so big you could put a SADDLE on him, continued to elude me.
> The CLIENT [Black Panther] and his personal entourage had, moments before, collectively leaped out of an open window, leaving me, EVERETT K. ROSS, Emperor of the Useless White Boys, to fend for himself among the indigenous tribes of tribes of The Leslie N. Hill Housing Project.
> ZURI was into the THIRD re-telling of how the great god T'Chaka ran the evil white devils from their ancient homeland.
> The bathroom had no door.
> I still had no pants [emphasis in original].

Ross is utilized as a foil for the Black Panther and the contrast serves as a commentary on white masculinity. While T'Challa is a cluster of masculine signifiers (muscular, black, superhero, king), he carries them as though they are natural. Ross acts with casual entitlement to his white masculinity and the authority and deference it provides. However, Ross is illustrated as short and lean but not muscular. It is also later revealed that his superior at work, to whom he is narrating, is a woman, Nikki Adams, and that they are also dating. All of these signifiers create the very image of the emasculated white American man: powerless in a situation of which he has little understanding and no control.

The contrast between Black Panther and Ross serves an important narrative purpose in a superhero comic book. Panther is always in a hypermasculine performance. Whether he is acting as a superhero or a king, he must always be hard, strong, reserved, and active; he is not allowed the safety valve of an alter ego. Dismissing the alter ego overvalues the hypermasculine, much as the extreme heroes of the early nineties had done. However, as a foil, Ross is able to fulfill the role of the alter ego. In the macho/wimp binary, Ross embodies the feminine side as he is soft, weak, emotional, and passive (Brown 173–175). Within the postmodern landscape of American manhood, wherein no man can perform all the types of masculinity, T'Challa and Ross complement each other and form a holism through a homosocial bond.

This not to say that Ross is not also a critique of white emasculation. As stated above, those who could not adhere to the model of the masculine mystique were not considered fully men. By the 1990s, many American males felt alienated from this ideal. "In the post-modern world lacking clear-cut borders and distinctions, it became hard to know what it meant to be a man and even harder to feel good about being one" (qtd. in Mahn 117). There needed to be a reevaluation of American society's definition of strength and success to create a new man that may maintain hegemonic power structures while incorporating the critiques of the modern ideologies (Chapman 235).

This new man was a counterpoint to the hard-bodied masculinity of the eighties, itself a reaction to second-wave feminism. Physical strength was no longer the dominant definition of manhood; the image of economic success was. Michael Goebal states: "First, there has been a move away from the traditional belief that white-collar working men are effeminate and emasculated because they do not use physical strength to earn a living, and corporate businessmen now define a 'new masculinity'" (184). The new man existed on the spectrum between the upwardly-mobile yuppie of the eighties and the metrosexual of the early 2000s: middle-class, heteronormative, but embracing feminine qualities like prioritizing relationships and participating in household chores and childcare. The new man affirms his economic success through the consumption of commodities. According the nuclear family dynamic, men earned and women spent; now men could present their masculinity by buying the image (Pagnoni Berns 84). The business suit, power tie, and new car became status symbols that reinforced masculinity. The officious Ross relies on the image of his suit and his new Mazda Miata, as well as the trappings of this position, to convey authority and societal position. Perhaps the ultimate demonstration of the power of consumerism to affirm masculinity is when the demon Mephisto offers Ross a new pair of pants, Ross having lost his previous pair in a women's mud wrestling match (*BP* #2). Though he regains his confidence, Ross quickly realizes that this is a devil's bargain as, even though he receives an infinite number of new pants, he may have sold his soul (*BP* #3).

This is indicative of the fact that there is something inauthentic about Ross's performance of the new man. His image is all style and no substance. His suit is ill-fitting, in contrast with T'Challa's, and hides his true self by making him look larger to compensate for his small frame and lack of height (Kate Darowski). As a means of a display, it is the masquerade of a projected persona. His two-seat Miata is inadequate for serving the Panther's entourage. His previously unchallenged privilege is constantly defied as he moves from his safe bubble as a Washington, D.C., insider to the neighborhoods of lower-class Brooklyn. Even his badge of office is easily stolen, illustrating how little authority is actually holds (*BP* #2). He only reacts to situations and is frequently in need of rescue. Throughout the first arc (*BP* #1–5), Ross is literally stripped, both physically during a women's mud wrestling match and emotionally when Mephisto forces him to relive childhood traumas (*BP #2; #4* [Feb. 1999]), to reveal his true self as an ineffectual man-child.

But this changes at the end of the first year of *Black Panther*. Having accompanied T'Challa to restore order to Wakanda, Ross is initially concerned only for his own safety. However, with the palace exploding, Ross realizes he cannot leave his friend in there. Ross recounts: "I was just trying to stay out of the way—when, suddenly, when I least expected it—I became a MAN" (*BP #12* [Oct. 1999]). In this moment, Ross moves from "feminized-passive" to "masculine-active," which he equates with real manhood. However, this experience does not dramatically change Ross. He does not suddenly become taller, stronger, and stoic, perhaps best illustrated when, as regent of Wakanda, he wears T'Challa's ceremonial Black Panther costume which is about twice his size (*BP #15* [Feb. 2000]). In gaining more confidence in himself while remaining weak and emotional, Ross enacts a hybrid masculinity, a type of "feminized-active," which internalizes manhood in a way that hues closely to the new man.

"Deadly Amazon High School Karate Chicks"

As progressive as Priest made *Black Panther*'s postmodern masculinity, the portrayal of women in the series is ultimately regressive rather than providing images of female empowerment. The key female supporting cast, consisting of the Dora Milaje, T'Challa's former fiancé Monica Lynne, and T'Challa's college girlfriend/Ross's current boss and girlfriend Nicole "Nikki" Adams, are defined by their relationships with men and lack autonomy. Throughout the eighties and nineties, female protagonists rode the crest of second-wave feminism to break boundaries, with several becoming action heroes in their own right. These women were no longer victims or prizes in need of rescuing but could be as powerful as their male counterparts.[18] In their assumption of masculine violence and aggression, the body became principle marker of difference between male and female (Brown 173). As women in comics books became tougher, they also became sexier, in what came known as Bad Girl art (Friem 181). Women who can act in the same roles as men demystify hegemonic power structures. The threat to the status of men is then mitigated by reinforcing heteronormativity, which places women in a subordinate position. The women in *Black Panther* become a hybrid of the old and new roles, being shown as strong and active but also serving as props for heteronormative masculinity.

The Dora Milaje are a quintessential example of this hybrid femininity as both tough and passive. Okoye and Nakia, introduced in issue #1, serve as T'Challa's chauffer, aides, and bodyguards. They are adept at both armed and unarmed combat and frequently accompany Panther on his missions. Ross describes them in action as "deadly Amazonian high school karate chicks," as well as "six feet tall and not quite legal age" (*BP* #1). Yet they are without agency; they are defined by their relationship with T'Challa, with whom they speak only in Hausa and act only at his command, silencing their will. Building out of the tribal concepts created by *Black Panther* writer Don McGregor, their ceremonial roles as the "adored ones" creates a détente among the Wakandan tribes as "brides-in-training," yet they are not to fall in love until they are released from service. Their heteronormative role is then to be sexualized without being sexual; a combination the stereotype of the black woman's dangerous sexuality with a throwback to the Victorian ideal of the angel of the home. Both desirable and chaste, it is a dynamic in which a man has control but may still feel tempted or threatened.

The dangers of this situation are explored when Mephisto casts an illusion on T'Challa who, thinking he is kissing Monica Lynne, is actually kissing Nakia (*BP* #3). The teenager becomes obsessed with the idea that T'Challa loves her and attempts to kill Lynne (*BP* #11). When this is discovered, she is cast out of the Dora Milaje, tortured by Achebe, and rehabilitated by Killmonger (*BP* #13 [Dec. 1999]). She returns as Malice, seducing and drugging men in to order to control them and gain access to T'Challa.[19] In the process she sets out to kill Lynne, who she views as an obstacle, but accidentally kills Nikki Adams instead (*BP* #24 [Nov. 2000]). As Malice, Nakia has become the stereotype of the harlot, using her sexuality as a weapon. In embracing her agency and power, she becomes a threat to the societal power structures and is therefore labeled a villain.

Nakia is replaced in the Dora Milaje by Chante Giovanni Brown or, as she prefers to be called, Queen Divine Justice (hereafter QDJ). An outspoken sixteen-year-old social activist from Chicago, Priest created QDJ in order to explore the subtext "that we—all African Americans—have a rich heritage far too many of us know nothing about" (Smith, "Pt. 2"). QDJ is suitably impressed by the freedom and equality for black people she sees in Wakanda, something she could only dream about in the United States. With her forceful personality, she bristles under the servile relationship of the Dora Milaje, speaking in English and falling in love with Vibraxas from *Fantastic Force*. But it is only in who she loves that she had autonomy. QDJ was chosen for the Dora Milaje for political reasons. As a descendent of the rebellious Jabari tribe, led by Boku the Man-Ape, QDJ's selection could bring the Jabari under T'Challa's control and strengthen the peace within Wakanda. As much as she might fight against it, QDJ's tough persona is coupled with a passive role in the series and she becomes more defined by her emotion than her intelligence.

As love interests for T'Challa and Ross, respectively, Monica Lynne and

Nikki Adams are defined by their relationships with men and, due to that, highlight the problematic practice of using violence towards women to motivate men to action. Commonly referred to as Women in Refrigerators, the trope has come under increased scrutiny since it was coined in 1999.[20] T'Challa and Monica Lynne had become engaged in the previous mini-series, 1991's *Black Panther: Panther's Prey*, but at the beginning of the series they have become estranged.[21] Throughout Priest's run, Lynne becomes a pawn of, in turn, Achebe, Hunter, and Killmonger to force Black Panther to respond according to their plans. Seemingly unable to escape T'Challa's orbit, Lynne functions as a damsel-in-distress and even refers to herself as a "hockey puck" for how she is passed around the villains. Not allowed to act on her own, she becomes a perpetual victim solely because of her relationship with Black Panther. In contrast, Nikki Adams is presented as a white woman in a governmental position of power. Priest described Nikki Adams as: "A strong-willed, get-it-done administrator who, inexplicably, fell in love with this half-pint bozo" ("Chapter 11"). As seeming success story of feminism, Adams appears to spend most of her time trying to get a coherent report out of her boyfriend Ross. When she is killed by Malice, Ross is forced to confront Black Panther both about T'Challa's former relationship with Adams and their own friendship. Rather than promoting female empowerment, the women in Panther and Ross's lives are there to passively support their masculine performances by confirming their heteronormativity and inspiring them to action.

The Other Black Panther

After a year under the Marvel Knights banner, *Black Panther* was moved back to the auspices of the Marvel Universe. Though the title had initially sold well, late shipments and rotating artists had chipped away at those numbers.[22] It seemed like the series was constantly on the brink of cancellation and a rotating cast of editors were brought in to improve the sales figures. While Marvel Knights had been more creator-driven, Marvel Comics was editor-driven and each editor had their own idea of what would improve the marketability of *Black Panther*. Numerous guest stars, participating in crossover events, and creating jumping-on points were tried without much success. Finally, it was decided that Priest had created too much continuity and complexity in the series to welcome new readers and what was needed was a complete revamp. Taking a page from the Dark Age, T'Challa would disappear and a new hip-hop, street (i.e., blacker) Black Panther, Kasper Cole, would appear in New York City.[23] A new creative team was considered, but ultimately Priest remained the writer with a new artist. The initial artist quickly changed to Jorge Lucas, but something of specific black popular culture references were lost in translation to the South American artist, resulting in important African American cultural subtexts missing from the stories (Smith, "Pt. 3"). Sales did not improve and *Black Panther* Vol. 3 came to end with issue #62 (Sept. 2003).

Kevin "Kasper" Cole represents the intersectionality of fractured identities in twenty-first century America. Cole is half African American/half Jewish (white) with a live-in pregnant Korean American girlfriend, Gwen. Living as a postmodern nuclear family, his mother and Gwen do not get along while his father, former police officer Jonathan Payton Cole, is in prison. Kasper explains his complex racial identity: "Called him [Jonathan] 'Black Jack' Cole because he was so dark. Just like they called his kid 'Kasper' because I was so light" (*BP* #50 [Dec. 2002]). Biracial, Kole cannot fully identify with either black or white masculinity, even in their hybrid forms. And he can't achieve the American Dream of work, income, and home ownership. Kole is introduced as a police officer on unpaid probation, living in his mother's apartment, and struggling to pay the bills as he counts the money in his bank account in the single-digits.

Cole is on probation due to a drug-bust gone wrong against the 66 Bridges Gang. Wishing to make detective with the job security and increased income it would bring, his choices seem to be joining the corrupt cops in his precinct or working with Internal Affairs to expose the corruption, which would be career suicide. Between a rock and a hard place, Cole chooses his own path by putting on a discarded Black Panther costume he found so that he could clean up the corruption without the good or bad cops being able to identify him. Adding a trench coat to the ensemble and armed with guns that shoot mercy bullets (knocking out rather than killing targets), Cole's appearance and actions are similar to the violent replacement heroes of the previous decade. However, even though his motives are selfish as he is suspicious of authority and disgusted with corruption, his actions also benefit the community, making him initially more of what E. Anthony Rotundo would describe as an existential hero than an anti-hero (286). Cole's mission puts him in the crosshairs of the step-brothers Hunter the White Wolf and T'Challa. As Priest explains, the story becomes: "about the war between The Black Panther (T'Challa) and the 'white panther' (Hunter) over the soul of this young kid" ("Black and White").

And it is a battle of the soul as the conflict sets Cole on a journey from an existential hero to forge his own masculine identity as a spiritual warrior.[24] Rotundo identifies this as a symbolic ideal of manhood that emerged in the late 20th century and sought to establish a personal spiritual connection through an immersion in ritual and mythology (287). Cole decides to undergo the trials to become the legitimate Black Panther. Through rituals physical (combat with Wakandan warriors), mental (tests of knowledge of Wakandan history), and spiritual (entering into the Panther Clan), Cole internalizes aspects of the warrior or soldier. Cleaning up the corruption in his police precinct become symbolic of clearing out the impurities in his heart and coming to a new morality.

All this helps prepare Cole for his impending fatherhood. The key to this new spiritual masculinity is a focus on the bonds between fathers and sons. Though he is unable to reestablish a connection with his own father, it is revealed that the narration in these issues is Cole chronicling his story for his unborn son. This is not to say that the spiritual warrior focuses on the family; it is rather a turning away from women and femininity (Rotundo 287). "The appeal of the hero is his freedom from women: the snares and entrapments of dependency and vulnerability. […] The male hero is in flight from women" (Rutherford 47). Cole regularly debates his future with his girlfriend, with its threat of domesticity, even as he becomes obsessed with Okoye of the Dora Milaje because she reminds him of his high school girlfriend. Cole eventual realizes he loves Gwen and is ready for all the challenges fatherhood will bring.

The final trial of the Black Panther is combat with the current head of the Panther Clan, in this case Killmonger, miraculously awoken from his coma. Recognizing that Cole cannot beat him, Killmonger offers him an alternative: to become an acolyte of the Panther Clan, the White Tiger (*BP* #62).[25] Given a white outfit similar to the Haute Zerze, the Wakandan Secret Police, Cole continues his crimefighting and completes the dismantling of the 66 Bridges Gang in the eight-issue series *The Crew* (July 2003–Jan. 2004).[26]

Conclusion

The end of *Black Panther* Vol. 3 would leave several plot threads unresolved, including: T'Challa's brain aneurysm; Killmonger as the head of the Panther Clan; and Kasper Cole's father's exact relation to the 66 Bridges Gang. Much of the continuity and characterization Priest created was erased by the next relaunch, *Black Panther* Vol. 4 (Apr. 2005–Nov. 2008). Everett K. Ross is no longer friends with T'Challa and only appears briefly as an expert on Wakanda. The Dora Milaje are no longer brides-in-training but the king's ceremonial bodyguards. Monica Lynne only appears once during the marriage of Black Panther and Storm.[27] Achebe and Hunter never existed and it is debatable whether Kasper Cole is part of Marvel continuity. Yet the world-building Priest developed has entered into the canon of the Marvel Universe and lives on not only in the critical-acclaim of his run but in the successful Marvel film *Black Panther* (2018).

Christopher Priest states: "Panther's ethnicity is certainly a component of the series, but it is not the central theme. We neither ignore nor build our stories around it" ("Chapter 11"). Likewise, gender is not a central theme but the performance of masculinity is a central component of Priest's *Black Panther* run. Modeling internalized masculinities through the lens of race, T'Challa, Everett K. Ross, and Kasper Cole suggest acceptable reconstructions following the deconstruction of the traditional masculine ideal. By negotiating progressive postmodern manhood that emphasized intelligence over physical power, Priest guided the Black Panther, and black superheroes, into the twenty-first century.

NOTES

1. Originally, this series was published as *Black Panther* Vol. 2, though at present Marvel codifies it as *Black Panther* Vol. 3, now including a 1988 mini-series as Vol. 2. Henceforth in this essay it will be referred to as Vol. 3.

2. Though *Black Panther* Vol. 3 ran for 62 issues, #57 and #58 were written by J. Torres. Priest additionally wrote one crossover issue, *Deadpool* Vol. 1 #44 (Sept. 2000), the story of which continued in *Black Panther* Vol. 3 #23 (Oct. 2000).

3. Sal Velluto drew thirty issues (48 percent) of *Black Panther* Vol. 3.

4. As documented elsewhere in this collection, Black Panther's solo adventures were chronicled beginning as a feature in *Jungle Action* #5–24 (July 1973–Nov. 1976). Jack Kirby returned to Marvel from rival DC Comics and launched *Black Panther* Vol. 1, which ran for 15 issues (Jan. 1977–May 1979); what would have been issues #16–18 were published as *Marvel Premiere* #51–53 (Dec. 1979–Apr. 1980). A Black Panther title would not return until 1988, when a four-issue miniseries was published. The character was then featured in the anthology *Marvel Comics Presents* #13–37 before receiving a final four-issue miniseries (Sept. 1990–Mar. 1991).

5. The history of superheroes has been divided into publication "ages," changing approximately every fifteen years. The naming convention was initially modelled after the history of man from the Roman poet Ovid's *Metamorphoses*: Golden, Silver, Bronze, and Iron; some, myself included, prefer to instead call latter one the Dark Age. I refer to the subsequent period (2000–approximately 2015) as the Baroque Age. Following the naming conventions of historical periods, the Dark or Middle Ages should be followed by the Renaissance; however, despite the high caliber of art and writing, it lacks the requisite innovation and originality to be considered a rebirth. Rather, the increasingly byzantine cycle of crossover events and relaunches, particularly by Marvel Comics, makes the term "Baroque" more appropriate.

6. The 1984 single "Do They Know It's Christmas?," the 1985 single "We Are the World," and the 1985 Live Aid concert were all fundraising initiatives for relief of the Ethiopian famine.

7. As defined by Edward Said in *Orientalism* (1978), Orientalim/Orientalist refers to the cultural construct of the East and its implications for the interaction between the "feminine" Orient and the "masculine" Occident. Said confined his analysis to the Middle East, but the characterization can be applied to the Far East and to Africa.

8. I will be using "black" as an all-encompassing term that transcends cultural context. Where appropriate to the character or context, I will specify "African" or "African-American."

9. Sales dropped 25 percent between 1996 and 1997 and a further 16 percent between 1997 and 1998. For comparison, in June 1997 only five comic books sold over 120,000 copies; only four years previous, in 1993, selling 120,000 would have barely cracked the top 100 comics sold (Sacks and Dallas 222, 242).

10. Superman was killed by Doomsday in *Superman* #75 and was temporarily replaced by four different heroes: Superboy, Steel, Cyborg-Superman, and the Last Son of Krypton.

Bane broke Batman's back in *Batman* #497 (July 1993), after which Azreal (Jean-Paul Valley) became the new Batman. Superman (Clark Kent) returned in *Adventure Comics* #505 (Oct. 1993) and Batman (Bruce Wayne) returned in *Batman: Legend of the Dark Knight* #63 (Aug. 1994). For an in-depth analysis of the Death and Return of Superman storyline, see "Searching for Meaning in 'The Death of Superman'" by Joseph J. Darowski in *The Ages of Superman*.

11. The Heroes Reborn line was fraught with problems behind the scenes. Though sales were high, they did not meet the expectations to justify Jim Lee and Rob Leifeld's high salaries. Liefeld's contract was terminated after six issues and creative control of the entire line was given to Lee for the last six issues (Sacks and Dallas 202).

12. In *Marvel Comics: The Untold Story*, Sean Howe recounts that these privileges included being set up in the penthouse at the Marvel offices, which contributed to the resentment felt by other Marvel editors (393). However, "An Oral History of Marvel Knights" reveals that this "penthouse" was really an annex built onto the rooftop access, making it the eleventh story of a ten-story building (Markus).

13. While Daredevil, Black Panther, and the Inhumans emphasized classic elements from their beginnings at Marvel Knights, the Punisher became a supernatural character for two four-issue mini-series as a literal avenging angel (*Punisher* [Nov. 1998–Feb. 1999]; *Wolverine/Punisher: Revelation* [June–Sept. 1999]). Writer Garth Ennis and artist Steve Dillon returned Frank Castle to his roots with a twelve-part maxi-series beginning in Apr. 2000.

14. African Americans Denys Cowan and Dwayne Turner had previously provided art for *Black Panther*. Denys Cowan penciled the 1988 four-issue self-titled mini-series (July–Oct. 1988) written by Peter B. Gillis. Dwayne Turner penciled and inked the four-issue *Black Panther: Panther's Prey* mini-series (Sept. 1990–Mar. 1991) written by Don McGregor.

15. "The Spy King: How Christopher Priest's Version of the Black Panther Shook Up Earth's Mightiest Heroes" by Todd Steven Burroughs in *The Ages of the Avengers* provides a contrast between Black Panther's active role in his own title and his passive supporting role in contemporaneous issues of *The Avengers*.

16. In his first press conference, Achebe uses a dog rescued from the fighting as a mascot and then declares National Biscuit Day, wherein citizens are to eat nothing but biscuits (*BP* #4); it is unclear whether biscuits is referring to dog biscuits. Saparmurat Niyazov of Turkmenistan (First Secretary 1985–1990, President 1990–2006) once encouraged his citizens to chew on bones for stronger teeth because that worked for dogs.

17. The visual similarities between Black Panther and Batman became more notable when Sal Velluto began drawing Panther's cape as full-length rather than shoulder-length, a change mirrored in the story with Ross commenting: "My second thought was along the lines of, 'What's the deal with the big cape?' I mean, okay, the little skippy half-cape WAS a tad Burt Ward, but now, OVERNIGHT, he'd gone totally Big Cape Guy" (*BP* #13).

18. For an in-depth analysis of transformation of female protagonists through the eighties and nineties, see *Dangerous Curves: Action Heroines, Gender, Fetishism, and Popular Culture* (2011) by Jeffrey A. Brown.

19. Nakia is the sixth Marvel character to take the codename Malice. The first was also a Black Panther villain, who aided Killmonger in *Jungle Action* #8 (Jan. 1974). The next villain to use the name appeared in *Ghost Rider* Vol 1 #25 (Aug. 1975). More famously, the name was used by Invisible Woman of the Fantastic Four when her personality was corrupted by Psycho-Man (*Fantastic Four* Vol. 1 #280 [Jul. 1985]). An evil doppelganger of Invisible Woman would later adopt the name. In *Uncanny X-Men*, a member of Mister Sinister's Marauders would also use the name Malice (*Uncanny X-Men* Vol. 1 #210 [Oct. 1986]).

20. The term Women in Refrigerators was created by comic book writer Gail Simone after Green Lantern Kyle Rayner discovers the dead body of his girlfriend stuffed in his refrigerator, leading him on a quest for vengeance (*Green Lantern* Vol. 3 #54 [Aug. 1994]).

21. T'Challa broke off the engagement because he knew he would eventually have an inoperable brain aneurysm. This revelation came when King Solomon's Brass Frogs from Jack Kirby's run, which have time travel capabilities, sent a version of T'Challa from the future who already had the aneurysm. Referred to as "Happy Pants Panther," this doppelganger mirrored Kirby's swashbuckling characterization. T'Challa chose to prepare Wakanda

and himself for the inevitable, which also explains his stoic and somber characterization during Priest's run.

22. *Black Panther* Vol. 3 initially averaged around 40th place on the sales charts in 1998 (Sacks and Dallas 248).

23. Despite Priest's extensive interviews and blog-commentaries on *Black Panther*, he does not recall who recommended replacing T'Challa and who decided on an urban, street-level approach (Priest, "What I Forgot to Mention"; Smith, "Pt. 3").

24. The spiritual warrior ideal has been linked to the men's movement of the 1990s, which does have connections to the men's rights and the alt-right/white supremacy movements, none of which is pertinent to this analysis.

25. Kasper Cole is the third of five characters to carry the codename White Tiger. The codename was created for Hector Ayala in *Deadly Hands of Kung Fu* #19 (Dec. 1975), who was granted special powers by a jade tiger amulet. Previous to Cole, the name was used by a literal white tiger evolved by the High Evolutionary in *Heroes for Hire* Vol. 1 (1997–99). Cole's tenure proved short-lived (no more than ten months) as the mantle and the jade amulet was taken up by Hector Ayala's niece, Angela del Toro, in *Daredevil* Vol. 3 #58 (May 2004). Hector's youngest sister and Angela's teenage aunt, Ava Ayala, also became the White Tiger beginning in *Avengers Academy* #20 (Dec. 2011).

26. The Crew consisted of an ethnically-diverse group, including: White Tiger (Kasper Cole); Jimmy Rhodes (sans War Machine armor); Josiah X, the son of the World War II black Captain America Isiah Bradley; and the Latino Junta (Danny Vincent), a freelance intelligence agent who had made several appearances in *Black Panther* Vol. 3.

27. T'Challa and Storm of the X-Men married after a short courtship in *Black Panther* Vol. 3 #18 (2006) and were divorced in 2012 during the *Avengers vs. X-Men* event. Priest established that they had a flirtation in their youth (*BP* #26 [Jan. 2001]), but with the intention that they would not actually get together (Smith, "Pt. 2").

Works Cited

Brown, Jeffery A. *Black Superheroes, Milestone Comics, and Their Fans*. University of Mississippi Press, 2001.

Chambliss, Julian C. "War Machine: Blackness, Power, and Identity in *Iron Man*." *The Ages of Iron Man: Essays on the Armored Avenger in Changing Times*, edited by Joseph J. Darowski. McFarland, 2015, pp. 148–163.

Chapman, Rowena. "The Great Pretender: Variations on the New Man Theme." *Male Order: Unwrapping Masculinity*, edited by Jonathan Rutherford and Rowena Chapman. Lawrence and Wishart, 1996, pp.225–248.

Coogan, Peter. *Superhero: The Secret Origin of a Genre*. MonkeyBrain Books, 2006.

Costello, Matthew J. *Secret Identity Crisis: Comic Books and the Unmasking of Cold War America*. Continuum, 2009.

Darowski, Joseph J. *X-Men and the Mutant Metaphor: Race and Gender in the Comic Books*. Rowan and Littlefield, 2014.

Darowski, Kate. Personal Interview. 1 July 2019.

Duncan, Randy, and Matthew J. Smith. *The Power of Comics: History, Form, and Culture*. Continuum, 2009.

Fingeroth, Danny. *Disguised as Clark Kent: Jews, Comics, and the Creation of the Superhero*. Continuum, 2007.

Friem, Nicole. "The Dark Amazon Saga: Diana Meets the Iron Age." *The Ages of Wonder Woman: Essays on the Amazon Princess in Changing Times*, edited by Joseph J. Darowski. McFarland, 2014, pp. 174–183.

Goebel, Michael. "Rethinking the American Man: Clark Kent, Superman, and Consumer Masculinity." *Ages of Heroes, Eras of Men*, edited by Julian C. Chambliss, William Svitavsky and Thomas Donaldson. Cambridge Scholars Publishing, 2013, pp. 182–195.

Howe, Sean. *Marvel Comics: The Untold Story*. Harper Perennial, 2012.

Kimmel, Michael. *Manhood in America: A Cultural History*. Oxford University Press, 2012.

Lee, Stan (w), and Jack Kirby (a). "The Black Panther!" *Fantastic Four Vol. 1* #52 (July 1966). Marvel Comics, 1966.
Mahn, Gerri. "Fatal Attractions: Wolverine, the Hegemonic Male, and the Crisis of Masculinity in the 1990s." *The Ages of the X-Men: Essays on the Children of the Atom in Changing Times*, edited by Joseph J. Darowski. McFarland, pp. 116–127.
Markus, Tucker Chet. "An Oral History of Marvel Knights." Marvel.com, 7 Jan. 2019, www.marvel.com/oral-history-marvel-knights. Accessed 5 July 2019.
Mercer, Kobena. *Welcome to the Jungle: New Positions in Black Cultural Studies*. Routledge, 1994.
Pagnoni Berns, Fernando Gabriel. "From Riches to Rags: The Rise and Fall of Wally West." *The Ages of the Flash: Essays on the Fastest Man Alive*, edited by Joseph J. Darowski. McFarland, 2019, pp. 80–90.
Priest, Christopher. "Black and White: A Crime Novel." *Digital Priest*, 10 Apr. 2003, digitalpriest.com/legacy/comics/panther/bw.html. Accessed 6 July 2019.
_____. "Chapter Eleven: Black Panther Series Commentary." *Digital Priest*, June 2001, digitalpriest.com/legacy/comics/panther/start.html. Accessed 4 July 2019.
_____. "What I Forgot to Mention." *Digital Priest*, 21 Sept. 2011, digitalpriest.com/comics/panther/. Accessed 6 July 2019.
Priest, Christopher (w), and Mark Bright (a). "Enemy of the State, Book Three," *Black Panther Vol. 3* #11 (Sept. 1999). Marvel Comics, 1999.
_____. "Enemy of the State: Conclusion," *Black Panther Vol. 3* #12 (Oct. 1999). Marvel Comics, 1999.
_____. "Beloved," *Black Panther Vol. 3* #24 (Nov. 2000). Marvel Comics, 2000.
_____ and Jim Calafiore (p). "Ascension, Part 4," *Black Panther Vol. 3* #62 (Sept. 2003). Marvel Comics, 2003.
_____ and Dan Fraga (p). "Tin Men in the Garden of Good & Evil," *Black Panther Vol. 3* #50 (Dec. 2002). Marvel Comics, 2002.
_____ (w), and Kyle Hotz (p). "Legacy," *Black Panther Vol. 3* #18 (May 2000). Marvel Comics, 2000.
_____ (w), Joe Jusko (p) and Amanda Connor (p). "That Business with the Avengers," *Black Panther Vol. 3* #8 (June 1999). Marvel Comics, 1999.
_____ (w), and Kenny Martinez (p). "Misery," *Ka-Zar Vol. 3* #17 (Sept. 1998). Marvel Comics, 1998.
_____ (w), and Mark Texiera (p/i). "The Client," *Black Panther Vol. 3* #1 (Nov. 1998). Marvel Comics, 1998.
_____. "Invasion," *Black Panther Vol. 3* #2 (Dec. 1998). *Marvel Comics, 1998.*
_____. "Original Sin," *Black Panther Vol. 3* #3 (Jan. 1999). Marvel Comics, 1999.
_____. "The Price," *Black Panther Vol. 3* #4 (Feb. 1999). Marvel Comics, 1999.
_____ (w), and Sal Velluto (p). "The End," *Black Panther Vol. 3* #13 (Dec. 1999). Marvel Comics, 1999.
_____. "Smash," *Black Panther Vol. 3* #15 (Feb. 2000). Marvel Comics, 2000.
_____. "Sturm Und Drang: A Story of Love and War Book 1: Echoes," *Black Panther Vol. 3* #26 (Jan. 2001). Marvel Comics, 2001.
_____. "Sturm Und Drang: A Story of Love and War Book 2: An Epidemic of Insanity," *Black Panther Vol. 3* #27 (Feb. 2001). Marvel Comics, 2001.
_____. "Return of the Dragon Book Two: Silent Stone," *Black Panther Vol. 3* #39 (Feb. 2002). Marvel Comics, 2002.
_____. "Enemy of the State II- Book Three: The Kiber Chronicles," *Black Panther Vol. 3* #43 (June 2002). Marvel Comics, 2002.
Rotundo, E. Anthony. *American Manhood*. New York: BasicBooks, 1993.
Rutherford, Jonathan. "Who's That Man." *Male Order: Unwrapping Masculinity*, edited by Jonathan Rutherford and Rowena Chapman. Lawrence and Wishart, 1996, pp. 21–67.
Sacks, Jason, and Keith Dallas. *American Comic Book Chronicles: The 1990s*. TwoMorrows Publishing, 2018.
Smith, Zack. "PRIEST on BLACK PANTHER, Pt. 1: 'Everyone Kind of Forgot Who PANTHER Was.'" *Newsarama*, 15 Feb. 2018, www.newsarama.com/25496-priest-looks-back-at-black-panther.html. Accessed 4 July 2019.

_____. "PRIEST on BLACK PANTHER, Pt. 2: 'It's Not Arrogance, It's Competence.'" *Newsarama*, 16 Feb. 2018, www.newsarama.com/25506-priest-on-black-panther-pt-2.html. Accessed 4 July 2019.

_____. "PRIEST on BLACK PANTHER, Pt. 3: 'Hubris and Arrogance' Would Kill BLACK PANTHER Movie." *Newsarama*, 21 Feb. 2018, www.newsarama.com/25518-priest-on-black-panther-pt-3-enemy-of-the-state-and-the-panther-film.html. Accessed 6 July 2019.

Svitavsky, William L. "Race, Superheroes, and Identity: 'Did You Know He Was Black?'" *Ages of Heroes, Eras of Men*, edited by Julian C. Chambliss, William Svitavsky and Thomas Donaldson. Cambridge Scholars Publishing, 2013, pp. 163–180.

Thomas, Roy (w), and John Buscema (p). "Death Calls for the Arch-Heroes!" *The Avengers Vol. 1* #52 (May 1968). Marvel Comics, 1968.

An Initiative for a More Fantastic Union
Prowling Around the PATRIOT Act

Peter W.Y. Lee

"America remains a nation at war," President George W. Bush declared on March 9, 2006, as he signed the USA PATRIOT Improvement and Reauthorization Act. "In the face of this ruthless threat, our nation has made a clear choice. We will confront mortal danger, we will stay on the offensive, and we're not going to wait to be attacked again" (Bush). Speaking five years after 9/11, the President pointed to the need for all Americans to remain vigilant against foes foreign and domestic, even—as critics alleged—at the cost of civil liberties.

For their part, Marvel's superhero community was anything but secure. Previous mega events of the 1980s and 1990s, such as *Secret Wars* or *Act of Vengeance*, featured crossovers between multiple titles, but were basically giant-sized team-ups with little relevance outside the four-color pages. In 2007, the mini-series *Civil War* and its clear 9/11 parallels shook the Marvel Universe to the core. Creators, characters, and fans questioned the need for national security via keeping tabs on all "Living Weapons of Mass Destruction," even if this meant eschewing the rights and privileges of American citizens.

As is typical for comic books, the Mighty Marvel Manner amped up the Superhuman Registration Act—its version of the PATRIOT Act—into a company-wide event as do-gooders challenged the necessity of Uncle Sam registering and regulating freedom fighters. The resulting squabble among the cape and cowl set turned into a Civil War, notably, in the company's title that started it all, the *Fantastic Four*. The foursome's first couple, Reed and Susan Richards, asked themselves which side they were on, and irreconcilable differences nearly ended their forty-year marriage. The FF shattered, with Sue opting for uncivil disobedience and Reed rallying around the flag. After the usual slugfest where the good guys wreak havoc in the name of justice, Reed and Sue turned to each other—and another power couple, the Black Panther and Storm—to pick up the pieces.

Reconstructing the First Family

In 1961, the Fantastic Four introduced the Marvel Universe to comic book pages, and in 2007 the FF could lead the recovery after Marvel's *Civil War*. With Marvel's House of Ideas reduced to a tumbling house of cards, the Baxter Building was a symbolic ground zero for the cynical public to face front and turn into true believers once again. *Civil War* concluded with the Fantastic Four's forty-fifth anniversary in issue #543 (April 2007), with nothing less than a celebratory retrospective into the self-styled world's greatest comic magazine. After interviewing everyone from badass hero-for-hire Luke Cage to the FF's ear-wiggling mailman, with fond reminiscences from 45 years of Marvel Bullpenners filling the letters page, the issue ended with a new lineup. Reed and Sue explain they need plan to transition from Civil War into a civil union via an extended honeymoon; after all, Americans had long positioned the family as the first line of civil defense throughout the Cold War, representing the foundation for home and country (May 20). But lest the Fantastic Four ended up neither fantastic nor a foursome, writer Dwayne McDuffie gave the FF new married leads: King T'Challa and Queen Ororo Munroe of Wakanda.

For Marvel, T'Challa is a ready-made half of a black power couple. His marriage to Storm was partly a marketing gimmick in which creators retconned an earlier meeting between the two in *Marvel Team-Up* #100 (December 1980) in favor of a blossoming childhood romance between a prince and a goddess in the heart of Africa that culminated in a royal wedding. The Wingless Wizard—a stout, semi-mental giant who leads the supervillain team the Frightful Four—even comments on Marvel's PR stunt, dismissing Black Panther and Storm as "C-listers with pretensions to relevance" who are "not even worth mentioning" (McDuffie "Chapter Five"). While the Wizard clearly exaggerated, given Storm's past leadership of Marvel's golden team, the flagship X-Men franchise, the Black Panther temporarily benefited from the extra fan exposure. His flagging series hung on until 2008. Additionally, Black Panther's nuptials gave the royal king street cred with comic book readers. His marriage to Ororo Munroe linked him to the mutant community that Americans love to hate and fear—a status that minority groups on and off the comics pages could readily identify with.

In the narrative world of Marvel Comics, at the conclusion of *Civil War* Black Panther needs the legitimacy the FF offers. The Wakandan king didn't shy away from superhero infighting, pleading with Captain America and Iron Man on his wedding day to not let "a piece of paper" disassemble Earth's mightiest heroes (Hamblin "Bride"). Both men walk out on T'Challa's nuptials. A bit less diplomatically, T'Challa bluntly tells Reed Richards—who supports enlisting super-humans as U.S. agents—that joining the hunt for dissident non-registrants isn't a fantastic idea. T'Challa informs Reed that policing costumed crime-fighters simply to boost public opinion won't involve Wakanda: "I don't like it when America interferes in Wakandan affairs. And I can only assume the feeling is *reciprocated*" (Millar "Untitled").[1] While T'Challa utters platitudes about national sovereignty, the Black Panther's scowl suggests he is already invested, especially given his wife's stormy reputation among the American public. After all, the X-Men were alternatively public enemies, misfits, and undesirables among the body politic—and the team officially turns their former leader down when Storm comes to them for help in combating superhuman registration. Queen Ororo doesn't help her husband's cause when she instigates an international incident in *Black Panther* #25 (April 2007), battling Reed's government-sanctioned clone of Thor and wrecking the Wakandan embassy in the process. The former African goddess's altercation with U.S. property ends in a stalemate, resolved only when the self-styled ladies' man, Hercules, steps in to "splunch" the faux Norse god of thunder. But the meteorological melee leaves the royal Wakandan couple homeless (Hudlin "War Crimes"). On their own, T'Challa's oppositional stance against strong federal damage control agencies remains fraught.

In the aftermath of Her Majesty's brawl, Richards offers them the Baxter Building while he and Susan head to an off-planet honeymoon. By participating in Marvel's first family as a temporary replacement, T'Challa gains legitimacy and respect from the American community. He takes advantage of his wife's "disagreement" with "Thor" to indirectly muster public support. Storm later reveals she and T'Challa capitalized on the incident, turning it into an opportunity, "allowing his two dear friends to go work on their marriage without worrying about their responsibilities to the team" (McDuffie "Chapter 6"). By giving the appearance of needing assistance, the Wakandan king pays back the comic title to which he owes his existence. After all, T'Challa made his debut in *Fantastic Four* and now he returns when they need him most. In a far greater ruse, T'Challa makes it appear that he needs a favor, enticing Richards to extend an open invitation as house guests, even though Wakanda benefits from American superhero celebrity culture.

In the public eye, the Fantastic Four makes for a better home for the Black Panther than the consistently disassembling Avengers or the uncannily untrustworthy X-Men. The Fantastic Four are Marvel's royal family. As celebrities, the FF had a movie under their belt as far back as issue #9 (September 1962), ran a licensing empire, and had respect in the public eye.[2] The Civil War had ripped the figurative superhero family apart, but Black Panther acts as an intermediary to rebuild their reputation in the public eye. After manipulating Richards to invite him to the team, T'Challa holds a press conference. He and Storm profess they aren't "officially" joining the group. Black Panther points out that the FF is a family, not a team with a roster. Storm adds that, as guests, they simply fill in should "circumstances" require it (McDuffie "Chapter 1"). While she later regards her comments as simple public relations work—Storm of the outlawed X-Men can mouth off freely while Queen Ororo must watch her words—she, her husband, and the Fantastic Four recognize the need to keep up appearances for the cameras. By hanging out with the FF, Black Panther and Storm bridge their opposition to disagreeable patriot acts as mainstream American idols.

Black Panther's assertion that he is not an "official member" of the FF dances around the shift in minority identity in the public eye. By the turn of the millennium, several social critics argued that the end of the Civil Rights era had abolished racism via legislation and all-round enlightenment, but other scholars have pointed out racism remained institutionalized and normalized in daily American politics and economics (Bonilla-Silva 89). The PATRIOT Act and other national security policies played on these codified forms of discrimination, justifying them through stereotypes about "Arabs" and other threatening minorities. As Chairman of the Joint Chiefs of Staff Richard Myers warned, the Middle Eastern detainees at Guantanamo Bay were "among the most dangerous, best-trained, and vicious killers on the face of the earth." These religious fanatics would "gnaw through hydraulic lines" in a plane just to "bring it down" (Mayer 183). In the light of such a threat, the Office of Legal Counsel advised the White House that "the government may be justified in taking measures which in less troubled conditions could be seen as infringements of individual liberties" (Mayer 46). Such inconvenient measures included carte blanche on wiretapping, unwarranted search and seizures, and anything else the executive branch deemed a hindrance in the War on Terror.

This coloring of jihadists and "enemy combatants" stigmatized minority groups, especially Muslims at home and abroad. The potential loss of freedom under an increasingly powerful police state turned into a nightmarish reality, as 762 people found themselves detained, questioned, and held for months in violation of due process (Herman 197, Brzezinski 104). Civil rights activists turned to voices of reform for encouragement, leading to Barack Obama's rapid rise in the Democratic Party on a theme of "hope and change" from the status quo. But the necessity of national security trumped civil liberties;

in 2007, as Marvel's *Civil War* concluded, Obama campaigned on a presidential platform to shut down the military prison at Guantanamo Bay and end torture as a way of extracting information (Savage 13–14). But his actions as president never lived up to those promises, leaving many disappointed. Even Captain America, the champion of American freedoms and opponent of superhero registration, found himself hauled off to jail in shackles once he surrendered to the authorities. Lest Black Panther wanted to confer with Cap behind bars—or in death, as a convoluted but popular storyline temporarily kills off Marvel's living legend—the Wakandan king distances himself from his opposition to superhuman registration. T'Challa's assertion that he is not an "official member" of the FF puts critics' minds at ease that he is not formally joining the U.S.'s superhero set, but he goes around these fear to partake in Americanism by literally joining the family.

Neither T'Challa nor Ororo are related to the Richards clan, nor do they sport numbers on their costumes. T'Challa's status as an outsider visiting the team's building positions him to remain in the public eye as a member of Marvel's premiere celebrities while not ruffling upsetting critics who wonder why the Wakandan king isn't staying in his own turf. The two certainly try their best to fill in for Reed and Sue. As Marvel's black power couple, Ororo and T'Challa take every opportunity to remind audiences that they are husband and wife, fit to lead the household. In lighter moments of familial melodrama, T'Challa warns Ben to not question the authenticity of Ororo's white hair and blue eyes, and uncharacteristically turns hysterical when his wife is endangered. For her part, Ororo relaxes her guard and calls her husband "honey" and "beloved," terms of endearment rarely casually uttered among the hardboiled X-Men. Ororo describes playing the part of a monarch as "challenging," but "a price I happily pay to have a life with the man I love" (McDuffie "Chapter 1"). Ororo's surrendering her usual outspokenness in exchange for loving submission under a stern king is a happy trade. As a queen and now part of the Fantastic Four, Storm has access to the best that the United States offers. She isn't hunted or hated in this comic magazine— no one even mentions the word "mutant" during her time with the FF. Instead, Storm enjoys diplomatic immunity as T'Challa's wife and basks in her role as the de facto successor to Susan Richards.

Black Panther and Storm gain legitimacy and respect by staying in the Baxter Building. But even as the two capitalize on the fame that American celebrityhood bestows upon the FF, the Black Panther remakes the team as his own. During a press conference, T'Challa claims the Baxter Building as "the official Wakandan embassy" while his cleanup crew rebuilds (McDuffie "Chapter 1"). Having repurposed the FF's home as foreign soil, T'Challa takes the liberty of filling the skyscraper with art and décor from his country. For their part, the remaining half of the FF, the Human Torch and the Thing, take T'Challa's makeover in stride. Ben Grimm jokes about His Highness making himself at home, and he and Johnny Storm don older black jumpsuits from the later 1980s and 1990s, even though the old uniforms lack the technowizardry of their modern garb. Ben quips about the niceties of color coordination as basic manners, but here, the FF adjusts to Black Panther's and Storm's costumes and skin tones, not the other way around. The FF will never have a Blue Panther, for instance, who sports the FF jumpsuit, or even a white or orange Panther befitting Johnny's and Ben's skin tones.

As part of the FF, King T'Challa publicly continues to work with the U.N. to counter the U.S. government's militarizing super-folk. Even though Civil War is over, T'Challa remains wary of government officials. After discovered bombs in his embassy's wreckage, he suspects S.H.I.E.L.D. director Tony Stark of masterminding a covert operation to destroy Wakanda's embassy—and possibly assassinate his royal self (McDuffie "Chapter One"). Stark declares his innocence and promises aid, but he also sees Black Panther's staying with the FF as an opportunity, asking Reed to reign in the meddlesome Wakandan king. Here, Reed draws the line, telling Stark he had supported registration of super-powered citizens, but he now disagrees with the administration's current conscription program—notwithstanding FF allies Hank Pym and She-Hulk moonlighting as trainers. Instead, he literally distances himself from the U.S. government by heading out for deep space, leaving T'Challa and Storm to head the new Fantastic Four.

Stark has good reason to be wary of what T'Challa might do while shielded by the popular FF brand. The Wakandan king clearly opposes increased militarization, which he sees as a sign of an emerging police state. He openly rebukes Stark's view of the FF and the team's role in the national narrative. In issue #543 (April 2007), Stark defends Reed's past support for superhero registration as part of his character. According to Stark, Richards is always "looking to the future, doing what needs to be done to secure our safety," restating the necessity of homeland security as part of a bright American future (McDuffie "C'Mon Suzie"). After all, as fanboys and comics scholars note, Richards had inaugurated the Marvel Age of comics in *Fantastic Four* #1 (Nov. 1961) by overseeing a rocket project in the name of national security, beating the Commies into exploring space. In Stark's nationalistic eyes, Richards continues to carry the flag forward.

However, T'Challa indirectly rebukes Stark's characterization of the FF by labeling them as American challengers of the unknown. Rather than focus on the FF as a family of uniformed security guards protecting national interests, in #543 (April 2007) T'Challa creates a parallels between the long-lived antagonism between Dr. Doom and Dr. Richards with the dangers of an authoritarian regime and the American family.[3] "He'll never defeat Dr. Richards," T'Challa proclaims before readers learn that he and his wife are in the process of moving into the Baxter Building. "He continues to make the same mistake most of the Fantastic Four's antagonists make. They aren't a team. They're a family" (McDuffie "C'Mon Suzie"). Again, T'Challa labels the FF as more than colleagues or citizen-soldiers. Shared blood runs thicker than the black ink of any law. The FF's familial ties give them strength to fight, and outlast, any assertion of government power—bonds that now extend to T'Challa himself. Sue, Johnny, and Ben all eventually sided against government registration, and their unity is greater than any security measure Stark can implement. The Black Panther says he isn't part of the FF's roster for the benefits of the cameras and the weary public, but the FF certainly treats him like a member of their household.

T'Challa's on-camera statements not only refute Stark's political aims, they also criticize the public for its failure to recognize the qualities of the U.S.'s celebrity heroes—just as the FF's rogue gallery's failure to see the same values led to their defeats. For the Fantastic Four, family ultimately comes first as the Richards clan actively heals the Civil War rifts that had divided them, with Reed even compromising his former support for government oversight. Indeed, Black Panther's consistently reminding the media (and the readers) that the team has no roster openly corrects the public's ignorance of not only how the FF operates, but reinforces the shared values that made the public idolize the team in the first place. As an outsider to the U.S., a guest in the FF's headquarters, and de facto family member, the Black Panther critiques the American public and government policies, even as he uses this association as a means to promote his Wakandan agendas.

From the Baxter Building, King T'Challa heads to the U.N. There, he informs the American delegates that government policies have created what T'Challa describes as a "remarkably unstable situation" (McDuffie "Chapter 4"). The U.S. drive to register, enlist, and regulate super powered military has driven marginalized communities to ban together to protect their own threatened sovereignty. Specifically, King T'Challa notes the American obsession with national security has led Wakanda to side with Latveria, Attilan, and Atlantis, all of which have menaced the U.S. in the past. T'Challa's teaming up with a European despot known for dooming dissenters, inhuman misfits from the moon, and blue-skinned fish people who have attacked surface dwellers doesn't create a formal alliance between them. As part of the FF, he will certainly step up should they actually invade American soil—but these powerful countries act as a unified front against American militarism. Nor is T'Challa's stance unprecedented; back in *Fantastic Four* #311 (February 1988), for instance, an exiled Doctor Doom seeks T'Challa's help to reclaim Latveria after an arrogant young brat usurps him. In that issue, T'Challa gains access to Doom's weaponry for services rendered. International relations take a turn in *Black Panther* #18 (September 2006), as Doom invites T'Challa and

Ororo to spend a honeymoon in Latveria and create an alliance in the face of crumbling American institutions: "If friends aren't who they used to be ... perhaps *enemies* aren't either?" (Hudlin "Bride"). In this case, their own endangered sovereignties have made the monarchs political bedfellows.

Black Panther initially rejects Dr. Doom's invitation to create an alliance but ends up doing so anyway. Doom bitingly and rhetorically asks if Black Panther and Storm trust the U.S. government, S.H.I.E.L.D., or Tony Stark, all of which he knows T'Challa does not. Black Panther rebuffs Doom, asserting that Captain America is his friend—a symbol of his adherence to American freedoms, even if Wakanda disagrees with the registration program. Black Panther boldly announces he will stand up "for the principles that I share with my comrades, *not* fear of losing my throne" (Hudlin "World Tour Part One"). Storm jumps in and adds that, should they surrender their principles, they have already lost. They demonstrate their point by thrashing Doom's robot army before leaving. But even though they spurn Doom's offer for an alliance against supposed American tyranny, Civil War draws Wakanda in. When kings Blackbolt of Attilan and Namor of Atlantis ask him to spearhead an international resistance movement against U.S. policy, Black Panther agrees to "defend the oppressed!" (Hudlin "World Tour Part Three"). The full splash page concluding the issue, with a full-figures Black Panther leading the way supposedly encourages the audience to cheer along.

Ironically, Black Panther's stance echoes the U.S.'s own behavior in waging war on terror. Reeling after 9/11, Americans invaded Afghanistan and then Iraq on the pretense of liberating the countries from Al Qaeda's tyranny and then embarking on a program of intense nation building to foster democracy. In the name of defending the oppressed, the Bush Administration sanctioned torture of prisoners, unwarranted surveillance on citizens, and ignoring constitutional safeguards. Black Panther and Storm side with Captain America and position Cap's (and their own) American values above Doom's autocratic regime, but they end up siding with him anyway, paralleling the hard decision that American officials made in and out of the comics pages. While Black Panther doesn't mimic Doom's form of rule for his own people—unlike the United States, Wakanda isn't ground zero for terrorists or supervillains—his alliance to autocrats shows the limits of his ideology. To defend the oppressed, he must work with oppressors. The superhero stuff ends with Captain America's arrest and death and T'Challa entering Four Freedoms Plaza as part of the new FF. T'Challa holds multiple roles as a foreign king, a member of the premiere American superhero family, and whose intricate diplomatic entanglements puts Americans ill at ease even as they mirror Homeland Security policy.

For his part, Doctor Doom has a few choice words for the FF anniversary bash in issue #543 (April 2007). Before the live cameras, Doom doesn't reject

T'Challa's assessment of his historical losing streak when it comes to battling the Fantastic Four, but after spewing forth the usual diatribe against his rival Reed Richards, Doom hit home with a biting indictment: Richards's "reckless adventuring in my and many other countries' internal affairs has destabilized the political balance of the entire world" (McDuffie "C'Mon Suzie"). Blasting Reed's failed attempt at nation-building, including his own Latveria,[4] Doom enumerates how the FF has undermined American national security: Richards has "built and maintained secret prisons," contributed "to the dissolution of your country's habeas corpus, and seeks now to export his evil to the rest of the world"(McDuffie "C'Mon Suzie"). His accusations reflect the criticism against the sweeping language of the PATRIOT Act and the War on Terror's turning inward to spy on American citizens. In the space of two panels, Doom subverts the American national narrative of the inclusive family, turning it from a source of national strength to a clan that breeds distrust and disunity. Doom ruins his point by elevating himself as an autocratic savior resisting the Fantastic Four's undermining American freedoms. Indeed, Ben tells Doom to "shuddup," throwing his popcorn bowl at the television to support his best friend when the monarch suggests a power-hungry Richards has deliberately failed to cure Grimm from his rocky skin condition. But for one brief moment, the Latverian monarch effectively cautions the American public that the superhero establishment Reed Richards had constructed way back in 1961 as a site of public idolization, and of which the FF continues to champion, are siphoning the people's liberties under their star-struck eyes and noses.

At the United Nations, T'Challa is careful to distance himself from Dr. Doom's bluster. Although Doom is correct that the U.S. Superhero Registration Act has upended international political balance, T'Challa insists he himself only speaks for his people of Wakanda, not for the FF, and certainly not for Latveria. Nevertheless, King T'Challa warns the American ambassador that the other kingdoms are "*far* more interventionist than my people" (McDuffie "Chapter Four"). This is an understatement; the Latverian monarch has tried to conquer the world on multiple occasions and the Atlanteans' various attacks, dating as far back as flooding New York with a tidal wave during World War II, were timely reminders of the constant threat Americans faced. Unfortunately for the Black Panther, due to the infinite crises of comic book madmen and despots, the need to fight dangers at home and abroad remains a top priority for Americans. With the U.S. government rallying super-powered beings to protect the flag, T'Challa recognizes the U.S. desire to shift from defense to offense, even, as the Latverian monarch had warned, at the cost of personal freedoms.

And that is why T'Challa's efforts are doomed to fail.

A Dark(er) Reign

By recognizing the precariousness of American national security and doing his part as a member of Marvel's First Family, T'Challa ultimately doesn't upset the establishment. He pushes buttons and tests Tony Stark's iron resolve, but the Black Panther doesn't overturn the structures that hold the Marvel Universe in place. After all, the Fantastic Four wants to return to normal and move on, not take Tony Stark down as the late Captain America did. Raw nerves remained throughout the superhero community post–Civil War. Scientist Henry Pym, now Stark's pencil pusher, holds a goliath-sized grudge against Black Panther for his not patriotically siding with the U.S.A., T'Challa's kingship and former Avengers membership notwithstanding. Even with the cosmos at stake in this storyline, Pym refuses to take orders from Black Panther, his fist clenched tight as he sinks low to strike at his highness. Pym's superheroing kicks in, overcoming his blind patriotism and his personal grudge against T'Challa to get the job done (McDuffie "Chapter Four"). But common sense aside, for Black Panther, hobnobbing with the FF doesn't give him the same standing among his powered peers as it did among the public.

Notably, creators Dwayne McDuffie and Paul Pelletier play it safe by sending Black Panther off the planet. For his part, McDuffie noted Marvel had shepherded Black Panther and Storm into the FF before his run began, and he juxtaposed T'Challa and Ororo into what he saw as the team's core concept: "the family of explorers who, while they're exploring, if they see someone getting screwed over, they try to fix it" (George). However, while paying homage to the FF's celebrated history of challenging the unknown, McDuffie directs the viewers' attention away from the "event" that had engulfed the Marvel Universe.

Rather than face problems on Earth, where Wakanda's king and queen can present a positive image of international cooperation against foes no single superhero can withstand, the Fantastic Four opt to leave terra firma during the creators' six-issue run. Reed and Susan Richards head to Titan for some fantastic foreplay while T'Challa takes Storm, Johnny, and Ben first to the moon, then into interstellar space, far beyond S.H.I.E.L.D.'s jurisdiction. They act on the behest of Deathlok, another outsider—in this case, a 1970s Robocop gone rogue—who now professes to be "cured," meaning he's fully human and integrated in the establishment he had once rebelled against. While the Fantastic Four are typically explorers and "imaginauts," the team's heading off into parts unknown ensures Black Panther is out of Stark's hair—just what the Director of S.H.I.E.L.D. wanted from Reed in the first place. For the readers, the FF is back in business as the new normal.

Furthermore, for all of Black Panther's leadership skills, he can't stretch his talents to fill Mr. Fantastic's shoes. When the team heads into space to confront the Watcher in #544 (May 2007), Black Panther starts to give exposition about the Watchers' passivity before his wife intervenes, saying that she knows about the observers already. The Human Torch jumps in, asking who hasn't heard of Uatu and his chrome-domed compatriots. The silent, static panel, echoed by FF readers who have followed the series for over four decades, renders Black Panther's briefing moot. Upon entering Uatu's house later that issue, the Black Panther brandishes the self-descriptive Ultimate Nullifier, threatening to erase the Watcher from existence should the bald behemoth refuse to cooperate—a move that turns out to be entirely unnecessary, since all he needed to do is ask.[5] Later, when T'Challa looks at silver age-old dossiers of villain Paste Pot Pete the Thing chides him for doing "*homework* on the bad guys" (McDuffie "Chapter Five"). The Human Torch again jumps in, summarizing the leader of the Frightful Four, the Wingless Wizard, with crossed eyes, a wagged tongue, and twirled finger against his ear in the universal sign of lunacy. The Black Panther may prep and do his homework, but he is one step behind the quartet and the fans.

King T'Challa also encounters resistance among his own ranks. Just as Reed's big brain led him to assume command, T'Challa thrusts his own scientific prowess as the head of the team. When the Black Panther uses his fancy instruments to measure "Reissner-Nordstrom metrics," Ben deadpans with a touch of sarcasm. "Things are so much easier without Reed to around ta confuse us with all the big words" (McDuffie "Chapter One"). But Ben's wishful thinking and nostalgia aside, he abides by family politics, often giving center stage to the scientist-king. However, even among "family," T'Challa pales beside Richards. When Reed is around, Ben looks to "Stretch" for approval before obeying commands from His Highness. Those more in sync with the U.S. government, such as Henry Pym, only turn to Mr. Fantastic. When Pym has an update on an immediate, sensitive crisis tearing the space time continuum apart, he looks over Black Panther's shoulders, immediately inquiring, "Is Reed with you?" (McDuffie "Chapter Six"). Only when Richards steps in and asks Pym to report does the other scientist relay his technobabble. McDuffie had regarded T'Challa as a superior strategist than Reed: "A lot of times Reed is just looking around, investigating. By the time Panther has arrived somewhere, he's figured out what his goal is, and he's figured out a set of plans and sub-plans to achieve that goal" (George). While McDuffie admired T'Challa's tactical mind befitting a head of state, American superheroes are warier. Even in a family of supposed equals, Black Panther is a second stringer.

The Black Panther's standing among the FF remains uncertain during his short time with the team. Despite the FF's welcoming the Black Panther and even changing their costumes to color-coordinate with his, the Black

Panther's leadership clashes with the Fantastic Four's established modus operandi. In their first run-in with the Silver Surfer in issue #545 (June 2007), T'Challa's first option is simply to turn tail, noting they lack the firepower to battle the sentinel of the spaceways or his master, Galactus, who wants to consume a living planet. Furthermore, as a passing space farer, the Black Panther abides by a personal prime directive; he respects sovereign entities just as he expects others to honor Wakandan jurisdiction, even if it means an entire world's death. The Thing and Human Torch, of course, with their long history of butting into others' affairs out of their moral righteousness, object to flight as an option. Indeed, given McDuffie's note about how the FF "fix" situations where people are "getting screwed," Black Panther's initial plan is out of line. In response, Storm, long accustomed to standing up for marginalized misfits and outcasts, takes her husband aside and threatens to "embarrass" him in front of the team. Even then, Black Panther initially gives the appearance of running away, with the Thing's jaw hanging loose and in wide blue-eyed astonishment. Even though Black Panther returns with a solution, the Wakandan king's unorthodox approach jarred with the FF's normal way of doing things.

Given the Black Panther's lingering outsider status, writer Dwayne McDuffie needs to redeem T'Challa as a full-fledged member of the Fantastic Four. McDuffie accomplishes this by turning to the past and reinforcing the historical narrative that originally defined the characters, specifically, T'Challa's origins. When the Frightful Four busts up the Richards' honeymoon in issue #548 (September 2007), the Wizard admits that the Fantastic Four have them outnumbered, with T'Challa and Storm making the FF into a six pack of trouble. To even the odds, the Wizard re-introduces a helping hand in the name of Klaw, a sonic being full of bad vibrations.

Clawing Apart Colonialism

Klaw's appearance isn't just by happenstance. As explained in the Black Panther's origin issue in *Fantastic Four* #52 (July 1966), Ulysses Klaue, originally a stereotyped European safari adventurer thrashing his way through the African continent, was on an odyssey to harvest valuable Wakandan vibranium. In a classic comic book turn, his supervillain origin metamorphoses him from man to monster, with a heavy dose of racism and neocolonialism added. Either in Wakanda or in the FF's NY HQ, Klaw, like all comic book baddies, meets defeat every time. But, as a killer of Wakandans, including T'Challa's father, he remained a thorn in T'Challa's side as a legacy of white supremacy.

Sound doesn't travel in a vacuum, but Klaw easily takes their longstanding feud into the heavens. Now in outer space, Black Panther must prove himself here as he did back in his stomping grounds of Africa's jungle action terrain. As a historical force of racism, Klaw denies T'Challa a voice in the final frontier, just as he did when he killed T'Challa's father way back in the 1960s, and just as Ben Grimm, Hank Pym, and Tony Stark now question the Wakandan king's legitimacy as a superhero and as a sovereign ally of the United States. Indeed, Klaw bursts forth from the Wizard's box, and lords over a battered Black Panther. "Reincorporated for less than a minute and I'm *already* tired of your ceaseless bluffing," Klaw scoffs as Black Panther struggles to get up (McDuffie "Chapter Six"). Nor is Klaw the only one who wants to silence the Black Panther's voice. Given that the American envoy at the U.N. easily lump T'Challa's country with Doom's as a potential axis of evil against U.S. national security, Klaw merely echoes the old racial fears of black legitimacy as a threat to the structures that make up American society, whether on terra firma or in deep space.

With his identity and agency at stake, Black Panther must re-affirm himself as a credible do-gooder. He orders the Thing to halt in his tracks when bashful Ben prepares to defend Black Panther as one of their own. "If he ain't up for the job today, we'll kick yer butt *for* him," the Thing says, eyes narrowed and teeth gritted in his best Yancy Street sneer (McDuffie "Chapter Six"). T'Challa cuts Ben off, declaring that he can fight his own battles. The Thing is taken aback, partly because his own role as the team's strong guy demands his taking front and center whenever it's clobbering time, but also because the FF stands up for their own, like a family should. But T'Challa vocally refuses Ben's aid. "Don't want to hear it, Grimm," Black Panther huffs as the Thing helps the king to his feet (McDuffie "Chapter Six"). T'Challa's declaration of independence is a refusal to submit to the self-styled master of sound who would keep.

For his part, Klaw draws on comic book history to demonstrate his superiority to the Black Panther. He privileges his knowing the Wakandan king better than his own superhero family does. In classic villain style, he briefly explains to Ben that the Black Panther stubbornly holds a grudge against him because he's "killed so many of his friends," presumably members of the Wakandan nation and the royal family (McDuffie "Chapter Six"). He recreates this history by sending shock waves through the FF, knocking them unconscious save for the Thing. After the Thing clobbers Klaw, he explains that the Black Panther slipped him vibranium earplugs to negate Klaw's sound bites.

Black Panther's sneakiness proves his worthiness as he defeats his archvillain by race-baiting. T'Challa relies on this tactic throughout McDuffie's run on *Fantastic Four*, appearing weak and need of assistance before his assembled white peers. He appeals to Reed for a place to stay, deceives the gleaming Silver Surfer into thinking he was fleeing a battlefield, and now appears helpless before an orange rock-pile and a purplish-skinned sound wave. By tapping into this trope, Black Panther renders the master of sound silent; indeed, Ben Grimm couldn't hear or feel a thing when he punched Klaw into oblivion. Even though Ben is uncomfortable with how the FF won the day—he tells T'Challa that the comments "Don't want to hear it" is a "little on the nose," meaning it was a bit abrasive for family—T'Challa excuses his language by saying he was "improvising" (McDuffie "Chapter Six"). T'Challa is a bit disingenuous, as minorities have played to stereotypes of needing white tutelage as a means of defiance and self-preservation for centuries. But in this case, the Black Panther gets a final dig at the establishment the FF represented.

Four No More (Sort of)

T'Challa learns that working as a team player ultimately pays off. Despite his stance against superhuman registration and the conscription program under the auspices of the U.S. government, the Black Panther bows before the status quo in the final act. McDuffie ends his run with a big bang, as the space-time continuum threatens to tear itself asunder. In *Fantastic Four* #550, the FF marshals their allies in a bid to literally save Eternity. However, given the large stakes, the Black Panther does little. While each of the Richards family and guest stars, like the Silver Surfer, Dr. Strange, and even the passive Watcher, have crucial roles in carrying out Reed's operation, Black Panther turns the narration—including the captions—over to a real outsider and rookie superhero: Gravity, a 19-year-old white kid from suburban Wisconsin.

Young Greg Willis is a relative newcomer to the cape-and-cowl set, having first debuted in 2005, but shortly died later in the line of duty. He appears in *Fantastic Four* #544 (May 2007) as a corpse. But McDuffie revives the kid as a cosmic champion to help the team battle the Silver Surfer. In his civilian alter ego, Gravity is more concerned about the housing association knowing his secret identity than saving said association from cosmic annihilation. But despite Gravity's preference for a quiet civilian life, and for all the good guys' pretense about obeying civil liberties and personal freedoms, the Fantastic Four literally conscript the teenager against his wishes, blow his secret identity before his neighborhood, and force him to play superhero. In short, Black Panther participates in what he has rejected all along: the tracking and enlisting of super-powered people to serve national (and intergalactic) security. Greg accepts his fate, breathlessly describing the action as "cool as all get-out" and concluding, "It was the hardest thing I've ever done" (McDuffie "Conclusion"). While Gravity might have found saving the cosmos ultimately satisfying, his lesson pales beside that of T'Challa.

The Black Panther finally realizes the futility of resisting to the norms of comic book patriotism and heroism. He accepts that the needs of the few—or the one—does not compare with the big picture, whether that means saving all of space-time, or providing protection for the folks/block association at home. Black Panther's silence in the face of Greg's conscription and ultra-cool climax that follows legitimatizes the necessity of any and all patriotic acts for the sake of king, country, and eternity. Gravity's secret identity is lost and the kid's life will never be the same, but the Marvel Universe lives to see another day.

With Black Panther's quietly acknowledging the need for superhero cooperation and self-sacrifice for the greater good, his international goals are temporarily frustrated and he has no reason to remain with the Fantastic Four. Government registration continues and the superhero training camps under Tony Stark and Hank Pym progress unabated. Instead, Black Panther gives a farewell dinner to the team, as he and Ororo treat the FF to a Wakandan royal feast that leaves the ever-lovin' blue-eyed Thing stuffed. Notably, the kid who saved the day—and presumably every day for eternity thereafter—Greg Willis, is not present. With his cover blown, perhaps the teenager resides at a military camp as a super solider in the making. No matter, for Black Panther also moves on as he vacates the Baxter Building in favor of his other hang-outs—his suspicion that the U.S. government played a part in the destruction of his New York's embassy goes unsolved and forgotten. After fighting the system for so long, T'Challa and Ororo finally yield and get S.H.I.E.L.D.

But Black Panther does not leave empty-handed. He and Storm gain legitimacy and a measure of celebrityhood as American superheroes, especially a brighter public image than they had before. Even though Black Panther spends most of his entire FF stint away from Earth, the Baxter Building's brief status as the Wakandan embassy adds a glossy shine to his country's reputation. For the Black Panther, his time with the Fantastic Four, his tough-guy persona and his good-husband interior, and even his very kingship, serve his needs and interests. Despite his protestations and activism, however, T'Challa, like other civil rights groups, ultimately falls in line with the government as an act of patriotism for a country still at war.

Notes

1. In 1961, the Fantastic Four point out that Marvel's comic books are supposedly adaptations from the heroes' real-life adventures. Government oversight of all superheroes' behavior is akin to the Comics Code, an industry creation in response to a Senate subcommittee's investigation of juvenile delinquency during the 1950s. The Comics Code sanitized stories, arguably turning them into juvenile kiddie fare. One can assume bureaucratic-run superhero teams would likewise make for stifling—if not dull—stories.

2. The team's beloved status among comic book New Yorkers is an ironic twist of fate, given how the franchise's cinematic productions have turned out in real life.

3. Ironically, in the sub-universe created by Reed and Sue's son, Franklin, the heroes are reborn with the U.S. government as a midwife; the team even take their jumpsuits from S.H.I.E.L.D.

4. Reed has dethroned Dr. Doom several times, once replacing him with a Latverian resistance leader (#200; November 1978) and another time assuming the throne himself after banishing Doom to hell (#500; September 2003). McDuffie also planned for Reed to use Civil War as a launching point to create a "utopia" within the Marvel Universe. While McDuffie did not bring this storyline to fruition, it foreshadowed the later "Future Foundation" in Jonathan Hickman's run.

5. Uatu gets the last laugh, hinting that the T'Challa's and Ororo's unborn children will have a remarkable legacy, leaving the Wakandan royal couple bug-eyed and speechless at the prospect of heirs. As of this writing, T'Challa has no children.

WORKS CITED

Bonilla-Silva, Eduardo. *White Supremacy & Racism in the Post-Civil Rights Era.* Lynne Rienner Publishers, 2001.

Brzezinski, Matthew. *Fortress America: On the Front Lines of Homeland Security—An Inside Look at the Coming Surveillance State.* Bantham Books, 2004.

Bush, George W. "President Signs USA PATRIOT Improvement and Reauthorization Act." *The White* House, 9 Mar. 2006, https://georgewbush-whitehouse.archives.gov/news/releases/2006/03/20060309-4.html Accessed 3 Aug. 2018.

Claremont, Chris, John Byrne and Bob McLeod. "Cry—Vengeance!" *Marvel Team-Up* #100 (December 1980). New York: Marvel Comics.

Englehart, Steve, Keith Pollard and Joe Sinnott. "I Want to Die!" *Fantastic Four* #311 (February 1988). New York: Marvel Comics.

George, Richard. "Fantastic Four Interview: Dwayne McDuffie Chats About Marvel's First Family." *IGN*, 13 Jun. 2007, www.ign.com/articles/2007/06/14/fantastic-four-interview. Accessed 9 Nov. 2018.

Herman, Susan N. *Taking Liberties: The War on Terror and the Erosion of American Democracy.* Oxford University Press, 2011.

Hudlin, Reginald, Manuel Garcia, and Jay Leisten. "World Tour Part Three: Aqua-Boogie." *Black Panther* #21 (December 2006). New York: Marvel Comics.

Hudlin, Reginald, Marcus To, Do Ho, and De Los Stanton. "War Crimes Part Three: Thunder and Lightning." *Black Panther* #25 (April 2007). New York: Marvel Comics.

Hudlin, Reginald, Scot Eaton, Kaare Andrews and Klaus Janson. "Bride of the Panther Part 5: Here Come a Storm." *Black Panther* #18 (September 2006). New York: Marvel Comics.

Hudlin, Reginald, Scot Eaton, and Andrew Hennessey. "World Tour Part One: Holiday in Latveria." *Black Panther* #19 (October 2006). New York: Marvel Comics.

Lee, Jim, Bandon Choi, and Scott Williams. "Repercussions." *Fantastic Four* vol. 2 #2 (December 1996). New York: Marvel Comics.

Lee, Stan, Jack Kirby, and George Klein. "The Fantastic Four!" *Fantastic Four* #1 (November 1961). New York: Marvel Comics.

Lee, Stan, Jack Kirby, and Dick Ayers. "The End of the Fantastic Four!" *Fantastic Four* #9 (December 1962). New York: Marvel Comics.

Lee, Stan, Jack Kirby, and Joe Sinnott. "The Black Panther!" *Fantastic Four* #52 (July 1966). New York: Marvel Comics.

May, Elaine Tyler. *Homeward Bound: American Families in the Cold War.* Basic Books, 1988.

Mayer, Jane. *The Dark Side: The Inside Story of How the War on Terror Turned into a War on American Ideals.* Doubleday, 2008.

McDuffie, Dwayne, Mike McKone, Andy Lanning and Cam Smith. "C'Mon, Suzie, Don't Leave Us Hangin.'" *Fantastic Four* #543. (April 2007). New York: Marvel Comics.

McDuffie, Dwayne, Paul Pelletier and Rick Magyar. "Reconstruction: Chapter One—From the Ridiculous to the Sublime." *Fantastic Four* #544 (May 2007). New York: Marvel Comics.

_____. "Reconstruction: Chapter Two—Don't Make Me Embarrass You in Front of Your Friends." *Fantastic Four* #545 (June 2007). New York: Marvel Comics.

_____. "Reconstruction: Chapter Four—Never Ask Her if She's Wearing Colored Contact Lenses." *Fantastic Four* #547 (August 2007). New York: Marvel Comics.

_____. "Reconstruction: Chapter Five—Kind of an Expensive Test." *Fantastic Four* #548 (September 2007). New York: Marvel Comics.

_____. "Reconstruction: Chapter Six—So I Guess You're Saying the Honeymoon's Over." *Fantastic Four* #549 (October 2007). New York: Marvel Comics.

_____. "Reconstruction: Conclusion—Should Eternity Perish." *Fantastic Four* #550 (November 2007). New York: Marvel Comics.

McDuffie, Dwayne, Paul Pelletier, Rick Magyar, and Scott Hanna. "Reconstruction: Chapter Three—Aw, That's Just Crude." *Fantastic Four* #546 (July 2007). New York: Marvel Comics.

Millar, Mark, Steve McNiven, Dexter Vines, and Mark Morales. Untitled. *Civil War* #3 (September 2006). New York: Marvel Comics.

Nama, Adilifu. *Super Black: American Pop Culture and Black Superheroes*. University of Texas Press, 2011.

Savage, Charlie. *Power Wars: The Relentless Rise of Presidential Authority and Secrecy*. Hatchette Book Group, 2017.

Waid, Mark, Mike Wieringo, and Karl Kessel. "Unthinkable Part Four." *Fantastic Four* #500 (September 2003). New York: Marvel Comics.

Wolfman, Marv, Keith Pollard, and Joe Sinnott. "When Titans Clash!" *Fantastic Four* #200 (November 1978). New York: Marvel Comics.

Secret Invasions, Lost Technology and 21st Century Learning Skills

How Black Panther Saved Wakanda Using the "Four C's"

Daniel J. Bergman

A 21st Century Crisis

The dawn of the 2000s provided a turning point to both reflect and refine educational goals for children in kindergarten through high school (K–12). It was also an opportune time for stakeholders from many realms to engage in conversation about school and education policy. In particular, several leaders in education, business, and technology collaborated to promote "21st Century Skills" for all K-12 students. Founded in 2002, this coalition of policymakers dubbed themselves "P21," for the Partnership for 21st Century Skills (changed later to Partnership for 21st Century Learning ["Our History"]).

P21's vision was relevance for the present and the future, and looked beyond students' mastery of fundamental content knowledge (English, math, science, history, etc.) to focus on skills deemed necessary for success in the coming century. This resulted in a two-year process to formulate the "Framework for 21st Century Learning" (National Education Association). The framework—shared in P21's "Action Guide" for state leaders in 2006—includes student outcomes such as Life and Career Skills; Information, Media and Technology Skills; and 21st Century Themes as well as the Core Subjects and the traditional "Three Rs" (reading, writing, arithmetic).

At the center of the framework, however, are Learning and Innovation

Skills, also known as the "Four C's": critical thinking, communication, collaboration, and creativity. The P21 coalition identified these four specific skills as the most important after multiple interviews with workforce and education leaders (NEA). P21 strategy consultant Bob Pearlman notes, "Just as the Three Rs serve as an umbrella for all core subjects, so the Four C's serve for all other 21st Century Skills" (10). While such skills may be applicable in multiple aspects of life, the 21st Century's "Four C" emphasis aligns with survey data about employer needs (Casner-Lotto and Barrington).

In 2008, the P21 group specifically targeted American education and "creating an aligned, 21st century public education system that prepares students, workers and citizens to triumph in the global skills race," pursuing this as "the central economic competitiveness issue for the next decade" (*Policy Guide* 1). P21's overt emphasis on winning the global economy competition is understandable given the coalition's founding organizations consisted mostly of technology-based businesses—Apple, Cisco Systems, Dell, Microsoft, and others—clearly outnumbering two education organizations (U.S. Department of Education, National Education Association) in the original group.

Language in P21 publications and materials frequently advocates for immediate action, citing trends in employment, the economy, and academic achievement via standardized assessments. Additional data noted in P21 documents are American demographic changes, noting the rise of population diversity. The National Center for Education Statistics projects that by 2024, minorities and traditionally underrepresented students will become the majority of high school graduates (NCES). The growth of underrepresented students is especially noteworthy given the historical gaps in achievement of Hispanics and African Americans compared to white students (Brownstein). As the P21 coalition states, "This accelerating diversification will challenge efforts to improve student performance and close achievement gaps" (9).

Student achievement gaps are frequently noted in the subjects of math and science, related to the continually expanding field of STEM (science, technology, engineering, mathematics). The 2007 Trends in International Mathematics and Science Study (TIMSS) indicates that, on average, African American and Hispanic students continued to score much lower than white students in both math and science, and in all grade levels tested, from kindergarten to high school (The Education Trust). "Thus, as larger numbers of underrepresented minorities are entering the STEM pipeline, many still are not progressing at a rate comparable to that of whites" (NAS et al. 5). In keeping with the P21 emphasis on global comparisons, the TIMSS 2007 study also shows that in both math and science, American 4th and 8th grade students scored lower than those in peer countries.

Such issues are not limited to K–12 education, as 2008 featured the ninth annual "Biology Education Summit" in Washington, D.C. (Musante). At this meeting, college educators met to share concerns and ideas for improving undergraduate and graduate biology education. Familiar topics were highlighted: underrepresented minorities in the sciences, workforce need, and global competition.

Also in 2008, physicist and Nobel Laureate Leon Lederman discussed "Scientists and 21st Century Science Education," noting that such challenges are not exclusive to the United States. Rather, there are "parallels in many nations" (398). Lederman elaborates further:

> Attitudes depend on a nation's history and culture, its *leadership*, and its industrial and scientific base. No matter which nation, however, there is a *common* incentive: the need to create and maintain an educational system that *encourages* its graduates to *innovate*, to be *creative*, and to *create* [emphases added].

Note the presence of words identical or similar to those of the Four C's in the 21st Century Skills. Also note the attention to universal themes, while still considering unique national and cultural identities. In his essay, Lederman continues with an eye toward schooling, as well as STEM and non–STEM connections:

> The education system, then, must provide a matching high level of preparation, not just in mathematics, science and engineering but also in reading, speaking, writing *and* history, economics, literature, and the arts [398, emphasis in original].

Lederman notes that in the U.S., at least, significant efforts toward educational improvement typically occur only after a "major crisis" (397). World War II, Sputnik, and 1983's *A Nation at Risk* report are all examples of events instigating drastic changes.

A 21st Century Hero

In 2008, the Marvel Comics universe experienced a crisis of its own, the "Secret Invasion" (Bendis and Yu). In this event, shapeshifting alien Skrulls had invaded planet Earth, with invaders masquerading as superheroes or other familiar Marvel characters. The mini-series event spanned nearly the entire year, with several other comic book issues presenting prelude, tie-in, and aftermath stories. Additionally, over a dozen separate Marvel titles featured stories based on the core *Secret Invasion* narrative.

In the *Black Panther* comic book series (*Volume 4*, Issues #39–41), King T'Challa's Wakandan home is the target of an invading Skrull army (Aaron and Palo). This particular attack is noteworthy due to Wakanda's legendary reputation as an unconquered nation, and the Skrulls' apparent advantages in size, technology, and subterfuge. The three-part "See Wakanda and Die" storyline is widely regarded as one of the best *Black Panther* comic book stories (Foxe; Gullickson; Huckabee; Lydon; Magnett; O'Reilly). The paperback trade collection of these three issues appeared on the very first "Graphic Books Best Seller List (Softcover)" released by the *New York Times* in March 2009 (Gustines).

In 2008, writer Jason Aaron was relatively new to Marvel Comics. He was best known for his critically-acclaimed series *Scalped*, a crime story based on a modern-day Native American reservation (CBR Staff; Hudson; Vertigo). Through his personal blog, Aaron wrote that the Black Panther story was "my first time working within a major company-wide crossover, and I'm pretty proud of how it turned out. Fun little sandbox to play in" (1). "[Marvel] editor Axel Alonso wanted the *Secret Invasion* tie-in issues of *Black Panther* to tell an epic war story, which is why he offered Aaron, the author of Vertigo's Vietnam War graphic novel *The Other Side*, a chance to write it" (Richards 1).

"See Wakanda and Die" demonstrates T'Challa's strengths not only as a superhero, but also as an inspiring leader and innovative thinker. In particular, Black Panther is an epitome of the 21st Century Learning and Innovation Skills. Through different and unexpected ways, he demonstrates the "Four C's"—collaboration, communication, critical thinking, and creativity—when all is seemingly lost. The following paragraphs examine each of "Four C's" depicted in this story, with examples, impact, and discussion of these skills with respect to 21st Century Learning documents.

Critical Thinking

At the dawn of the 1900s, educational leaders first began articulating the importance of critical thinking, exemplified by John Dewey's book *How We Think* in 1910. Over the course of the 20th century, numerous researchers and educators presented different definitions and perspectives of critical thinking. Summarizing these efforts, Norris concludes that critical thinking is "rationally deciding what to do or believe" (40). Working from cognitive science research, Sternberg further defines critical thinking as "the mental processes, strategies, and representations people use to solve problems, make decisions, and learn new concepts" (*Critical Thinking* 3). The P21 organization provides an overview of critical thinking research, as well as tools for assessing and teaching this skill (Dilley et al., *Critical Thinking*). They conclude with recommendations for including explicit critical thinking instruction throughout all age levels and subjects, with proper modeling of these skills by teachers.

In their guide for educators, the National Education Association (NEA) notes the importance of critical thinking both now and in the years to come:

Today's citizens must be active critical thinkers if they are to compare evidence, evaluate competing claims, and make sensible decisions. Today's 21st century families must sift through a vast array of information regarding financial, health, civic, even leisure activities to formulate plausible plans of action. The solutions to international problems, such as global warming, require highly developed critical thinking and problem-solving skills [8].

The Black Panther models critical thinking during the Skrull invasion, demonstrating rational thought, speech, and action throughout the ordeal. Although "See Wakanda and Die" was a relatively brief three-issue story, the example here is applicable to students, citizens, and families living throughout the 21st century.

Black Panther #39 (Jul. 2008) opens inside a Skrull spacecraft as it enters Wakandan airspace. The alien officers discuss the upcoming battle, confident of an easy victory. As one lieutenant states, "The Wakandans may have staved off invasion up until now, but they've never faced an enemy quite like us." This element of the unknown is common in stories featuring the shapeshifting Skrulls, typically able to assume the identity of anyone from anonymous stranger to prominent leader. In this case, Skrull sleeper agents "began infiltrating every aspect of Wakanda's power structure," including advisors to T'Challa and his inner circle. The theme of hidden enemies and lurking dangers occurs throughout the entire story, similar to present and future challenges facing society. "Life today is exponentially more complicated and complex than it was 50 years ago" (NEA 5).

During the opening battle between Skrulls and Wakandans, Black Panther comes face-to-face with an especially difficult enemy—a "Super Skrull." This "secret weapon" is an enhanced warrior possessing additional powers copied from various superheroes and villains. Moreover, the enemy boasts to Black Panther, "I have trained my entire life to face you." In contrast, T'Challa responds with a disposition of critical thinking: "Then you have already lost. For I have trained my entire life to face the unknown." The ensuing duel occurs over the course of *Black Panther* #40 (Aug. 2008), where T'Challa demonstrates critical thinking in action. Further insight comes from captions narrating Black Panther's thoughts during the fight.

Early on, T'Challa mentions prior knowledge of the Skrulls from his past years studying the aliens. Content understanding is a key foundation for critical thinking. "You can't think critically about topics you know little about or solve problems that you don't know well enough to recognize and execute the type of solutions they call for" (Willingham 12). Cognitive scientist Daniel Willingham has written extensively about 21st Century Skills, and critical thinking in particular, noting research about the ongoing importance of content knowledge. "Without content knowledge we often cannot use thinking skills properly and effectively.... But all content knowledge is not equally important to mathematics, or to science, or to literature. To think critically, students need the knowledge that is central to the domain" (Rotherham and Willingham 18).

In this case, T'Challa uses his knowledge of Skrull anatomy to target his attack at a painful pressure point. However, this initial prediction must be revised when the Black Panther learns of the Super Skrull's impenetrable skin. Critical thinking occurs as T'Challa reflects on this new experience and revises his understanding. Through internal narration, Black Panther describes recognizable attacks from friend and foe—Wolverine, Iron Fist, Bullseye, and more. As the battle continues, he demonstrates further critical thinking (and application of knowledge) to devise a solution: "There's no way I can outfight him. But then, I don't have to outfight him. All I have to do is just survive long enough to figure out his weakness" (12).

All of this thinking occurs while T'Challa spars with the Super Skrull. Although outwardly it appears Black Panther is losing the fight, he is actually gaining the advantage. All the while, he demonstrates characteristics of a critical thinker: focusing, testing first impressions, distinguishing choices, basing conclusions on evidence (Murawski). Through this process, Black Panther determines that the Super Skrull has "tells," revealing patterns or moments of weakness. Again, T'Challa describes his conclusions about the adversary:

> He can't use all of his powers at once, so he has to switch between them. And when he switches, he has tells. A subtle shift of weight. A slight change in posture. They're small and hard to detect, but once I have them down, they tell me everything I need to know [13].

Armed with this insight, Black Panther needs only three quick strikes to disable and defeat the Super Skrull.

The greater battle is not over, but T'Challa earns victory through critical thinking. Murawski's description of critical thinker characteristics matches those of the Black Panther:

> They become more adept in their thinking by using a variety of probing techniques which enable them to discover new and often improved ideas. More specifically, critical thinkers tend to see the problem from many perspectives, to consider many different investigative approaches, and to produce many ideas before choosing a course of action. In addition, they are more willing to take intellectual risks, to be adventurous, to consider unusual ideas, and to use their imaginations while analyzing problems and issues [26].

Problems and issues will continue to arise throughout the 21st century. Individuals who find success are those who practice and develop critical thinking skills, intertwined with foundational knowledge (Rotherham and Willingham).

Collaboration

Success is seldom a solo event. It often depends on collective effort, and the Black Panther achieves his victory through collaboration. Simply put, collaboration is "the activity of working together towards a common goal" (Hesse et al. 38). Plucker et al. advocate for educators to consider collaboration as both a process and product: "the value of collaboration ... has been assumed for many years, but until recently, policy makers have not singled out the ability to collaborate as an important outcome in its own right.... Collaboration is not merely a means to an end, but crucial to enhance" (*Collaboration* 1). Kuhn's research is used by P21 to articulate two views of collaboration: first the traditional action itself and secondly the outcome—considered a 21st Century Skill.

In their battle against the Skrull army, the Wakandans demonstrate collaboration aligned with both categories. At key moments, several supporting cast members take action to collaborate with Black Panther. In the initial attack, Chief of Security W'Kabi and Chief of Operations S'Yan work with their king inside the Wakandan command center. T'Challa's sister Shuri leads Wakandan soldiers in the battle's final charge. Fighting alongside Black Panther—at both the very beginning and end—is his wife at the time, Ororo ("Storm" from the X-Men). Storm uses her mutant ability of weather manipulation to rain a deluge on the enemy, and later to signal allies with lightning.

More plentiful than recurring characters, however, are the numerous "faces in the crowd" of Wakanda. These individuals come from all walks of life, yet each has joined the fight, each donning a panther mask and armor to conceal their leader among the ranks. Although the Skrulls are initially confused by the multitude, T'Challa displays "collaborative leadership" as he fights alongside his companions. This includes attention to the "human element" and "personal relationships" (Goman), recognizing individuals among the fallen soldiers. During the battle, Black Panther shares the names and personal stories of the casualties:

> Even from across the battlefield, I feel them. Guedado the miner. Son of Gahiji. Husband of Rashida. Dead at 22. Lisimba the palace guard. His newborn daughter will never know her father's embrace. Bassey the fisherman from Black Warrior Creek. His wife is at home right now, praying to the panther god to keep him safe. I feel each one as they slip away [#40, Aug. 2008, 5].

Outnumbered three to one, the Wakandan army manages to hold their own against the Skrull invaders. Their primary tactic is synergetic, a collaborative outcome which has been called "collective intelligence" (Palca 4) or "the wisdom of crowds." The latter term is from journalist James Surowiecki, who writes, "Under the right circumstances, groups are remarkably intelligent, and are often smarter than the smartest people in them" (xiii). Whereas the Skrulls had considered Wakanda "one little African country," "backwoods," and "isolated [with] barely a single superpowered protector" (#39, Jul. 2008), they soon understand the challenge of defeating a unified and collaborative people.

Research indicates that collaboration in the classroom also yields powerful results. Active student cooperation and teamwork correlates with improved student engagement, motivation, relationships, and retention (Johnson and Johnson; Prince). Students at various ability levels benefit from collaborative groups (Lou et al.), including expert students teaching information to peers (Webb et al.) as well as novices working together to find information (Smith et al.). While these studies examine academic achievement and learner engagement, a parallel exists with the fictional Wakandan collaboration, an ideal as both process and outcome.

Communication

King T'Challa inspires his people to collaborate through his effective skill in communication. Competent communication is characterized as the "ability to pass along or give information; the ability to make known by talking or writing" (McCroskey and McCroskey 109). In this comic book story, most communication between characters is spoken dialogue, although it is implied other messages are sent through writing, transmission, or—as mentioned previously—signals via Storm's weather manipulation.

Communication is closely linked to collaboration (Brown and Duguid; Seefeldt), and Black Panther explicitly states the need for unity among his people. This desire for uniformity is not only in superficial appearances, but in a cohesive spirit. Before the armies meet in battle, T'Challa rouses his Wakandan fighters with a lengthy speech (#40, Aug. 2008, 2–3). Note the initial reference to "friends," as the king instills a sense of camaraderie and equality:

> We've been down this road before, my friends. Countless times over the years has an army massed outside these gates, looking to subjugate us. Looking to pillage our resources or wipe us from the face of the earth. We see their weapons in our museums. We dredge up their bones when we till our fields. They are but ghosts, while Wakanda remains [Aaron].

After reviewing their nation's past, he focuses on the present predicament:

> Now a new army has arrived, unlike any other we have ever faced. They are a race of deceivers and murderers who have crossed the very skies to come here, raping a thousand worlds along the way. And here is where they will die [Aaron].

T'Challa is truthful about the challenge awaiting the Wakandans. But rather than dwell on the difficulty, he quickly redirects their attention toward the future:

> A hundred years from now, when our grandchildren till these same fields, and they dredge up the strange shattered bones of these Skrulls, they will remember the stories of this day and the names of all who fought here. Who bled here. So that Wakanda might endure [Aaron].

Black Panther clearly communicates his goal—victory and survival of their nation—which he confidently imparts to his fellow Wakandans. Furthermore, T'Challa finishes his address by once again conveying the idea of collaboration as both a process and outcome:

> Regardless of what you were yesterday—miner, shepherd, farmer—today, you are all soldiers of the panther god. Today we are all the Black Panther! And today we will fight as one! [Aaron].

The Wakandan army responds with the cry "For Wakanda!" echoing their leader's intent for unity and victory.

Compare this speech with the one given by the Skrull commander in #39 (Jul. 2008, 12), yelled to his warriors before the first ground battle. Although the setting and timing are similar, the attackers' mood comes across as much more fraught than that of the defenders:

> You all know what we fight for here today! You all know the prophecies! You know that if we lose this battle, there is no going home! For there is no home left for us to go back to! This is where we make our final stand! But I'm not asking you to fight for a prophecy here today! I'm asking you to fight for the Skrull next to you! Your brother! As he will fight for you! [Aaron].

In the Skrull's speech, familiar themes emerge about the past, the urgency to win, even unity among warriors. However, the rest of his words shift significantly from Black Panther's address. In fact, the commander turns his complete attention toward T'Challa himself:

> You see this man? You see how he mocks you! How he mocks an empire that has laid waste to a thousand galaxies! This one puny earth man! Bring me his head so we might toast the empress with a drink from his skull! Without their arrogant king, the rest of the Wakandans will fall in line like the weak little humans they are! Kill the Black Panther and the day is ours! [Aaron].

In place of cooperative effort and widespread strategy, the Skrull narrows his army's focus onto a single target. Moreover, his speech slips away from an honest assessment of the situation. This error in judgment results in distrust. A Skrull lieutenant responds to the commander's appeal for victory with a timid, "Uh, Sir, that might not be as simple as it sounds" (Aaron). The entire alien army also shows less enthusiasm than the Wakandans. Rather than a collective battle cry, we see a single Skrull shout "For the empire!" (Aaron).

Trust is an essential component of successful communication. "Trust is a feeling of security you have, based on the belief that someone or something is knowledgeable, reliable, good, honest, and effective" (Hoff 1). Throughout the Skrull invasion, T'Challa urges his fellow Wakandans to trust their plan for victory. This includes counterintuitive choices—creative tactics explained further below—and patience for precise timing and teamwork. Again, connections exist among all four 21st Century Skills of communication, collaboration, critical thinking, and creativity.

Although enduring since the dawn of civilization, communication is not as extensively researched as other skills in education (Dilley et al., *Communication*). The presence of effective classroom conversations is clearly linked to better student comprehension and critical thinking (Applebee et al.; Fall et al.; Murphy et al.). Successful classroom communication depends on several factors, including invitational non-verbal behaviors and posture (Babad; Neill and Caswell), student-focused teacher questions and responses (Ashmann and Berg; Weimer), and seating arrangements that promote equity and engagement (Marx et al.; Rosenfield et al.). Citing workforce demands, the NEA notes the growing need in effective communication due to cultural and technological shifts: "The power of modern media and the ubiquity of communication technologies in all aspects of life make teaching strong communication skills even more important" (13). However, purposeful teaching of communication skills has lagged, perhaps due to a belief that students acquire these abilities simply through implicit means and daily interactions. Yet with expanding globalization and technology, explicit attention and instruction are needed even more. "As our society evolves, we can no longer assume that communicative competence is something that our students will learn 'on their own'" (Dilley et al. *Communication* 1).

Lack of communication can lead to lead to disaster, though hopefully not as grim as what happens to the Skrull invaders. On the last page of the first issue (#39, Jul. 2008), the Skrull commander reproves his lieutenant's suggestion to contact their superiors and request reinforcements. Reasons for the refusal include hubris as well as fear of retribution—"We might as well write our own death warrants, lieutenant" (22). Interestingly, the final issue (#41, Sept. 2008) is framed by narration from a letter the Skrull commander is writing to his wife back home. Juxtaposed with these words of confident victory are images of countless dead Skrulls, fallen from the Wakandans' final attack. As he breathes his last, the dying commander transmits his letter. However, the definitive message comes from the Black Panther, written in Skrull blood inside their returning spacecraft: "This is what happens when you invade Wakanda." In its guide for educators, the NEA states,

"Communication cannot be effective unless the message is received and understood" (14). The Skrulls' defeat is due, at least in part, from ineffective communication. Even without advanced technology, the Wakandans are better at clearly sending, receiving, and understanding messages.

Creativity

Creativity is the fourth of the "Four C's," and is exemplified by the battle plan Black Panther had been communicating and collaborating to accomplish. In a seemingly *non*-21st century move, the first step in T'Challa's plan is eliminating all electronic technology. The Wakandans use a "long-range energy disruptor" to destroy the Skrull armory, then hack into the alien systems to paralyze their vehicles. In doing so, however, all Wakandan power is also lost. As Chief of Security W'Kabi explains, "All our automatic defenses are down. And anything within a five mile radius that even remotely resembled a gun has been rendered utterly useless" (#39, Jul. 2008, 10). Black Panther's response is "We've got them exactly where we want them" (Aaron).

As mentioned before, T'Challa must ensure trust among his people. In each issue, at least one Wakandan refers to sticking to the plan. When advisor S'Yan asks early on, "If this doesn't work, what next?" the king's response is "There is no what next" (#39, Jul. 2008, 8). Even so, wife Ororo explains that T'Challa "always knows what he's doing. He has contingency plans for every eventuality" (#40, Aug. 2008, 18). Black Panther's creative skill as a planner and strategist is reiterated by writer Jason Aaron. In an interview he explains, "The Black Panther has a contingency plan for everything, including an alien invasion. So he's never going to be caught unaware" (cited in Richards 2). This preparedness is evident in the story's climax, when it appears the Skrulls have ambushed and imprisoned T'Challa and Ororo.

In an ironic twist, the heroes have masked themselves among the shapeshifting aliens. The prisoners are actually captured Skrulls, made to resemble Black Panther and Storm with implanted "vocal manipulators" and "flesh transmuters." Using the same tools, the heroes infiltrate the command ship and attack from within. Now with forces both inside and out, the Wakandans achieve a quick and decisive victory.

In contrast, the Skrulls admit to being fooled completely, unprepared and oblivious to their impending doom. While not as ominous, the absence of creativity in education can lead to unfortunate struggles. "If students leave school without knowing how to continuously create and innovate, they will be underprepared for the challenges of society and the workforce" (NEA 24). P21 documents also highlight the importance of creativity for students with respect to ubiquitous technology. "In an age when much of the world's information can be quickly accessed on a smartphone, a premium is placed on the ability to use that knowledge in creative ways to produce valuable outcomes and solve complex problems" (Plucker et al. *Creativity* 1).

With the exception of their final ploy, Black Panther and his allies purposefully avoid the use of technology. Creativity, then, is not limited to technological applications. This stands to reason, considering what counts as creative work. While individual definitions differ, two common ingredients for creativity are novelty and usefulness (Plucker et al. *Educational Psychologist*; Stein). Neither criterion is exclusive to electronic devices. In fact, in today's digital era, an unplugged tool or off-the-grid idea may be truly unique and advantageous.

Conclusions and Commitment

Ultimately, the Wakandans' use of hidden technology does sway the battle in their favor. In this way, a sort of *deus ex machina* resolves the climax just when things seem most desperate. While this makes for a good story, the same cannot be said for schools and students. A common lament in education is that its numerous challenges are not solvable by a "magic bullet" (Cepeda; Peterson) or "quick fix" (Harste and Leland; Robinson; Sharma). Even so, many of these issues are not exclusive to the 21st century. Educators and stakeholders have scrutinized and debated matters of equity, accessibility, quality, relevance, and more for as long as there have been students and schools.

Likewise, Rotherham and Willingham note that "21st Skills" are not necessarily new. "What's actually new is the extent to which changes in our economy and the world mean that collective and individual success depends on having such skills" (16). They argue that schools do not need a radical overhaul, but "must be more deliberate" in teaching skills such as communication, collaboration, critical thinking, and creativity. In a way, T'Challa's most essential trait for success may not be one of the "Four C's," but rather his intentionality and determination. Or to propose a fifth "C," Black Panther demonstrates *commitment*.

The skills discussed here are not simply items to add to one's repository of talents. While each can be practiced and expanded, they are greater than mere attributes to acquire. Instead, such "skills" are more akin to an outlook, or even an ethic. One can and should certainly work to improve their abilities, but lasting impact relies on values to guide external actions. In describing "successful individuals," psychologist Robert Sternberg summarizes both the interdependence of skills as well as underlying principles:

Successful individuals are those who have creative skills, to produce a vision for how they intend to make the world a better place for everyone; analytical intellectual skills, to assess their vision and those of others; practical intellectual skills, to carry out their vision and persuade people of its value; and wisdom, to ensure that their vision is not a selfish one [*Wisdom, Intelligence, and Creativity Synthesized*, cited in NEA 24].

Though rooted in the early 21st century, these ideals have timeless application. Whether one is a king or commoner, a superhero or student, they can find inspiration from Black Panther and his fellow Wakandans.

WORKS CITED

Aaron, Jason. "Black Panther #39 Out Today." 30 July 2008, http://jasoneaaron.blogspot.com/2008/07/black-panther-39-out-today.html.

Aaron, Jason (w), and Jefte Palo (a). "See Wakanda and Die, Part One." *Black Panther (Vol. 4)* #39 (July 2008). New York: Marvel Comics.

_____. "See Wakanda and Die, Part Two." *Black Panther (Vol. 4)* #40 (Aug. 2008). New York: Marvel Comics.

_____. "See Wakanda and Die, Part Three." *Black Panther (Vol. 4)* #41 (Sept. 2008). New York: Marvel Comics.

Applebee, Arthur, et al. "Discussion-Based Approaches to Developing Understanding: Classroom Instruction and Student Performance in Middle and High School English." *American Educational Research Journal*, vol. 40, no. 3, 2003, pp. 685–730.

Ashmann, Scott, and Craig Berg. "An iPad App for Classroom Observation." *National Social Science Technology Journal*, vol. 3, no. 3, 2013, pp. 1–10.

Babad, Elisha. "Teaching and Nonverbal Behavior in the Classroom." *International Handbook of Research on Teachers and Teaching*, edited by Lawrence Saha and A. Gary Dworkin, Springer, 2009, pp. 817–827.

Bendis, Brian Michael (w), and Leinil Yu (a). *Secret Invasion*. New York: Marvel, 2009.

Brown, John Seely, and Paul Duguid. *The Social Life of Information*. Boston: Harvard Business School, 2000.

Brownstein, Ronald. "The Challenge of Educational Inequality." *The Atlantic*. 19 May 2016, https://www.theatlantic.com/education/archive/2016/05/education-inequality-takes-center-stage/483405/.

Casner-Lotto, Jill, and Linda Barrington. *Are They Really Ready to Work? Employers' Perspectives on the Basic Knowledge and Applied Skills of New Entrants to the 21st Century U.S. Workforce*. New York: The Conference Board, 2006.

Cepeda, Esther. "Technology Is No Magic Bullet for U.S. Schools." *Las Vegas Review-Journal*. 12 March 2017, https://www.reviewjournal.com/opinion/comentary-technology-is-no-magic-bullet-for-u-s-schools/.

Comic Book Resources Staff. "Best 100 Comics of 2008: Master List." *Comic Book Resources*. 4 January 2009, https://www.cbr.com/best-100-comics-of-2008-master-list/.

Dewey, John. *How We Think: A Restatement of the Relation of Reflective Thinking to the Educative Process*. Boston: Heath, 1910/1933.

Dilley, Anna, et al. *What We Know About Communication*. Washington, D.C.: Partnership for 21st Century Learning, 2015.

_____. *What We Know About Critical Thinking*. Washington, D.C.: Partnership for 21st Century Learning, 2015.

The Education Trust. *Highlights from Trends in International Mathematics and Science Study (TIMSS) 2007*. Washington, D.C.: National Center for Education Statistics, U.S. Department of Education, 2008.

Fall, Randy, et al. "Group Discussion and Large-Scale Language Arts Assessment: Effects on Students' Comprehension." *American Educational Research Journal*, vol. 37, no. 4, 1997, pp. 911–942.

Foxe, Steve. "'See Wakanda and Die' Tells You Everything You Need to Know About Black Panther." *Paste Magazine*. 16 February 2018, https://www.pastemagazine.com/articles/2018/02/see-wakanda-and-die-tells-you-everything-you-need.html.
Goman, Carol Kinsey. "8 Tips for Collaborative Leadership." *Forbes*. 13 February 2014, https://www.forbes.com/sites/carolkinseygoman/2014/02/13/8-tips-for-collaborative-leadership/#794a9d275fd9.
Gullickson, Brad. "5 Great Black Panther Comics to Read Before February." *Film School Rejects*. 14 June 2017, https://filmschoolrejects.com/great-black-panther-comics/.
Gustines, George Gene. "Introducing the New York Times Graphic Books Best Seller Lists." *The New York Times Arts Beat*. 5 March 2009, https://artsbeat.blogs.nytimes.com/2009/03/05/introducing-the-new-york-times-graphic-books-best-seller-lists/.
Harste, Jerome, and Christine Leland. "No Quick Fix: Education as Inquiry." *Literacy Research and Instruction*, vol. 37, no. 3, 1998, pp. 191–205.
Hesse, Friedrich, et al. "A Framework for Teachable Collaborative Problem Solving Skills." *Assessment and Teaching of 21st Century Skills*, edited by Patrick Griffin and Esther Care, Springer, 2015, pp. 37–56.
Hoff, Naphtali. "The Importance of Building Trust." *Huffington Post*. 3 March 2016, https://www.huffingtonpost.com/naphtali-hoff/the-importance-of-buildin_1_b_9366838.html.
Huckabee, Tyler. "10 Best Black Panther Comic Books." *IGN*. 13 February 2018, https://www.ign.com/articles/2018/02/13/10-best-black-panther-comic-books.
Hudson, Laura. "The 2011 Eisner Awards." *Comics Alliance*. 8 April 2011, http://comicsalliance.com/2011-eisner-awards-nominees/.
Johnson, David, and Roger Johnson. "An Educational Psychology Success Story: Social Interdependence Theory and Cooperative Learning." *Educational Researcher*, vol. 8, no. 5, 2009, pp. 365–379.
Kuhn, Deanna. "Thinking Together and Alone." *Educational Researcher*, vol. 44, no. 1, 2015, pp. 46–53.
Lederman, Leon. "Scientists and 21st Century Science Education." *Technology in Society*, vol. 30, 2008, pp. 397–400.
Lou, Yiping, et al. "Within-Class Grouping: A Meta-Analysis." *Review of Educational Research*, vol. 66, no. 4, 1996, pp. 423–458.
Lydon, Pierce. "10 Must-Read Black Panther Stories." *Newsarama*. 15 February 2018, https://www.newsarama.com/38600-10-greatest-black-panther-stories-of-all-time.html.
Magnett, Chase. "The 10 Best Black Panther Comics of All Time." *Comic Book*. 16 February 2018, https://comicbook.com/comics/2018/02/16/best-black-panther-comics/#6.
Marx, Alexandra, et al. "Effects of Classroom Seating Arrangements on Children's Question-Asking." *Learning Environments Research*, vol. 2, no. 3, 1999, pp. 249–263.
McCroskey, James, and Linda McCroskey. "Self-Report as an Approach to Measuring Communication Competence." *Communication Research Reports*, vol. 5, no. 2, 1988, pp. 108–113.
Murawski, Linda. "Critical Thinking in the Classroom … and Beyond." *Journal of Learning in Higher Education*, vol. 10, no. 1, 2014, pp. 25–30.
Murphy, P. Karen, et al. "Examining the Effects of Classroom Discussion on Students' High-Level Comprehension of Text: A Meta-Analysis." *Journal of Educational Psychology*, vol. 101, no. 3, 2009, pp. 740–764.
Musante, Susan. "Critical Conversations: The 2008 Biology Education Summit." *BioScience*, vol. 58, no. 8, 2008, pp. 685–689.
National Academy of Sciences, et al. *Expanding Underrepresented Minority Participation*. Washington, D.C.: National Academies Press, 2011.
National Center for Education Statistics. "Table 219.30. Public High School Graduates, by Race/Ethnicity: 1998–99 through 2025–26." https://nces.ed.gov/programs/digest/d15/tables/dt15_219.30.asp?current=yes.
National Education Association. *An Educator's Guide to the Four C's: Preparing 21st Century Students for a Global Society*. Washington, D.C.: NEA, 2012.
Neill, Sean, and Chris Caswell. *Body Language for Competent Teachers*. London: Routledge, 1993.

Norris, Stephen. "Synthesis of Research on Critical Thinking." *Educational Leadership*, vol. 42, no. 8, 1985, pp. 40–45.
O'Reilly, Tim. "Black Panther Essential Reading: Who Is Black Panther?" *Comicsverse*. 20 February 2018, https://comicsverse.com/black-panther-essential-reading/.
Palca, Joe. "Collaboration Beats Smarts in Group Problem Solving" *National Public Radio*. 30 September 2010, https://www.npr.org/templates/story/story.php?storyId=130247631.
Partnership for 21st Century Skills. *21st Century Skills, Education & Competitiveness: A Resource and Policy Guide*. Tucson: Partnership for 21st Century Skills, 2008. http://www.p21.org/storage/documents/21st_century_skills_education_and_competitiveness_guide.pdf.
_____. *A State Leader's Action Guide to 21st Century Skills: A New Vision for Education*. Tucson: Partnership for 21st Century Skills, 2006.
Partnership for 21st Century Learning. "Our History." http://www.p21.org/about-us/our-history.
Pearlman, Bob. "From Students to Learners: New Learning Environments for 21st Century Skills." 21st Century Learning Summit, 13 October 2010, Rosemont, IL. Conference Presentation.
Peterson, Steven. "There's No Magic Bullet to Improve Education." *Penn Live*. 31 May 2011, https://www.pennlive.com/editorials/index.ssf/2011/05/theres_no_magic_bullet_to_impr.html.
Plucker, Jonathan, et al. *What We Know About Collaboration*. Washington, D.C.: Partnership for 21st Century Learning, 2015.
_____. *What We Know About Creativity*. Washington, D.C.: Partnership for 21st Century Learning, 2015.
_____. "Why Isn't Creativity More Important to Educational Psychologists? Potential, Pitfalls, and Future Directions in Creativity Research." *Educational Psychologist*, vol. 39, no. 2, 2004, pp. 83–96.
Prince, Michael. "Does Active Learning Work? A Review of the Research." *Journal of Engineering Education*, vol. 93, no. 3, 2004, pp. 223–231.
Richards, Dave. "Total War: Aaron Talks Black Panther Secret Invasion Tie-In." *Comic Book Resources*. 14 May 2008, https://www.cbr.com/total-war-aaron-talks-black-panther-secret-invasion-tie-in/.
Robinson, Kimberly. "No Quick Fix for Equity and Excellence: The Virtues of Incremental Shifts in Education Federalism" *Stanford Law and Policy Review*, vol. 27, 2016, pp. 201–250.
Rosenfield, Peter, et al. "Desk Arrangement Effects on Pupil Classroom Behavior." *Journal of Educational Psychology*, vol. 77, no. 1, 1985, pp. 101–108.
Rotherham, Andrew, and Daniel Willingham. "21st Century Skills: The Challenges Ahead." *Educational Leadership*, Sept. 2009, pp. 16–21.
Seefeldt, Carol. "Helping Children Communicate." *Early Childhood Today*, vol. 19, no. 1, 2004, pp. 36–42.
Sharma, CB. "There Is No Quick Fix in Education." *The Pioneer*. 30 November 2017, https://www.dailypioneer.com/2017/columnists/there-is-no-quick-fix-in-education.html.
Smith, Michelle, et al. "Why Peer Discussion Improves Student Performance on In-Class Concept Questions." *Science*, vol. 323, no. 5910, 2009, pp. 122–124.
Stein, Morris. "Creativity and Culture." *The Journal of Psychology*, vol. 36, no. 2, 1953, pp. 311–322.
Sternberg, Robert. *Critical Thinking: Its Nature, Measurement, and Improvement*. Washington, D.C.: National Institute of Education, 1986. Available at http://eric.ed.gov/PDFS/ED272882.pdf.
Sternberg, Robert. *Wisdom, Intelligence, and Creativity Synthesized*. Cambridge: Cambridge University Press, 2007.
Surowiecki, James. *The Wisdom of Crowds*. New York: Anchor, 2005.
Vertigo. "Jason Aaron." Talent Directory. https://www.vertigocomics.com/talent/jason-aaron.
Webb, Noreen, et al. "Productive Helping in Cooperative Groups." *Theory Into Practice*, vol. 41, no. 1, 2002, pp. 13–20.

Weimer, Maryellen. *Learner-Centered Teaching: Five Key Changes to Practice.* San Francisco: Jossey-Bass/Wiley & Sons, Inc., 2002.
Willingham, Daniel. "Critical Thinking: Why Is It So Hard to Teach?" *American Educator,* Summer 2007, pp. 8–18.

Gender in Wakanda

Exploring Intersectionality and Hyper-Sexualization in Princess Shuri's Tenure as Black Panther

HOLLIE FITZMAURICE

The world of superhero comic books has been largely male-centric, resulting in stories where female characters are frequently underrepresented. But, the women of Wakanda—from the Dora Milaje to Princess Shuri—are shown to be strong, smart, and fearsome. These women stand as equals with, and oftentimes ahead of Wakanda's male heroes. Yet their representation is not without its flaws. While these women can stand toe-to-toe with the most famous heroes, and defeat the most fearsome of enemies, they are also hyper-sexualized, undervalued, and—particularly in the case of the Dora Milaje—they are treated as though they are disposable. The Dora Milaje were introduced in 1998 in the *Black Panther* run by Christopher Priest and Mark Texeira. Shuri was created by Reginald Hudlin and John Romita, Jr., in 2005. The 2009 storyline *Deadliest of the Species* by Reginald Hudlin and Ken Lashley sees Shuri taking over from T'Challa as the new Black Panther. It was reissued in 2018 as *Shuri: Deadliest of the Species* due to the popularity of the character in the Marvel Cinematic Universe, yet the portrayal of the character in Hudlin's arc has little resemblance to the live action Shuri. Hudlin's portrayal of Shuri adopting the moniker of the Black Panther provides a complex and unique representation of women in comics, as well as providing a new legacy to one of the most famous black heroes to date.

    This essay aims to explore the representation of the women of Wakanda throughout Shuri's tenure as the Black Panther, as well as Shuri's development as both the leader of her country, and its greatest warrior. As a female character taking over the role of a historically male character, and as a woman of color, intersectionality is at the heart of her representation. The importance and effectiveness of this intersectionality, and its relation to the women of Wakanda will also be explored. Shuri herself is not the only woman impacted by her tenure, as the complexity of the cultural narrative ties directly into the larger representation of women in Wakanda.

While the representation of women in superhero comics has generally been unimpressive when compared to the representation of men, the representation of women of color has been worse. Many female characters adopt stereotypical roles like that of the romantic interest, or the damsel in distress, however women of color are rarely seen, even in this narrow, stereotypical space. With just a handful of non-white female superheroes in the biggest publishing houses, Shuri's representation becomes even more important. For better or worse, gender and culture are at the fore of her story arc simply because of the lack of representation in previous decades. Shuri is part of a larger trend of improvement in this area. As Neal Curtis and Valentino Cardo note "There has been a noticeable change in superhero comics over the last five to ten years that has done a great deal to address their notoriously poor record on representation" (Curtis & Cardo 381).

This rise in the number of heroes represented from cultural minorities, including more of those characters who are female, breaks the boundaries that had been set by previous creators. "The increase in female characters, a rise in the number of female-led titles..., the gender-swapping of traditionally male characters to female, and a significant increase in the number of women writing and drawing comics have all been recent developments in this area" (Curtis & Cardo 381). Without more development of intersectional characters, comic books have the potential to reinforce racism by debasing minority characters (Curtis & Cardo 382). There have been positive steps taken, nevertheless, it is important not just to have inclusivity with the characters created, but with the creators themselves. Shuri is a black hero who has her introduction told by a black creator, giving her a sense of depth and realism that many characters lack.

Deadliest of the Species introduces Shuri as the new Black Panther, but the transition is far from easy. The legacy of Black Panther comics is complicated, fraught with racial tension. The character of CIA Agent Everett Ross was introduced as a way to placate "company fears that a primarily white readership would not relate to the African king" (Howard 126). While there was undoubtedly a readership there for the Black Panther stories, it was overshadowed by market fears. Yet, working within these constraints, Hudlin is largely credited as the man who reframed the character of the Black Panther. Sheena C. Howard explains, "Hudlin's Black Panther ... embraces an identity that refuses to accommodate these types of racialized market fears" (Howard 126). Hudlin showcases a version of Africa untouched by colonialism, where the people can thrive based on their own volition and use their country's resources without the need for outside influence. Hudlin's Black Panther is one that sits firmly in the modern world, while still paying homage to African tradition. When Hudlin introduced Shuri as Black Panther, he once again refused to accommodate market fears, creating a female hero who embraces intersectionality, while telling her story in a way that acknowledges the complexity of this new hero's journey.

Shuri's Growth as the Black Panther

In mainstream superhero comic books, there was an increase in the representation of women in the 1960s and 1970s, yet this representation lacked intersectionality. "Historically under- and misrepresented, women superheroes became more prevalent in the 1960s and 1970s, when more and more female-led titles … and powerful female characters appeared in a male-dominated world" (Curtis & Cardo 382). This increase in female characters still "failed to challenge the long-standing prejudice that the feminine ideal was white" (Curtis & Cardo 382). Shuri, on the other hand, breaks away from the status quo, rejecting Western ideals in favor of a more diverse African hero. "However, feminist concerns remain around what Michelle R. Finn calls 'a vision of female empowerment' which, she argues, has been missing since the Golden Age" (Curtis & Cardo 382). Shuri is a powerful black woman, yet her portrayal still raises concerns. With intersectionality as such an important aspect of modern feminism Shuri's role and portrayal becomes even more significant.

The mantle of the Black Panther becomes available when T'Challa is injured. "Tradition and the safety of our nation demand a new Black Panther. The only question is who" (Hudlin "Ch. 1"). Shuri is next in line for the throne, yet she is not the first person put forward for the role. Even Shuri's own mother looks towards others, viewing Shuri as unworthy of the title, despite the rigorous training that was an integral part of her youth. Training that was on par with her brother's.

A preferred option is Storm, a hero in her own right, and a strong woman of color. She is established from the onset as an outsider in the country, newly minted as a Wakandan Royal through marriage. In the opening pages, before a new Black Panther is needed, her trust, loyalty, and authority are questioned. Yet she is called upon by the Queen Mother to take on the role of the Panther despite this. Storm herself points out that a Wakandan woman is more suited to the role.

> T'Challa's condition makes me Queen of Wakanda, not the next Black Panther candidate by default.… To find the new Black Panther we need not leave this room. It is up

to the Panther God to make the final choice, but it is my belief that she stands among us. Someone who's been training her whole life for this moment [Hudlin "Ch. 1"].

Storm recognizes the struggles Shuri faced. She also sees the resistance the people of Wakanda display when it comes to her potential as the new Black Panther. While the remainder of the council believed Storm was the next obvious choice, Storm herself is acutely aware of the tenuous position she holds in Wakandan society. Even so, the Queen Mother is still uncertain, once again reinforcing the notion that Shuri is an unworthy candidate. Yet it is not out of any form of charity that Storm nominates Shuri, rather it is an acknowledgment of the expectations of her upbringing. When Shuri shows Storm gratitude, Storm rebukes her, "Do not thank me, sister. And more important, do not fail" (Hudlin "Ch. 1"). The move was not placatory, it was tactical. Storm may have the powers to protect T'Challa, but she does not have the training or experience to protect Wakanda. Wakanda needed a Wakandan protector.

Being nominated as the next Black Panther is only the first in a succession of obstacles Shuri must face. She must convince the people of Wakanda that she is capable of leading them in a time of upheaval and prove to the Panther God that she is worthy. Unlike T'Challa, Shuri is not expected to succeed as the Black Panther. She faces physical and mental trials on her way to face the Panther God, and displays a certain cockiness in her attitude, yet even she does not truly believe she is worthy. She disguises this with negatively stereotyped traits that can hark back to racial tension seen in early popular culture. From the 1800s there has been a stereotype of Black women being portrayed as "sassy, emasculating, and domineering. [...] This trope depicted African American women as aggressive, loud and angry" (NMAAHC).

This stereotype is still somewhat pervasive in popular culture today, including comic books. "Comic books, and particularly the dominant genre of superhero comic books, have proven fertile ground for stereotyped depictions of race" (Singer 107). Shuri often displays these traits, particularly early in her development, but unlike the majority of stereotyped characters she is not defined by these tropes. Instead they are used to show her development as a hero. Rather than remaining the boastful, brash Princess, she grows, learning to become a more balanced leader. Shuri's journey is not about her inherent traits or even her instincts, it is about learning and developing into the Black Panther Wakanda needs. While she never truly loses these traits, she learns to channel them into her heroics. Her anger fuels her, her arrogance is a mask to hide her vulnerability, and her so-called sassiness develops into a sharp sense of humor, all of which aid her as a leader. While many characters and creators fall into the trap of stereotyping, here Hudlin has turned the tables, using the negatively perpetuated stereotypes as positive attributes throughout Shuri's tenure. Instead of tokenizing Shuri through these characteristics he turned her into a capable leader, unencumbered by Western perceptions of what black or African culture is.

One of the more creative ways these stereotypes are called into question is through the Shuri's interaction with the Panther God. While the aforementioned stereotypes develop and change over Shuri's time as the Black Panther, the Panther God openly calls them into question, deeming Shuri as unworthy while she still perpetuates the negative idea. Although Shuri herself is certainly not the most stereotyped black character, the negative traits are present enough to give the Panther God pause. There is a certain amount of humbleness to Shuri in the presence of the Panther God, yet it is hindered by her desire to prove herself. "I've prepared my whole life for this moment ... to be ready to face you ... to request your blessing" (Hudlin "Ch. 2"), yet this humble nature is quickly lost.

> I am ready. Ready to step out from my brother's shadow. Ready to walk my path. Ready to embrace my destiny. To be what I was born to be! I'm ready. Give me what I need to save my people [Hudlin "Ch. 2"].

It is this moment that cements Hudlin's Wakanda as one that breaks from Western stereotypes of what black or African identity is. "The stereotypes through which American popular culture often interprets and represents racial identity operate not only as tools of defamation but also as vehicles for far more subtle manipulations of race" (Singer 107). Hudlin breaks away from this Westernized portrayal of a homogenized African culture, creating a new version of Wakanda that is free from the manipulation and context placed by white writers. While Shuri had shown a humble attitude, she quickly fell back into familiar patterns. Her demands of the Panther God are in stark contrast with everything else the reader has been shown about Wakanda. The Panther God rejects her brashness, questioning this sense of entitlement that is prevalent within Shuri's arc, dismissing the arrogance that is intertwined with her character in the earliest part of the story.

The first hints of heroism also bring to the fore a hyper-sexualized image that is an all too familiar sight within the world of comic books. From the moment the role of Black Panther becomes available to Shuri, she contorts herself into unnatural poses. She is clad in form fitting clothing that leaves her seeming exposed and vulnerable, unlike T'Challa, whose armor left him appearing strong and protected. The sexualization of women within the comic book genre is certainly not new, with controversy surrounding the depiction of women being a common cause of debate. A common trope within comic books is presenting women with "breasts the size of heads or larger," while "a lack of obvious muscles as representative of femininity has remained constant across the seven decades of superhero comics" (Gavaler 188). It is true that while there are a minority who do not fit this gendered stereotype, the majority do. While the visual narrative does rely on some instantly identifiable features to make characters particularly recognizable, the manipulation of the female anatomy is pervasive and damaging. "Comics rely upon visually codified representations in which characters are continually reduced to their appearances, and this reductionism is especially prevalent in superhero comics, whose characters are wholly externalized into their heroic costumes and aliases" (Singer 107). In the case of Shuri, that means that her race and sexuality are linked with her role as a superhero. From the moment she dons the costume her sexuality becomes a defining characteristic of her role as the Black Panther. Her visual portrayal is created distinctly through the male gaze, contorting her into unnatural poses, showing every identifiably feminine part of her body at once, lest the reader forget their hero was a woman.

While the trials she faces are on par, if not greater than those her brother faced, they are somewhat devalued by this constant reminder to the reader that Shuri is female. It suggests, in some ways, that her achievements are only great because she is a woman facing these foes, rather than just being a hero. This visual representation is directly at odds with what is written, which tells the reader that Shuri, in spite of the very stereotypical traits she initially displays, is a worthy hero, as capable as her brother. She is capable of making the most difficult decisions, yet this is detracted from based on the way her body is portrayed, and the discourse that surrounds it. The notion of the superhero has itself become a gendered concept. "The word 'superhero' pretty much assumes that the hero in question is male, and white, and heterosexual, and able-bodied" (Cocca 6). When discussing superheroes, many people "don't generally feel the need to say 'male superheroes' but tend to clarify when they are talking about 'female superheroes' or 'black superheroes' or 'queer superheroes' or 'disabled superheroes'" (Cocca 6).

As a superhero who is both black and female, Shuri must prove herself more than most. As Hudlin departs the franchise, Shuri's tenure continues. Yet the growth of the character does not remain on the same trajectory. Where the discourse had not actively discussed her abilities as a hero based on her gender in *Deadliest of the Species*, now this is to the fore. She is no longer the Black Panther who defended her country against a supernatural foe in spite of her lack of superpowers, though this is one of the more positive stereotypes relating to black women in popular culture. "Perceived as strong without super powers, Africana (African diaspora) women are also viewed, and often view themselves, as queens without crowns" (Harris 1). Nevertheless, Shuri is looked at as simply being a spoiled, immature princess, incapable of being the leader of Wakandan defense, and unworthy in the eyes of the public to don the mantle. While public unrest and lack of faith is not unusual within comic books, it is seldom a gendered complaint. Shuri, however, faces unrest simply based on her femaleness.

The Dora Milaje

Shuri is not the only female warrior prominently featured in Black Panther. While the Dora Milaje are depicted as fierce warriors, there is still a problem in their representation. Introduced by Christopher Priest in 1998 as warriors and wives in training, their early representation was somewhat dismissive, as was their later representation. The Dora Milaje are at least partially based on the real life Dahomey Amazons, a group of female warriors in West Africa, so named by the French after the female warriors of Greek mythology (Coleman). In the 19th century "'an estimated 4,000 women ... were among the Dahomey military ranks." In times of war Dahomey female warriors "were the last line of defense between the enemy and the King ... and were prepared to sacrifice their lives to protect him" (Coleman).

Part of the legacy of the Black Panther franchise is its ability to combine historical and cultural significance with the most popular and fantastical elements of the genre, and the Dora Milaje are no exception. The Dora Milaje, and the entirety of Wakanda offers a perspective on a society unaffected by stereotypical patriarchy and colonialism. Yet in spite of this distinct shirking of the patriarchy the Dora Milaje are still portrayed through the male gaze, hypersexualized in much the same way as Shuri. While Shuri is portrayed in a skintight suit or armor, the Dora Milaje are scantily clad, and therefore unprotected. While the Dahomey Amazons were not clad in armor, Wakanda's technological advancements should theoretically allow more protection for the nation's warriors. The over-exaggerated hyper-sexualization presented in the comic books is at odds with the historical significance of the Dahomey Amazons, as well as with the male warriors presented within the series. It suggests that while they are a distinctly African part of comic books, the overreaching narrative still leans heavily towards the predominantly white male fanbase.

Many male warriors are depicted in *Deadliest of the Species*, battling beside Shuri and the Dora Milaje. Unlike the Dora Milaje, however, the male warriors are given distinct features and identities, and clad in an advanced armor likely to protect them from the majority of attacks, even when they are unnamed and never seen again. The Dora Milaje, on the other hand, are presented as almost faceless, a generic mass of female warriors without any distinct personalities or characteristics. While most individual Dora Milaje do not play a significant role within this particular story arc, the collective is vital to the survival of Wakanda. As a result, it is not essential to have distinct or developed personalities, yet it does somewhat take away from the impact of a group of female warriors. This dehumanizing of the Dora Milaje, combined with the unimpressive uniform, leads the reader to question the role of these women in Wakandan society. While the Dora Milaje are clearly feared and revered, they are also faceless, nameless in the greater scheme of things. "Ayisi and Brylla (2013, p. 125) asserted that the media output of Western societies 'consistently constructed cinematic images of African life and society that are reductive and even offensive.' They added that as a result of Africans being perceived and portrayed as inferior to Whites, there tended to be an absence of culturally affirming representations" (Harris 2). This notion is certainly true in the case of the Dora Milaje. While their representation has drastically improved in recent years, most notably in the Marvel Cinematic Universe, here they are reduced to side characters without any real development. The intersectional representation is diminished due to the underdevelopment of the individual as well as the collective. They may be intended to be the greatest warriors in the nation, yet their representation fails to follow through, instead stereotyping them, hindering the ability they possessed to be a culturally significant and affirming representation for years to come.

While the Dora Milaje are protecting their King, and later Wakanda as a whole, they are presented in increasingly unnatural poses, with their uniforms becoming increasingly revealing. Like Shuri, it is as though the artist is concerned that the reader will forget these warriors are women if they are not showing every aspect of their feminine bodies, even if these poses put them in more danger. A fierce collection of warriors such as the Dora Milaje are far more likely to be concerned with the effectiveness of their skills in battle and the ability of their armor to protect them, rather than showing their curves to their best advantage. Shuri's run as the Black Panther shows only a handful of individual Dora Milaje identified as more than just a silhouette in the background. Many of those select warriors are seen as tertiary characters, there to validate Shuri and her team. While they may have been inspired by the Dahomey Amazons, the Dora Milaje certainly do not meet the same potential as their real-life counterparts while Shuri is in power. Having a powerful female character in the title role is an impressive step, but it comes at the expense of the other women in the story. By creating characters with a real life historical significance and reducing them to blank faces on a page it takes away from the cultural significance of such a series.

Intersectional Necessity in the World of Comic Books

"Intersectionality ... was my attempt to make feminism, anti-racist activism, and anti-discrimination law do what I thought they should—highlight the multiple avenues through which racial and gender oppression were experienced" (Crenshaw 2014). Although the representation of the female hero is changing, both on and off screen, more needs to be done to make it an inclusive and intersectional change. It is not enough to tell the story of one race or gender, as was prevalent prior to the 1960s and 1970s. Throughout popular culture race and gender are used to stereotype a character instead of considering the need for individual identities. "Race, gender, and other identity categories are most often treated in mainstream liberal discourse as vestiges of bias or domination ... intrinsically negative frameworks in which social power works to exclude or marginalize those who are different" (Crenshaw 1242). While representation matters, it is also important to represent minorities in a way that is not insulting, demeaning, nor in a way that makes them seem like they are a token character in order to have real intersectionality within the genre. "This system of visual typology combines with the superhero genre's long history of excluding, trivializing, or 'tokenizing' minorities to create numerous minority superheroes who are marked purely for their race: 'Black Lightning,' 'Black Panther,' and so forth" (Singer 107).

Much of the research into the role of race in comic books focuses on characters in the decades before Shuri donned the Black Panther armor, a time in which female characters were few and far between. Yet much of what was explored is still relevant. While there are now an increasing number of female characters, as well as an increasing number of women of color within comic books, very few of those women are black. There is an awareness of the importance of intersectionality within popular culture, and steps are being taken. However, there is also a complicated relationship regarding the creators and the characters. As Blair Davis puts it; "Given that white writers and artists created the majority of black superheroes these characters ... can therefore be seen as touchstones for how white American society regards black identity... in any given period" (Gavaler 184). While Shuri manages, for the most part, to break away from the stereotype portrayed within Western comics, she is not immune, nor are the Dora Milaje. If the stereotype of aggressive black women is within the pages of the Black Panther comic books, the Dora Milaje embody it as a collective. As warriors they are depicted as relishing the aggressive nature of battle, showing a bloodthirsty nature that Shuri herself develops throughout her time as the Black Panther, after Hudlin's departure. Yet even here there is a certain embracing of this stereotype, and turning it into something advantageous for the characters. This aggressive, domineering nature shown by the Dora Milaje undoubtedly aids in protecting them, keeping them alive in battle, and allowing them to protect Wakanda.

When exploring Shuri's tenure as the Black Panther, historical context of race and comic books is vital. While there has always been a certain amount of the genre that has been radical, the representation of minorities has not been.

> Black superheroes, a nonexistent category for the first thirty years of the superhero comics genre, emerged in the late 1960s, suffered reductive racial conceptions and poor sales in the 1970s, and, as more black creators gained influence, grew in prominence and complexity during the 1980s, 1990s, and early twenty-first century [Gavaler 156].

When T'Challa's Black Panther was introduced to the world there is no doubt that he fit with these generic ideals of what both a hero and a person of color are, by Western standards, yet the character grew over his publication history. The legacy of the Black Panther does not rest solely with T'Challa, but rather with the notion that any Wakandan can become a hero. Black Panther offers representation for men and women alike who had previously been denied that experience. "Rebecca Wanzo writes 'for many people of color in the United States, the experience of consuming comic book heroism ... has involved reconciling themselves to representing the antithesis of heroic ideals'" (Galaver 155). Black Panther, either male or female, provided an alternative to this. While the inescapable ideal is still that of the able bodied white male, characters do exist who challenge the status quo and bring intersectionality to the fore of the genre.

Within the Dora Milaje and Shuri's complex representations there are many positive aspects. They collectively represent a strong, uncolonized African nation, unaffected by Western patriarchy. Although Shuri struggles to find her place as a Black Panther, and struggles with her value as Wakanda's protector, she also represents some of the most positive aspects of the Black Panther legacy. As a hero she breaks away from the preconceived notions of what she should be. She faces adversity not just from enemies, but from her own people who do not believe in her. Yet she overcomes this and succeeds where none believed she would. While many heroes, even female heroes, focus on the primarily white ideals of Western ideology, Shuri embraces her African identity. Shuri is not a great hero in spite of her race or her gender. They are not weaknesses, not flaws in her armor. She is a great hero because of them. They are as much a part of her heroism as they were for T'Challa. Her desire to prove herself as a strong leader largely comes from her need to prove herself as a woman of her people. The questions of her authority are focused on her gender, and as a result so is her determination. Her devotion to the mantle of the Panther comes from the cultural legacy that she has been provided with. She, along with the Dora Milaje cement continental African cultures as part of the Marvel Universe and encourage greater development of characters that break away from the norm of comic book culture. Not every hero has to be a white American. Not every hero has to be a man. With a more consistent representation the Dora Milaje and Shuri could form the foundation of a strong legacy of intersectional characters throughout the world of comics.

Works Cited

Cocca, Carolyn. *Superwomen: Gender, Power, and Representation*, Bloomsbury 2016.
Coleman, Arica L.. *There's a True Story Behind Black Panther's Strong Women. Here's Why That Matters*. Time.com, http://time.com/5171219/black-panther-women-true-history/
Crenshaw, Kimberlé. *Mapping the Margins: Intersectionality, Identity Politics, and Violence against Women of Color*. Stanford Law Review, Vol. 43, 1991, pp. 1241–1299.
_____. *Why Intersectionality Can't Wait*. Washington Post, 24/9/2015 https://www.washingtonpost.com/news/in-theory/wp/2015/09/24/why-intersectionality-cantwait/?noredirect=on&utm_term=.6d15a9176a9e.
Curtis, Neal, and Valentino Cardo. *Superheroes and Third Wave Feminism*, Feminist Media Studies, 24/7/2018, pp. 381–396.
Gavaler, Chris. *Superhero Comics*, Bloomsbury 2018.
Harris, Heather E. *Queen Phiona and Princess Shuri—Alternative Africana "Royalty" in Disney's Royal Realm: An Intersectional Analysis*. MPDI Social Sciences 20/10/2018.
Howard, Sheena C. *Encyclopedia of Black Comics*. Fulcrum Publishing 2017.
Hudlin, Reginald (w), and Ken Lashley (a). *Deadliest of the Species*. Marvel, 2016.
NMAAHC. *Popular and Pervasive Stereotypes of African Americans*. National Museum of African American History & Culture, 2018, https://nmaahc.si.edu/blog-post/popular-and-pervasive-stereotypes-african-americans.
Singer, Marc. *Black Skins and White Masks: Comic Books and the Secret of Race*, African American Review, Spring 2002, pp. 107–119.

Black Panther, Namor and Mimetic Violence in Jonathan Hickman's *New Avengers*

MATTHEW BRAKE

Jonathan Hickman's run on *New Avengers* (2012–2015) chronicles the tales of the Illuminati, a group of leaders within the Marvel Universe—Iron Man, Mr. Fantastic, Namor, Beast, Dr. Strange, Black Bolt, and Black Panther—as they work to prevent the destruction of their world, and ultimately, the multiverse itself. Hickman's run, culminating in the event comic *Secret Wars*, begins and ends with a focus on T'Challa, the Black Panther. While the tale of the multiverse's destruction is the primary plot point, there is a running subplot involving a conflict between himself and fellow Illuminati member Namor.

In a previous event comic, *Avengers vs. X-Men*, a cosmically powered Namor flooded Wakanda and killed many of its people in a bid to cow them into cooperating with his world-domineering intentions. Hickman picks up on the lingering effects of that event in his run with Black Panther biding his time to take revenge. Throughout Hickman's run, there is a back and forth between T'Challa and Namor as each seeks to strike the final blow against the other and the kingdom that each represents—Wakanda decimates Atlantis, Namor misleads a group of supervillains into invading Wakanda, Black Panther attempts to kill Namor, and so on. Namor's original offense against Wakanda sets off a cycle of violence and revenge. Even though readers may sympathize with Wakanda's right to retaliate, one also sees how the greater good of the world (and the multiverse) is sacrificed by the refusal to make peace.

This cycle is akin to the philosophical anthropology of René Girard and his theory of mimetic violence. For Girard, without a mechanism to curb and channel the desire for revenge elsewhere, violence spreads like a contagion in a never-ending cycle. Unfortunately, however justified, the actions of Black Panther and Wakanda provide an example of how this cycle works in the superhero genre. Girard himself warns that oppressed peoples, by engaging in the cycle of violence, only serve to bolster the mimetic cycle, and while the oppressed can overcome their oppressors, they may simply switch places with them and perpetuate the cycle. How does one overcome oppression while also avoiding the cycle of mimetic violence? The oppressed must most certainly be liberated, but how can this happen without perpetuating a cycle of violence?

In this essay, I will evaluate the problem of retaliation by oppressed peoples through the lens of Girard's mimetic theory. In lieu of violent revolution and retaliation, which for Girard would only perpetuate mimetic violence, I will look at the writings and teachings of nonviolence advocated by Mahatma Gandhi and Martin Luther King, Jr.

Setting the Stage

Avengers v. X-Men was a 2012 event comic pitting the Avengers against the X-Men. It centers around the return of the Phoenix force to Earth. The Phoenix, who had previously possessed the X-Man Jean Grey and had corrupted her into the Dark Phoenix, now sought to possess the new mutant Messiah—a girl named Hope. At this point in X-Men history, the mutant population had been decimated, reduced to a mere 198 people. With the return of the Phoenix, the X-Men leader Cyclops believed that if it possessed Hope, it would lead to the reemergence of a vibrant mutant population. The Avengers (joined by T'Challa), by contrast, are concerned about the Phoenix's history of corrupting its hosts and destroying entire planets. They go on a twofold mission to both destroy the Phoenix and place Hope within protective custody, ultimately leading to conflict between the two teams.

While the Avengers are ultimately successful in apprehending Hope, their efforts to destroy the Phoenix split it into five pieces, each possessing a different member of the X-Men: Cyclops, Emma Frost, Colossus, Magik, and Namor. The "Phoenix Five" begin to remake the world, creating a utopia on Earth, even as they succumb to the Phoenix's corrupting power while fighting a shadow war with the Avengers in order to search for Hope. Finding out that Hope is hidden in Wakanda and believing that extreme measures are needed against the Avengers, Namor does the unthinkable—he floods Wakanda to force the Avengers out of hiding, killing thousands of innocent

Wakandans in the process. This event establishes the enmity between T'Challa and Namor throughout Hickman's *New Avengers* run and provides us with an opportunity to consider the destructive nature of violence and revenge, however justified that violence or revenge might be.

Violence, Revenge and Contagion

For René Girard, violence plays a key role in the establishment of all human culture (*Battling to the End* 105). One of the reasons for this is that humans are "mimetic" or imitative by nature. This rule applies not only to actions, but to desire itself. Human desires do not arise spontaneously, but "our desire comes from others" in a process Girard calls "mimetic rivalry" (*Scandal* 5). He explains:

> The rival desires the same object as the subject.... Rivalry does not arise because of the fortuitous convergence of two desires on a single object; rather, *the subject desires the object because the rival desires it*. In desiring an object the rival alerts the subject to the desirability of the object [*Violence and the Sacred* 145].

As Girard points out, "Two desires converging on the same object are bound to clash. Thus, mimesis coupled with desire leads automatically to conflict" (146).

It isn't difficult to see the conflict in *Avengers v. X-Men* in this light. While the two sides may not have understood their conflict in this light, part of Girard's theory is that the human actors involved are unaware of the actual nature of their conflict (146). For Girard, it is a form of mythological thinking to believe that one can settle the question about the origin of a conflict by pinning it on one party. To think that the responsibility for violence falls on one side is a mistake that keeps the true cause of conflict, i.e., mimetic desire, hidden. By contrast, tragedy is much more revealing of the true nature of human violence. In tragedy, "[n]obody ... incarnates the true oppressor or the true oppressed." There are no settled "good guys" and "bad guys." Instead, there are merely "revolving oppositions ... reversal as such" (150). No matter who may strike the first blow, Girard states, "One cannot exert violence without submitting to it: that is the law of reciprocity" (245), for "whoever uses violence will in turn be used by it" (261). The history of mutants in the Marvel Universe is one of oppression, and Namor's actions to retrieve Hope ultimately serves the purpose of preventing mutant oppression from ever returning. However, Girard's analysis puts aside the question of right and wrong and asks us instead to see violence as a form of contamination that must be contained (28).

Violence unleashes a cycle of revenge. The violence unleashed is about "the balancing of the scale, not of justice but of violence" (45). But with vengeance, "every reprisal calls for another reprisal" (14). Girard writes, "Only violence can put an end to violence, and that is why violence is self-propagating. Everyone wants to strike the last blow, and reprisal can thus follow reprisal without any true conclusion ever being reached." (26). This ongoing self-propagation and its escalation is the danger of violence, leading Girard to say that "evil and the violent measures taken to combat evil are essentially the same" (37). However much we may sympathize with the Wakandans and their suffering at Namor's hands, we can certainly see Girard's warnings about violence and revenge play out in the Wakandan response.

New Avengers #1 begins with the focus on T'Challa in Wakanda. When Black Panther discovers that the multiverse is dying as Earths from across the multiverse are colliding and taking their respective universes out with them, T'Challa assembles the Illuminati, a secret group of leaders from all the super-team corners of the Marvel Universe. Included in this group are Mr. Fantastic of the Fantastic Four, Captain America and Tony Stark of the Avengers, the mystical hero Dr. Strange, Beast from the X-Men, Black Bolt of the Inhumans, and Namor, King of Atlantis.

The group meets in Wakanda at the Necropolis, the City of the Dead over which T'Challa rules while his sister Shuri reigns as queen of Wakanda (this involves a lot of complex comic book backstory we won't go into). The guards of the city, the Dora Milaje, are perplexed by T'Challa's decision to allow Namor into Wakanda. Despite the greater threat, their focus is on revenge. As one of them tells T'Challa, "The walls were broken. Blood was spilled. Thousands of Wakandans died" (*New Avengers* #1). This fact is not lost on T'Challa, who tells Namor himself, "But one last thing. You have the blood of my people on your hands. So when this is done—when my wants have replaced my needs, I'm going to kill you" (*New Avengers* #1).

One can see Girard's thought about violence and contagion come to life in these exchanges. Girard writes:

> Two men come to blows; blood is spilt; both men are thus rendered impure. Their impurity is contagious, and anyone who remains in their presence risks becoming a party to their quarrel. The only sure way to avoid contagion is to flee the scene of violence. There is no question here of duty or morality. Contamination is a terrible thing, and only those who are already contaminated would willfully expose themselves to it [*Violence and the Sacred* 28].

As Girard makes plain, morality and justice are not at stake in conflicts like those between Wakanda and Namor. Rather, the language of "infection" is more apt (28). He says, "Violence has been transformed into a sort of seminal fluid that impregnates objects on contact and who diffusion, like electricity … is determined by physical laws" (28). Girard indicates that archaic religious notions of ritual impurity reflect this recognition of the infectious nature of violence and such religious rules about impurity serve a concrete social function to keep the contagion of violence in check (28).

Doubling and Escalation

The story in *New Avengers* #7 opens one month after the first arc in the series. Tony Stark and Reed Richards speak to each other about the looming multiversal crisis as well as a number of other significant trouble spots in the Marvel Universe. However, one trouble spot stands out among the rest—the escalating conflict between Wakanda and Atlantis. Richards recounts to Stark:

> A Wakandan strike team captured several Atlantean generals and plans to try them for war crimes against their capital city. In retaliation, the Atlanteans tried to arrest the Wakandan ambassador to the U.N. Something went wrong and the ambassador and his entire entourage were killed. Things escalated further. Wakanda responded, but the intelligence they were acting on was bad. It was a ruse, and sixty elite Wakandans were killed [*New Avengers* #7].

The fight between the two fictional powers engulfs entire nations. No longer are the threats shared simply between T'Challa and Namor, but between Wakanda and Atlantis as a whole. This fits Roberto Farneti's contention that Girard's mimetic scheme applies not just to individuals, but to political entities and the dynamics of politics as well (Farneti 28). Girard himself would say "that violence is what structures our collective sense of belonging and our personal identities" (*Scandal* 31).

The conflict extends beyond Namor and two communities are falling into a cycle of revenge and reciprocal action that Girard says ultimately escalates towards extremes (*Battling to the End* 104). In fact, the more conflict intensifies, the more the opponents become "doubles" of one another in a process that Girard calls "undifferentiation." In other words, the more they fight and trade blows in the process of reciprocity, the more the two sides come to resemble each other in their violence (Farneti, 11). As Girard writes:

> Doubling occurs as soon as the object has disappeared in the heat of the rivalry: the two rivals become more and more concerned with defeating the opponent for the sake of it, rather than obtaining the object, which eventually becomes irrelevant, as it only exists as an excuse for the escalation of the dispute. Thus, the rivals become more and more undifferentiated, identical: doubles [*Evolution and Conversion* 57].

The original object of the conflict between Atlantis and Wakanda, Hope Summers, has disappeared from view and is never once mentioned in Hickman's entire Avengers run. All that remains is the conflict itself as it grows and contaminates all bystanders (57). Whereas modern political science focuses on "the object" in issues involving international dispute, the fight between

Wakanda and Atlantis illustrates what mimetic theory knows—the object does not matter as much as the conflict itself and the reciprocal imitation that is its cause (Farneti, 35–36). Everyone loses sight of the original reason for the conflict (87).

Wakanda Strikes Back

As Farneti claims, "conflicts arising over an original act of injustice ... develop a mimetic momentum after the original deed and resist a settlement arranged by a third party" (85). One can certainly sympathize with Wakanda in this conflict. Namor ruthlessly drowned thousands of their citizens in his attempt to reclaim Hope Summers. However, as the cycle of reciprocal violence escalates, "mimesis dissolves the discourse of victimhood," and both parties "can be seen as both good and evil, both perpetrator and victim, depending on perspective" (46).

Namor saw himself as having a good reason for the initial blow. Girard writes "no one ever sees himself as casting the first stone. Even the most violent persons believe that they are always reacting to a violence committed in the first instance by someone else" (*Scandal* 18). Namor certainly saw the Avengers' resistance and taking of Hope as an action worthy of reprisal, and he believed that in war, one ought not to hold back. Girard himself points out, "Faced with ... realism about violence, we have to admit that honorable combat is only an intellectual point of view" (*Battling to the End* 93). One could even talk about how the actions of the Phoenix Five were predicated on the past actions of humans against mutantkind. Getting to the bottom of the chain of reprisals is difficult. When analyzing a cycle of reprisals, violence makes the two parties resemble each other so much that the idea of justice is lost as one can see that vengeance operates by its own logic (*Violence and the Sacred* 46–47, 51).

In *New Avengers* #7, Namor comes to T'Challa offering a ceasefire, and encourages T'Challa to urge his sister, Queen Shuri, to accept Namor's terms. Given the larger crises on the horizon, Namor tells T'Challa, "Regardless of how you feel about me, you know we have better things to be doing than spilling blood." And yet according to Girard's logic, once parties have been contaminated by the spilling of blood, it is very difficult to stop the spread of the infection. This concept is literally expressed when T'Challa advocates for Namor's peace proposal to Shuri and her council, and he is told by one of the council members, "Blood demands blood." While T'Challa makes clear that the man responsible for the crime against Wakanda, Namor, will be dealt with, he is told in response, "This is not about retribution. Or a man paying the blood price. We must send a message."

Here, we see the mimetic cycle at work, gaining its own momentum and engulfing Wakanda and Atlantis as a whole. T'Challa seems to recognize this and says, "If we start a war, it will not end until one of our nations has fallen." Regretfully, Shuri takes the advice of her council over T'Challa and goes to war with Atlantis, and in the process, sows the seeds of Wakanda's own destruction. As Girard writes, "If men wish to prevent an interminable outbreak of vengeance (just as today we wish to prevent nuclear war), it is not enough to convince their fellows that violence is detestable," for "every reprisal calls for another reprisal" (14–15). It is this "multiplication of reprisals" that "instantaneously puts the very existence of a society in jeopardy" (15). Still, T'Challa recognizes the value of sending a strong message, stating, "I understand avoiding violence by appearing violent." Indeed, Girard notes, "it is precisely because they detest violence that men make a duty of vengeance" (15). This is how mimetic conflict works—there is the hope that *this* blow will be the final blow that puts an end to violence and brings peace, but "reprisal can thus follow reprisal without any true conclusion," thus making violence self-propagating (26).

Later at the Necropolis, T'Challa speaks with Namor, who has been told that Shuri is seriously considering his ceasefire. T'Challa bemoans, "This thing you started ... this thing between you and I—it's poison for our nations. Two giants battling each other completely unaware of the world—the lives—they are destroying around them. You were right, our people should be spared ... but that is not the world." T'Challa then reveals that Namor has been lied to, and Wakanda unleashes a surprise attack on Atlantis, devastating the city, killing innocent lives the same way that Namor did in Wakanda. Girard is again helpful here, noting, "to back down refuses combat and admits weakness. That vulnerability in fact provokes the conflict that it was supposed to avoid, and the clash will be all the more fearsome because it had been suspended by backing down" (*Battling to the End* 55).

Namor finds his city in ruins, with a majority of the city's population slain. Making matters worse, it is at this moment that the galactic supervillain Thanos launches an attack of Earth as part of the *Infinity* event. One of Thanos's Black Order, Proxima Midnight, arrives at Atlantis, poised to attack but finding the city already in ruins. Namor yields, and Proxima Midnight asks where one of the infinity gems is. She intends to redirect the bulk of Thanos' forces in pursuit of the gem. Namor lies and tells her it is in Wakanda. And the mimetic revenge cycle carries on. Eventually, Thanos and a group of supervillains take over and devastate Wakanda, Black Panther finds out about Namor's treachery and, at this point unsurprisingly, vows revenge.

Violence and the Duel

In his book *Battling to the End*, Girard asserts, "The real principle that is latent behind the alternating victories and defeats … is … the duel … *a merciless battle between twins*" (41). As discussed earlier, as opponents engage in the cycle of revenge, they come to resemble each other in their violence. The ultimate form, or structure of this conflict, is the duel (57). In the hand-to-hand combat of the duel, one nears "the heart of violence, which is murder" (93). Violence and revenge are seen for the bloodthirsty thing that they truly are.

When Namor tells T'Challa in *New Avengers* #23 that he is the one who sent Thanos's forces to Wakanda, the page is painted red to reflect T'Challa's blood rage. Even though the other members of the Illuminati break them up, the two have a final confrontation in *Avengers* #40. T'Challa stabs Namor and leaves him on a doomed planet that is about to be destroyed, and he says, "I want him to know … it's over. To fully realize there's no forgiveness for what he's done. That there is a price and he's finally going to pay it—that there's no mercy for men like him, and even if there was, he doesn't get any."

At this point in the story, both men's kingdoms have been destroyed and turned to ash. What started as an original act of atrocity by Namor, itself predicated on past injustices to mutants and attempts to prevent more such injustices, has ended with an attempted murder. Whatever T'Challa's original intentions and whatever genuine desire for justice may have existed, violence overmasters those who use it. Justice is thrown to the wayside and all that is left, even in the face of the apocalypse, is a desire for blood, to strike the final blow.

Injustice and Non-Violence

One can certainly understand T'Challa's desire for revenge against Namor. An injustice was committed against the people of Wakanda. Our own world is a world full of similar injustices: racism, genocide, and oppression of many kinds. One cannot necessarily say that the outrage of victims is undeserved. Many acts of modern international terrorism can be seen as a form of revenge against the West and "a response to the oppression of the Third World as a whole" (*Battling to the End* 211). This is not to justify terrorism but simply to recognize that "mimesis is the true primary engine" that drives history (213). But portrayed in the story of Namor and T'Challa, the back and forth of mimetic conflict can reap devastating results.

Do acts of injustice not call for some kind of vindication or comeuppance? Girard's own answer is clear:

> We are dealing with people who wish to infuriate us, to draw us into a cycle of escalating conflict. They do everything they can, in order words, to provoke a response that will justify them in retaliating in turn; to manufacture an excuse for legitimate self-defense. For if we treat them as they treat us, they will be able to disguise their own injustice by means of reprisals that are fully warranted by the violence we have committed. It is therefore necessary to deprive them of the negative collaboration that they demand of us [*Scandal* 19–20].

Girard's advice is to avoid allowing oneself (or perhaps even one's country) to be drawn into the mimetic cycle of violence and revenge by one's persecutors or oppressors. To engage in that cycle allows one's antagonist to excuse further aggression and escalate the cycle of violence. That's well and good for Girard to say, but when one considers the plight of people of color and formerly colonized peoples in our own world, does the voice of a Western white European provide much comfort or solace?

Thankfully, there are other voices from among historically marginalized and oppressed people who affirm Girard's own critiques of violence. Both Mahatma Gandhi and Martin Luther King, Jr., condemn the destructive power of violence and advocate ways of addressing injustice that bypass the mimetic cycle by avoiding the negative collaboration that Girard speaks about. In 1922, Gandhi felt the need to temporarily suspend the activities of his movement in response to an outbreak of violence by those who claimed to be a part of it ("Chauri Chaura" 33). In this, he recognized the contagious nature of violence and sought to eliminate it before reengaging in further activity. Informed in part by his Hindu faith and the belief in a universal self that all are a part of ("Civility" 49), Gandhi believed that "to return injury for injury does harm both to ourselves and our enemy" and that by pursuing even peaceful ends by violent means opens us up to the possibility that we might "replace one evil by another and a worse" ("Preface to Tolstoy" 38–39).

Whatever gains made by violence would only be temporary ("On the Verge of It" 43). This same idea about violence's temporary effects was taken up by Gandhi's admirer Martin Luther King, Jr., who noted:

> A…way that oppressed people sometimes deal with oppression is to resort to physical violence and corroding hatred. Violence often brings about momentary results. Nations have frequently won their independence in battle. But in spite of temporary victories, violence never brings permanent peace. It solves no social problem; it merely creates new and more complicated ones ["Stride Toward Freedom" 482].

Like his hero, Dr. King went on to condemn violence even more unequivocally, and in his critique, one can hear the echoes of Girard's mimetic theory:

> Violence as a way of achieving racial justice is both impractical and immoral. It is impractical because it is a descending spiral ending in destruction for all. The old law

of an eye for an eye leaves everybody blind. It is immoral because it seeks to humiliate the opponent rather than win his understanding; it seeks to annihilate rather than to convert. Violence is immoral because it thrives on hatred rather than love. It destroys community and makes brotherhood impossible. It leaves society in monologue rather than dialogue. Violence ends by defeating itself. It creates bitterness in the survivors and brutality in the destroyers [482].

In Dr. King's words, one can see a social truth that was subsequently illustrated through Jonathan Hickman's story about Namor and T'Challa. It is true that Namor committed an act of injustice against T'Challa and his people. However justified a violent response was, it inevitably led to the destruction of both men's societies, leaving bitterness and brutality in its wake. Any apparent victories by either side were only temporary and gave way to greater violence at a later time.

Renouncing Revenge

The superhero genre is inextricably associated with violence. However, depending on how that violence is depicted, the tales can be a celebration or a condemnation of violence. Readers should be mindful of the destructive potential of all violence. The conflict between Namor and T'Challa demonstrates the potency of Girard's mimetic theory and views about the contagious nature of violence. Even when that violence seems justified in light of past injustices, violence can overflow its intentions and cause unforeseen destruction, and the cycle of revenge may never end until both parties are destroyed. As Girard says, "[O]ne can only say to the combatants: Make friends or pursue your own ruin" (*Violence and the Sacred* 51). For T'Challa and Namor, it is only after their kingdoms and the entire multiverse is destroyed that they are able to recognize the destructiveness of their conflict and work together. For all of his egotism, Namor eventually became repentant for his wrongs, his conscience having been pricked by the greatness of the evils he had perpetrated. For his part, T'Challa seems to have forgiven Namor, and the two of them were able to work together, but only after being overwhelmed by the enormity of universal violence and destruction. We ourselves may only overcome the violence in our own world by allowing our consciences to be pricked, and our hearts to forgive.

Works Cited

Dalton, Dennis (ed.). *Mahatma Gandhi: Selected Political Writings*. Indianapolis: Hackett Publishing Company, Inc. 1996.
Farneti, Roberto. *Mimetic Politics: Dyadic Patterns in Global Politics*. East Lansing: Michigan State University Press. 2015.
Girard, René. *Battling to the End: Conversations with Benoit Chantre*. Trans. Mary Baker. East Lansing: Michigan State University Press. 2010.

_____. *Evolution and Conversion: Dialogues on the Origins of Culture*. Ed. P. Antonello and J.C. de Castro Rocha. London: Continuum. 2008.
_____. *The One by Whom Scandal Comes*. Trans. M.B. DeBevoise. East Lansing: Michigan State University Press. 2014.
_____. *Violence and the Sacred*. Trans. Patrick Gregory. Baltimore: Johns Hopkins University Press. 1977.
Washington, James M. (ed.). *A Testament of Hope: The Essential Writings and Speeches of Martin Luther King, Jr.* New York: HarperOne. 1986.

A Different Nation

Continuing a Legacy of Decolonization in Black Panther

JULIAN C. CHAMBLISS

"The protagonist can't just exist outside of context, it needs to be a textured, built out world."

In the media campaign attached to the launch of the *Black Panther* series written by Ta-Nehisi Coates, he speaks these words to suggest how his take on the iconic character will be different. An evolutionary engagement with question of identity and power from proto–Afrofuturism in the 1960s to contemporary concerns about race and power define *Black Panther* (Lackaff). A driving force for this progress has been the emergence of black creative voices linked to the character. These black writers have envisioned *Black Panther* in a manner that affirms the Afrofuturism label applied to the character. Reynaldo Anderson describes Afrofuturism discourse as "…a counternarrative that intersects history, progress, tradition, innovation, memory, the authentic and the engineered and analogue and digital within spaces of African-diasporic culture" (Anderson). Thus an African American *Black Panther* would necessarily challenge assumptions of power, community, and identity posited by whiteness as the baseline of American culture. Rebecca Wanzo suggests that the decolonization of *Black Panther* has been a long process that decentered "the white perspective from the construction of the character." Thus, Coates—who gained fame as the national correspondent for *The Atlantic* writing about topics such as race, gentrification and reparations—was positioned to provide the latest and greatest *Black Panther* series that centers blackness as never before. The decision to approach Coates, a 2015 MacArthur Fellowship (commonly known as the Genius Grant) winner, to write the Black Panther, the most famous black comic character in the United States, could be read as Marvel taking their historic black character seriously. Coates' writing puts a sharp focus on injustice around race and power and it was logical to assume broader concerns U.S. society would be reflected in *Black Panther* (Coates "The Black Family...," "Obama, Ferguson..."). Moreover, Coates' personal biography (his father was a member of the Black Panther Party) primed the public for a "woke" perspective in this series. In many ways, Coates has delivered on expectations, but he also remains constrained by the limitations of the superhero genre.

In this essay, I will discuss the legacy of the Black Panther and discuss how Coates' interpretation builds on expectations since the 1960s while engaging with contemporary critical interpretations linked to race and gender in the United States. Coates' *Black Panther* leverages his understanding of contemporary black activism and protest to continue a pattern of evolutionary rather than revolutionary engagement with blackness through *Black Panther*.

The Sensational Black Panther

When asked about Black Panther, like many fans Coates goes back to the character's fabled introduction, "The first time you see him, he's tricked the Fantastic Four and he defeats the Fantastic Four, and he's this genius, this athlete with these heightened senses and these heightened physical abilities, and he's depicted there in all his glory" ("Ta-Nehisi Coates..."). Coates' fandom is meaningful in two ways. First, he sees himself writing the Black Panther within Marvel's broader narrative continuity. As a result, he is deeply engaged in the narrative landscape of previous runs of the character in shaping his story. Second, as we shall see, he sees the historic benchmarks linked to the character within a broader framework of popular culture. Therefore, his concern with the first appearance of the Black Panther as a potent symbol is to be expected. As he explains, "...I don't think people should lose sight of what it meant to create an African, a black superhero in the 1960s. It happens within the midst of the civil rights movement, but I think if you search pop culture at that particular time for somebody like the Black Panther, you would come up really short" ("Ta-Nehisi Coates...").

The origin of Black Panther hints at the complexity linking race, representation, and pop culture. Sean Howe writes that the original idea for a black character called "Coal Tiger," which was part of a wider push by Martin Goodman, owner of Marvel Comics, to get more comic books on the shelf to respond to competition in 1965, was forestalled due to distribution problems (70). Nonetheless, the black character, renamed the Black Panther, debuted in 1966, becoming the first black superhero in modern comics.

Stan Lee and Jack Kirby's motivation for creating the Black Panther remains contested. Adilifu Nama rightly points out that the character transformed depictions of Black characters by providing a character in pop culture cast "beyond the confines of enslavement, Jim Crow segregation, social subservience, and the inner-city blues of the black ghetto" (39). Often linked to the Lowndes County Freedom Organization's use of a black panther as its symbol for black political liberation and further politicized by the emergence of the Black Panther Party for Self-Defense in the same year, the comic book character has no direct connections to these pivotal black political milestones. Instead, a broader recognition of the political landscape around civil rights in the United States is a better explanation. Indeed, if Stan Lee's comments to the *New York Times* in 1966 suggest anything, it was that Marvel did not want alienate readers and risk advertising dollars. Lee makes it clear the widest audience possible was his goal (Sloane). For his part, Jack Kirby would later talk about a desire to engage on questions of race. Reflecting on the creation of the Black Panther in a 1990 *Comic Journal* interview, he stressed he "came up with the Black Panther" after recognizing he "had no blacks" in his strips. He goes further, saying "I needed a black. I suddenly discovered that I had a lot of black readers" (Groth). Thus, Marvel's introduction of a black character was less racial progressivism and more a recognition of sociopolitical reality. Whatever the motivation, the result captured the shifting expectation around blackness created by decades of civil rights activism. Martin Lund writes that Black Panther's introduction, especially within the context of the *Fantastic Four*, served to emphasize Cold War themes common in Marvel Comics (and U.S. media) in the 1960s and captured fears linked to the process of decolonization in Africa (Lund).

Taken in this light the Black Panther is a proxy for an imagined African experience for the white American reader. The key to this decontextualization is an imaginary exploration of an African world that might have existed if freed from the economic exploitation and cultural domination linked to European colonialism. Lund writes "Lee and Kirby's Wakanda is a composite of colonial imaginary" that affirms a broader understanding of anti-colonialism grounded more in Cold War competition than concerns about black liberation. Thus, it is not revolutionary, it affirms the established public narrative within the United States. As Lund indicates, for much of the 1960s, the generic label of "Third World" encompassed Africa and Asian countries formerly captured in the imperialism system. The true concern for the American public was whether or not these countries would be "won over to the NATO bloc" or at the very least rest in an "non-alignment" stance that would put them outside the Cold War binary. In this context, the United States government could not and did not ignore popular culture. Under the auspices of the United States Information Agency (USIA) the government pursued pro–American narratives abroad and domestically. An outgrowth of the Smith-Mundt Act (1948), which allowed the United States to spread positive messages to foreign countries, the USIA could not ignore civil rights. In the 1960s President Kennedy appointed Edward R. Murrow to lead the organization and increased its budget. Under Murrow the USIA created film such as *The March*, which focused on the organization and planning of the March on Washington, and *Hollywood Roundtable* (1963), which brought together Harry Belafonte, Marlon Brando, Charlton Heston, Sidney Poitier, Joseph Mankiewicz, James Baldwin and David Schoenbrun to discuss civil rights (Green). The USIA published comic books abroad, but could rely on comic book publishers in the United States to follow the guidance of the Comics Code Authority (CCA), which regulated social commentary to affirm a broadly pro–American consensus (Cull 8–9). While Marvel's introduction of a black character appeared as a transformative turn in media depictions of blackness, it was grounded in a pro–American and broadly assimilative narrative that many white readers could accept and black readers could laud. As one reader wrote in 1968, "You ... are doing more than entertaining the masses, for you are promoting human respect and bringing about a better world" (Harper). Having established the essential black superhero character, Marvel struggled with what do with him. Coates says, "I think what happened after that [is] there were various high points in the '60s, '70s and '80s, but a lot of low points..." ("Ta-Nehisi Coates...").

A Public Black Consciousness

The defining high point in the 1970s that Coates refers to grew from the tension over black power politics re-shaping the American political landscape. In this moment writer Don McGregor and artists Gil Kane and African American artist Billy Graham featured Black Panther in the pages of *Jungle Action*. On the face of it, this decision was not a harbinger of innovation. *Jungle Action* was originally published by Atlas Comics in 1954 and featured jungle characters similar to Tarzan. Thus, the heritage of racial stereotypes linked to primitive tribes and white heroes that mastered their skills is explicitly evoked with this title (Carpenter; Chambliss and Svitavsky). Indeed, MacGregor characterizes *Jungle Action* as "blond jungle gods and goddess saving the native populace from whatever threat" (Howe). After reviewing previous adventures in the publication McGregor decided to focus on Wakanda. As he explained in the introduction to *Marvel Masterworks: The Black Panther Volume 1: Jungle Tales Nos 6–24*, "I immediately felt that the stories had to be about Wakandans, that already the Black Panther character had been *compromised*"(emphasis added) (McGregor vii). Indeed, he recalled being "appalled" that Marvel offered the kind of stereotypes found in the pages of *Jungle Action*. He approached his writing duties with the intention of correcting these distortions. True to his initial impulses, McGregor wrote "Panther's Rage," a story grounded in Wakanda and the political problem of a king in Africa. "That meant, if the stories were situated in Wakanda, all the major characters would have to be Wakandan. And that meant all of the characters save one would be black" (McGregor vii). This decision crystalized the uniqueness of the story, but caused tension with his editor. Indeed, he writes, "….I can't recall a single, encouraging word from editorial during the entire run of the series" (McGregor vii).

While editors might have been indifferent, McGregor's story grabbed readers. McGregor's creation of an Afrocentric world freed the Black Panther from expectations linked to superhero stories in the period. Indeed, by shifting the narrative to Africa and concentrating on geopolitical concerns, McGregor provided the foundation that shaped the Black Panther in the popular black imagination and matched the broader narrative in the United States. By 1972 black popular culture was ripe with powerful voices linked to black power politics. Yet, equally important was cultural enrichment of blackness inspired by Black Power. Summarizing the moment, historian Peniel Joseph notes that American imagination defines black power through "fleeting images" that include "…gun-toting Black Panthers to black-gloved sprinters at the 1968 Mexico City Olympics" and that continue to resist a single narrative (751–2). Despite this, one clear element from this period was a rejection of the racial liberalism associated with the postwar civil rights movement. In its place, Black Power politics sought structural transformation in the 1960s and 1970s, and this systemic approach disrupted expectation around culture as much as politics. From black student protest leading to black studies programs, to grassroots campaigns to elect black public officials, to black women's articulation of a black feminist vision, the culture of black power wove the experience of oppressed black and brown people in the United States into a wider narrative. For social critics, a culture of oppression that recognized global racial concerns were linked was inescapable. Within this landscape the importance of the arts as a tool to re-shape the public discourse about black people and their concerns was central. A direct engagement with African themes and concerns transformed popular discourse. In McGregor's tale T'Challa is a king first and a hero second. This essential point has become the template for writers to understand the Black Panther. While mini-series such as *Black Panther: Cry the Accursed Country* (1988) or *Panther's Prey* (1991) allowed the Black Panther to engage with questions of instability growing from globalization, the character's role as a political force gained renewed focus in the hands of Christopher Priest.

A Cultural Critique in Black Panther

Coates argues that Priest "was probably the first writer in our modern times to really, really take Black Panther seriously and try to put him on a level with other superheroes. Where he wasn't just a wallflower, he wasn't just sitting in the back as kind of decoration, but actually a protagonist in his own book and that was revolutionary" ("Ta-Nehisi Coates..."). The *Black Panther* series (1998–2003) written by Christopher Priest and illustrated by Mark Texeira was a direct inheritor to McGregor's stories. Yet, as the first black writer given the reins of the character, Priest was in a unique position. Prior to getting the job Priest was first the black writer to work full time at Marvel and DC Comics (Reisman). Priest was given the opportunity to recreate the Black Panther and return him to what he saw as his former glory. Like Coates, Priest's approach to the character seized on the potential of the introduction. "The Panther, as I understood him, was this incredibly wily strategist who beat the crap out of the Fantastic Four, largely on the strength of Ben Grimm's arrogance in assuming he'd be no threat to them" (Priest). Priest's version of T'Challa emphasized his actions and outlook through a "real politik" lens and made him as counterpoint to white heroes and white concerns. As a result, Coates, like many fans, sees Priest's time writing *Black Panther* as "the classic run" because of the work he put into thinking about "who and what Black Panther was" (Riesman).

Priest's more complicated and racial take on the character expanded the world in other ways as well. He added the Dora Milaje, seeing it as an extension of McGregor's "brilliant concepts of tribal castes within Wakanda" (Smith). Priest framed them as "brides in training" and bodyguards that allowed the Black Panther to manage potential tensions. "How does Wakanda avoid the kind of splintering and tribal warfare that riddles the continent? He keeps a representative from the two major tribes ... Wakanda's tribal factions remain in a state of détente" (Priest). Priest's Panther is a power player, and this was a deliberate engagement with expectation. As he explained in a 2015 Oral History of the series, "...somebody had to give voice to the expectation of a dull and colorless character who always got his butt kicked or was overshadowed by Thor and Iron Man suddenly knocking out Mephisto with one punch" (Priest). His Black Panther operated in a manner that challenged white assumptions about black culture and realized the potential of an African king operating in the fictive universe. Following the tone set by Priest, the subsequent *Black Panther* series written by Reginald Hudlin from 2005 to 2008 continued to explore the ground Priest established. The opening story arc, "Who is the Black Panther?" featured a re-imagining of the origin story and a pointed critique of the George W. Bush administration's preemptive invasion ideology (Hudlin). The collective effect of these and subsequent stories written by Jonathan Hickman in the pages of *Avengers* placed the Black Panther at the center of power in Marvel's fictive universe. As pressures around race and representation have mounted in the media, the importance of Black Panther as a signature character for Marvel has only increased. Acting as the ultimate outsider *and* insider, the character has grown in importance. Thus, the stakes were incredibly high when Coates debuted his series in 2016.

A Black Panther for Today

When Marvel announced that Ta-Nehisi Coates would write *Black Panther*, how he would approach the character and his world were obvious questions. Coates quickly established himself as a knowledgeable about comics, writing in *The Atlantic* about "the realization of my dreams as a 9-year-old" (Coates, "The Return…"). Indeed, Coates marked comics as a heavy influence, arguing that the way "…past writers had been shaped by the canon of Fitzgerald, Hemingway, and Wharton, I was formed by the canon of Claremont, DeFalco, and Simonson" (Coates, "The Return…"). The first story arc, "A Nation Under Our Feet," returned to ground previously established by McGregor, Priest, and Hudlin by thinking political stability in Wakanda was the central challenge. Like his counterparts in the 1970s, this story offers Coates the chance to highlight sociopolitical themes in *Black Panther*. Moreover, Coates paints a picture of turmoil rooted in questions about monarchical rule (McEniry). Coates explains that his research into the previous story highlighted two things, that perhaps "T'Challa does not like being a king … [and] maybe Wakandans have come to believe they don't need a king" ("Ta-Nehisi Coates…"). While the storylines from the '70s, '80s and '90s drew from the sociopolitical landscape of those periods, I think we can see Coates' approach is informed by ideological frameworks growing from Critical Race Theory (CRT) and Black Feminist Theory (BFT). The emergence of BFT, which emphasizes the need to understand the interlocking systems of oppression linked to race and gender, challenges the neglect of voices of black female thinkers dating back to the 1960s. Black female social activism, in the words of Robin D.G. Kelley, often imagined a "different future" with an "emancipatory vision" that was "more radical and inclusive" than its counterparts (6). Prior to publication, Coates recognized the feminist critique of comics was one element defining the popular dialogue and sought to "escape" the depiction of women defined by male desire and lust ("Ta-Nehisi Coates…"). Indeed, when asked by a fan in January 2017 where feminism intersected with his work, he answered, "Right now, it's most prominently in my comic books." He goes on to argue that facts of "sexual plunder, a society ignoring that plunder, and the fact of resistance to it…" run through every issue of his *Black Panther* run (Coates, "Ta-Nehisi Coates on Comic Books…").

In some ways, this should come as no surprise. Coates' description of the common thread between his work at *The Atlantic* and comic book writing was that the "big/small approach to literature" defined by a marriage of the "absurd and surreal" to the "concrete and tangible" that allowed comic books to work, "undergirded much of my approach to writing" (Coates, "The Return…"). Situating a Black Panther story in an era of #BlackLivesMatter created and led by female activists requires an engagement with intersectionality. Defined by Kimberle Crenshaw in the 1980s, the idea of mapping the ways overlapping oppression affects the lives of minorities, especially black women, has become a defining part of modern critiques of power. Moreover, as part of academic engagement with popular culture, critical assessment of how these imaginary worlds replicated normalizing restrictions around race and gender has led to a growing body of literature examining comics, horror, and science fiction (Gatewood; Brooks; Orthia; Carrington; McGrath; Rosenberg).

Coates' *Black Panther* was not confined to the single publication. Indeed, the ideological landscape he created played out across titles such as the *World of Wakanda* co-written with Roxane Gay and Yona Harvey and *Black Panther and the Crew* co-written with Yona Harvey (Coates, Gay, and Harvey). While *Black Panther* provides political rule as its central focus, the other titles extended the ideological examination to emphasize how expectations linked to gender and identity in Wakanda were challenged by a search for a more inclusive world. In this process, reading *Black Panther* provided a clear story, but *World of Wakanda* and to a lesser extent *Black Panther and the Crew*, which tackled contemporary questions about race, gentrification, and power, provided greater depth and context to characters and motivation offered in *Black Panther*.

Coates' main story in the pages of *Black Panther* incorporated an understanding of structure and power that highlighted Critical Race Theory (CRT) by suggesting how we need to recognize how seemingly "normative" social practice reproduces inequality and how law can easily fail to address power imbalance that creates injustice. Coates' work in *The Atlantic* is heavily influenced by this ideological framework and in the pages of *Black Panther* he applies an awareness of this practice of power from the beginning. While T'Challa has faced challenges to his rule in previous narratives, Coates differs in his approach by moving the critique away from challengers to the throne to a people's revolution. Thus, T'Challa's challenge is as much revolutionary thought as subversive action. Yet, in the course of the story, Coates is careful not to confuse the former for the latter. Indeed, the real engagement from the story comes from Coates' ability to use the framework of revolutionary action as a way to discuss new expectations around freedom and autonomy that have developed since the 1970s. In the first issue T'Challa's own monologue highlights this reality. "I came here to praise the heart of the country.... For I am their king and I love them as the father loves the child. But among my children, all I found was hate" (*Black Panther: A Nation*). The cause of this hate is unknown, but in the next scene, a trial presided over by the Black Panther's mother, Ramonda, outlines another threat to order. "...Wakanda is in chaos, mother. Roads are infested with robbers. Farmers are cut down in their fields. Villainy rules. Justice is a slave." These words are offered by Ayo, a Dora Milaje, pleading for the life Aneka (who will later be revealed as her lover), another member of the Dora Milaje, who is charged with murder. Yet, her crime is framed in terms that resonate with contemporary gender politics. Ayo explains, "There are no assassins among the Dora Milaje, mother. The Dora Milaje are the nation." In recounting the crime, she goes further, "The chieftain's outrages upon the girls of his village were known. Yet his lechery was unopposed. *Aneka spoke to him as fathers and brother should have spoken long before*" (emphasis added, Coates, *Black Panther: A Nation*).

Aneka and Ayo's rebellion and their queer relationship offers a vehicle to critique Wakanda and systemic exploitation of women. Guided by an intersectional feminism that recognizes women's twin oppression in the home and in the street, these characters and their story become a proxy for international debate about gender equality as a means to enhance global society ("#Envision2030 Goal..."). While comics depicting queer characters existed in broad mainstream, the presence of queer characters in the *Black Panther* has a longer history which highlight how Coates seeks to update the progressive framing of the character. Don McGregor intended Taku and Venomm from his *Jungle Action* run to be homosexuals but was prevented from presenting their relationship as such (Dar). In contrast, Aneka and Ayo's relationship and their evolution into renegades leading a women's centric revolution against the throne elevate the story and provide nuance to Wakandan society. Once Ayo steals two prototypes of battle armor and breaks Aneka out of prison, Aneka embraces Ayo's defiant vision saying, "I am tired of living and dying on the blood-right of one man." Ayo concurs, answering simply, "No one man should have that much power" (Coates, *Black Panther*). This subplot of about the de-legitimization of monarchical power is personified by T'Challa. He uses the language of fathers and children to describe his feeling toward Wakanda's citizens and in doing so, Coates is able to highlight the broader feminist critique.

This is a theme that Gay further develops in the companion series *World of Wakanda*. Offering a parallel storyline that explores the culture of Dora Milaje, the series follow Aneka and Ayo as they fall in love and use their relationship to explore gender inequality. Their turn toward rebellion does not happen in a vacuum and Gay shows how moving women's concerns and a vision of a just society to the center of the narrative added depth and complexity to Black Panther's world. In interviews she stressed she wanted "black women of all ages to see ourselves doing heroic things" and "see ourselves have healthy and loving relationship" (Vega). Using queer characters' struggles as a vehicle to signify the societal disruption shifted the political narrative in *Black Panther* and the related titles in significant ways. Using the queer experience to challenge the assumption of normality within Wakanda and positioning those characters as rebels immediately signals to the readers the challenge to the Black Panther would not be easily resolved. By the second issue, the slogan "No One Man" blazes on field as women rescued by Aneka and Ayo, now known as the "Midnight Angels," promise to punish those men victimizing women in Wakanda.

In a similar vein, the subversive action of the revolutionary army of the "People" led by Tetu and Xenzi represents a threat more aligned with traditional counterrevolutionaries offered in the page of previous *Black Panther* volumes. Cut from a mode that references previous villains in the comic, Tetu is presented as rooted in a Shamanic tradition that T'Challa's technology-driven vision of Wakanda has abandoned. Indeed, he sees himself as true Wakandan, guided by the natural world, and T'Challa as an outsider. In this manner, he joins a long line of African characters linked to the natural world. While confronting T'Challa in the series' third issue he boasts, "…a day is coming Wakanda will be ruled by Wakandans … and the era of kings shall end" (Coates, *Black Panther*). Clearly the true villain of the story, Tetu's goal is the destruction of the established order to be replaced by his rule. Xenzi, Tetu's female co-conspirator, is less defined. While her power to bring out "all the awful feelings that we have hidden away" fuels "The People" and makes them an also unstoppable fighting force, her identity is never fully defined. Some hints of past wrongs by Wakanda's kings and unfairness in their rule are suggested, but her power seems her justification for being in the story.

Tetu and Xenzi are given added dimension, in part, by the ideological critique of Changamire. A Wakandan philosopher and former tutor at the royal court, Changamire's criticism of the absolute power invested in the monarchial system is cited as the "heart" of the revolutionary drive behind Tetu's uprising. Introduced in issue #2 teaching a lecture, his parable on power to that class is offered as a companion to the turmoil created by the revolutionaries in the story. Coates uses Changamire to attack the structure of institutional power. Indeed, his lecture suggests resistance to such power is required.

> The injury and the crime is equal, whether committed by the wearer of a crown or some petty villain … because they are too big for the weak hands of justice in this world, and have the power in their possession, which should punish offenders….

> What is my remedy against the robber, who so broke into my house? [Coates, *Black Panther*].

As he later explains in issue #3, "Wakanda has all the intelligence any advanced society would want, and none of the wisdom that any free society needs" (Coates, *Black Panther*). Changamire's philosophy is called into question for the reader as it is revealed that Tetu is Changamire's former student. When he visits Changamire seeking his blessing for the violent revolution he has spawned based on his teaching, their exchange highlights a chasm between mentor and student:

> CHANGAMIRE: These days I hear tales of your associations with brutal men sworn to the knife.
> TETU: What I do, I do for a better country.
> CHANGAMIRE: And is **that** enough? Once I thought you were better than that. Why have you come here Tetu? [Coates, *Black Panther*].

Much like the generational schism in the 1970s around the path for black activism, Coates provides many of the same concerns in the pages of *Black Panther*. As the story continues, the institutional critiques offered by Ayo and Aneka's women's revolution and by Tetu and Xenzi converge and overlap in the series' second story arc. In "A Sword for Lions" Coates takes care to make a distinction between the two revolutionary forces facing the Black Panther. This story arc is noteworthy for Coates' decision to incorporate black heroes, including Storm (T'Challa's former queen), Luke Cage, Misty Knight and Manifold. The inclusion of these characters points the way toward narrative climax as the ideology and the action in Coates' *Black Panther* seek to establish T'Challa as a new kind of monarch.

Building on an idea offered in the first story arc, this ideological turn is encapsulated by a pivotal conversation between T'Challa and Changamire. As in Coates' writing in *The Atlantic*, history is the entry way for this discussion. Having come to Changamire to force his help in stopping Tetu's army, the two men discuss the classic history book *American Slavery, American Freedom* by Edmund S. Morgan (Coates, *Black Panther*). First published in 1975 and still in print, Morgan's book becomes a backdrop for the two men to understand the meaning of freedom. Changamire explains, "That book chronicles the attempt to raise an entire race of kings. And every year thousands of them were born and charged with keeping thousands more underfoot" (Coates, *Black Panther*). It is impossible to know how many readers searched out the book and found it a classic historical work that explains how the Virginia colony made the decision to go from a society with slaves to a slave society after white settlers who were promised freedom and property rebelled during Bacon's Rebellion in 1676, but the implication for Black Panther in the story is clear: denying freedom leads society down dark paths.

In crafting this narrative, Coates takes familiar concerns linked to the Black Panther that readers would recognize and creates a new context to engage with those ideas. The Black Panther is royalty figuratively and literally in comics. As we have seen, as the first black superhero, his blackness has always been tinged with elements of aspiration for racial transcendence for whites and the possibility of liberating power for blacks. He has served and continues to serve as a kind of guidepost for black superheroes, many of whom have their origins in the 1970s black power aesthetic. Thus, Luke Cage and Misty Knight, two characters modeled on blaxploitation films (*Shaft* and *Coffy*) have remained linked to the character (Guerrero). Not surprising, in the confines of Coates' story, these characters, along with Storm and Manifold, become allies in the Black Panther's struggle. Here too, Coates does an intriguing job of weaving together several elements of contemporary black ideology. While Wakanda has been described as xenophobic in previous stories, this series subtly shifts that narrative. T'Challa embraces support from these black heroes and brings them into the fight for Wakanda's future. At the same time, this group becomes the focal point of *Black Panther and The Crew*, where a mystery rooted in Wakanda's connection to historic struggle for black freedom and contemporary concerns are explored. A story that mirrors elements of Reginald Hudlin's *Captain America/Black Panther: Flags of Our Father* World War II era story, Coates' Wakanda has a bigger presence in the world and that legacy inspires contemporary action. The awareness of a shared diaspora is not new to the pages of *Black Panther*, but the implication that *Black Panther and The Crew* would tackle questions more rooted in black America again elevated the story.

Perhaps the final and most important contribution in Coates' story is his attempt to reconcile the tension between tradition versus modernity in *Black Panther*. Indeed, reconciling these concepts is the key to victory for T'Challa. Finding what to retain and what to discard in a rapidly changing world is a common theme in contemporary cultural debates. In this process, his sister Shuri, first seen in the first arc of the story in a coma and then revealed to be on a spiritual journey in The Djalia, a mystical plane of Wakandan memory, is key. Shuri's journey of understanding in the spirit world mirrors the insight T'Challa experiences in the real world. As her guide, Griot, explains, "…I am … a caretaker of all our histories now lost to the acolytes of machine and the prophets of the metal age" (Coates, *Black Panther*). The rejection of Eurocentric industrial ideology and an embrace of the system rooted in African ideology allow Coates to weave Afrofuturism and feminist themes into the story. In issue #3 the griot figure instructs Shuri and pushes her to see her tribal traditions as lost knowledge.

> I do not mock you … you have become lost. As were the men who rule before you. You have forgotten the old ways, my queens. You have lost your soul. Here we will

arm you, not with the spear, but with the drum, for it is the drum that carries the greatest power of all ... the power of memory, daughter. The power of our song [Coates, *Black Panther*].

Returned from her sojourn to the Wakandan dreamscape, Shuri offers a framework of thinking that emphasizes reconciliation as a path that cannot be ignored. Coates' decision to allow Shuri, who served as Black Panther in previous stories written by Reginald Hudlin, to give voice to ancestral knowledge allows her to draw on stories and parables that often center women's perspectives and concerns. In doing so, Coates acknowledges social justice views grounded in the black feminist epistemology. Deeply inspired by the work of feminist thinkers such as bell hooks, the critical examination of black women's experience highlights how race, sex, class, and heterosexism obscure pathways for freedom. Hooks' writings about the failure of black leaders "to acknowledge black male sexist oppression of black women" call out one element of the critique black power politics of the 1970s. As she explains, the "…emphasis on the impact of racism on black men has evoked an image of the black male as effete, emasculated, and crippled" (hooks). The net result is popular representations of black masculine figures that emerged in the 1970s under the guise of the Black Power and Black Art Movements arguably overcompensated in their depictions of positive black masculine power. In comics, Luke Cage's persona is an obvious example of this, but the Black Panther's role as ruler, scientist, warrior, and leader is a shrewder version of this same trope. Coates' story acknowledges deficits and seeks to create a balance between the masculine and the feminine. Unlike T'Challa, who had been shown communing with former Black Panthers (Priest, *Black Panther*), Shuri voices the folk knowledge of the people. As a result, she sees the key to victory is allowing society to change while recognizing tradition.

The superhero battle that ends "A Nation Under Our Feet" is secondary in my mind to the broader question about freedom Coates wants to engage with. In the course of the inaugural storyline, he questions the certainty of power linked to Black Panther, challenges how that power marginalizes women, and offers links between Wakanda and the wider world that will shape future stories. Positioned over and over again as a commentary on blackness, the struggle for anyone writing *Black Panther* is to hold on to the aspirations inherent to the creation of a black superhero. At the same time, for a black writer, the need make the black hero's journey resonate with decolonization inherent to contemporary race politics cannot be ignored. Thus, Coates' writing is a dialogue between the comic past and our expectation for the future. The evolution of Wakanda toward a constitutional monarchy may be forgotten, but Coates' efforts to transcribe the concerns linked to race, gender, and power are noteworthy. As a result, a narrative landscape with greater complexity around questions of identity, community, and power exists in *Black Panther*. Coates' *Black Panther* built on the historic legacy of the character, while acknowledging contemporary sociopolitical concerns linked to the black experience. With the success of Marvel Studios' *Black Panther*, interest in the character and his world continues to grow. However Marvel Comics seeks to capitalize on these efforts, we can be assured a recognition of the legacy of race and representation will continue to matter.

Works Cited

Anderson, Reynaldo. "Critical Afrofuturism: A Case Study in Visual Rhetoric, Sequential Art, and Postapocalyptic Black Identity," in *The Blacker the Ink: Constructions of Black Identity in Comics and Sequential Art*, ed. Professor Frances Gateward and John Jennings (New Brunswick, NJ: Rutgers University Press, 2015), 182.

Brooks, Kinitra D. "The Importance of Neglected Intersections: Race and Gender in Contemporary Zombie Texts and Theories," *African American Review* 47, no. 4 (2014): 461–75.

Carpenter, Stanford W. "Ethnographic Investigations Into the Creation of Black Images in Comic Books," in *Storied Inquiries in International Landscapes: An Anthology of Educational Research*, ed. Tonya Huber-Warring, Teaching-Learning Indigenous, Intercultural Worldviews (Charlotte, NC: Information Age Publishing, 2010).

Carrington, André. "SF and the Consciousness of Race," *Science Fiction Studies* 39, no. 2 (July 2012): 336–38.

Chambliss, Julian C., and William Svitavsky. "The Origin of the Superhero: Culture, Race, and Identity in US Popular Culture, 1890–1940," in *Ages of Heroes, Eras of Men: Superheroes and the American Experience* (Newcastle: Cambridge Scholars Publishing, 2013), 6–27.

Coates, Ta-Nehisi. "The Black Family in the Age of Mass Incarceration," *The Atlantic*, October 2015, http://www.theatlantic.com/magazine/archive/2015/10/the-black-family-in-the-age-of-mass-incarceration/403246/.

_____. *Black Panther: A Nation Under Our Feet* (Marvel, 2016).

_____. "Barack Obama, Ferguson, and the Evidence of Things Unsaid," The Atlantic, November 26, 2014, http://www.theatlantic.com/politics/archive/2014/11/barack-obama-ferguson-and-the-evidence-of-things-unsaid/383212/.

_____. "The Return of the Black Panther," *The Atlantic*, April 2016, http://www.theatlantic.com/magazine/archive/2016/04/the-return-of-the-black-panther/471516/.

_____. "Ta-Nehisi Coates on Comic Books and Feminism," *The Atlantic*, January 13, 2017, https://www.theatlantic.com/notes/2017/01/on-comic-books-and-feminism/513023/.

Coates, Ta-Nehisi, Roxane Gay, and Yona Harvey. *Black Panther: World of Wakanda*, 1st Edition (New York: Marvel, 2017).

Coates, Ta-Nehisi, and Yona Harvey. *Black Panther & the Crew: We Are the Streets* (New York: Marvel, 2017).

Costello, Matthew J. *Secret Identity Crisis: Comic Books and the Unmasking of Cold War America* (New York: Bloomsbury, 2009).

Cull, Nicholas J. *The Cold War and the United States Information Agency: American Propaganda and Public Diplomacy, 1945–1989*, 1st edition (Cambridge: Cambridge University Press, 2009), 179, 207.

Dar, Taimur. "Marvel's Earliest Gay Characters Introduced in Don McGregor's Black Panther Comics," The Beat, February 12, 2018, http://www.comicsbeat.com/marvels-earliest-gay-characters-introduced-in-don-mcgregors-black-panther-comics/.

"#Envision2030 Goal 5: Gender Equality | United Nations Enable," accessed July 30, 2018, https://www.un.org/development/desa/disabilities/envision2030-goal5.html.

Frances Gateward et al.. *The Blacker the Ink: Constructions of Black Identity in Comics and Sequential Art*, ed. Frances Gateward and John Jennings (New Brunswick: Rutgers University Press, 2015).

Green, Richard. "Hollywood Roundtable," The Unwritten Record, September 21, 2012, https://unwritten-record.blogs.archives.gov/2012/09/21/hollywood-roundtable/.

Groth, Gary. "Jack Kirby Interview," *The Comics Journal* (blog), May 23, 2011, http://www.tcj.com/jack-kirby-interview/2/.

Guerrero, Ed. "The Rise and Fall of Blaxploitation," in *The Wiley-Blackwell History of American Film* (American Cancer Society, 2011), https://doi.org/10.1002/9780470671153.wbhaf063.

Harper, Jackie. "Collegians Go for Comics—The Baltimore Sun," Newspapers.com, February 6, 1968, http://www.newspapers.com/image/376912487/?terms=%22Black+Panther%22+Marvel.

hooks, bell. *Ain't I a Woman: Black Women and Feminism*, 2nd edition (New York: Routledge, 2014), 87–89.

Howe, Sean. *Marvel Comics: The Untold Story.* New York: Harper Perennial, 2013.

Hudlin, Reginald. *Black Panther Vol. 1: Who Is The Black Panther* (New York: Marvel, 2006).

_____. *Captain America/Black Panther: Flags of Our Fathers* (New York: Marvel, 2018).

Joseph, Peniel E. "The Black Power Movement: A State of the Field," *Journal of American History* 96, no. 3 (December 2009): 751–52.

Kelley, Robin D.G. *Freedom Dreams: The Black Radical Imagination* (Beacon Press, 2002), 6.

Lackaff, Derek, and Michael Sales. "Black Comics and Social Media Economics: New Media, New Production Models," in *Black Comics: Politics of Race and Representation* (New York: Bloomsbury Academic, 2013), 67–68.

Lund, Martin. "'Introducing the Sensational Black Panther!' Fantastic Four #52–53, the Cold War, and Marvel's Imagined Africa," *The Comics Grid: Journal of Comics Scholarship* 6, no. 1 (May 23, 2016), https://doi.org/10.16995/cg.80.

McGrath, Karen. "Gender, Race, and Latina Identity: An Examination of Marvel Comics' Amazing Fantasy and Araña," *Atlantic Journal of Communication* 15, no. 4 (December 2007): 268–83.

McEniry, Matthew J. "An Archetype or a Token? The Challenge of the Black Panther," In *Marvel Comics into Film: Essays on Adaptations Since the 1940s.* Ed. Matthew J. McEniry, Robert Moses Peaslee and Robert G. Weiner. Jefferson, NC: McFarland, 2016.

McGregor Don et al. *Marvel Masterworks: The Black Panther*, 1st edition. New York: Marvel Enterprises, 2010.

Morgan, Edmund S. *American Slavery, American Freedom*, Reissue edition. New York: W.W. Norton & Company, 2003.

Nama, Adilifu. *Super Black: American Pop Culture and Black Superheroes.* Austin: University of Texas Press, 2011.

Orthia, Lindy, ed. *Doctor Who and Race.* Intellect Ltd, 2013.

_____. "The Death of the Black Panther: Quesada's Bitch Survives the Mean Season," DigitalPriest.com, 2008, http://digitalpriest.com/legacy/comics/panther/panther_death.html.

Riesman, Abraham. "The Man Who Made Black Panther Cool," Vulture, January 22, 2018, http://www.vulture.com/2018/01/christopher-priest-made-black-panther-cool-then-disappeared.html.

Rosenberg, Robin S., Peter Coogan, and A. David Lewis. *What Is a Superhero?*, 1st edition. New York: Oxford University Press, 2013.

Sloane, Leonard. "Advertising: Comics Go Up, Up and Away," *New York Times*, July 20, 1967, sec. Business & Finance, http://search.proquest.com.ezproxy.rollins.edu:2048/hnpnewyorktimes/docview/117480712/abstract/D403F7BD2B264CEFPQ/1?accountid=13584.

Smith, Zach. "PRIEST on BLACK PANTHER, Pt. 2: 'It's Not Arrogance, It's Competence,'" Newsarama, February 16, 2018, https://www.newsarama.com/25506-priest-on-black-panther-pt-2.html.

"Ta-Nehisi Coates Hopes 'Black Panther' Will Be Some Kid's 'Spider-Man,'" NPR.org, accessed August 5, 2018, https://www.npr.org/sections/codeswitch/2016/04/06/473224606/a-reluctant-king-ta-nehisi-coates-takes-on-marvels-black-panther.

Vega, Tanzina, Ethan Oberman and Dana Roberson. "After 'Black Panther': Roxane Gay on What's Still Missing from the Marvel Universe | The Takeaway | WNYC Studios," wnyc

studios, February 15, 2018, https://www.wnycstudios.org/story/after-black-panther-whats-still-missing-marvel-universe/.
Wanzo, Rebecca. "And All Our Past Decades Have Seen Revolutions: The Long Decolonization of Black Panther by Rebecca Wanzo," *The Black Scholar* (blog), February 19, 2018, http://www.theblackscholar.org/past-decades-seen-revolutions-long-decolonization-black-panther-rebecca-wanzo/.

About the Contributors

José **Alaniz** is a professor in the Department of Slavic Languages and Literatures and an adjunct in the Department of Comparative Literature at the University of Washington–Seattle. He authored *Komiks: Comic Art in Russia* in 2010 and *Death, Disability and the Superhero: The Silver Age and Beyond* in 2014, both published by the University Press of Mississippi.

Ivon **Alcime** received a Ph.D. in intercultural communication from Howard University. His research focuses on listening and conflict management. He is an assistant professor of communication in the Department of Communications at Alabama State University.

Daniel J. **Bergman** is a professor and program chair of science education at Wichita State University in Kansas. His research interests include teachers' interactive classroom behaviors and the role of popular culture in science and teacher education. He has published over 50 articles, including an essay in *The Ages of the Flash*, and writes at www.teachlikeasuperhero.blog.

Matthew **Brake** has a master's of divinity from Regent University and an MA in philosophy and interdisciplinary studies from George Mason University. He is the founder of the blog Pop Culture and Theology, the series editor for the Theology and Pop Culture series from Lexington Books and the series coeditor (with A. David Lewis) of the Religion and Comics series from Claremont Press.

Burton P. **Buchanan** is an assistant professor of mass communication at Alabama State University. He has taught mass communication classes full time at the university level for 20 years. His research interests include media portrayals of masculinity and male body image. He earned his Ph.D. from the University of Southern Mississippi.

Julian C. **Chambliss** is a professor of English at Michigan State University. His publications on comics and related culture include *Ages of Heroes, Eras of Men* (2013), *Assembling the Marvel Cinematic Universe* (2018) and *Cities Imagined* (2018).

John **Darowski** is a doctoral candidate in comparative humanities at the University of Louisville. His research is on the superhero Gothic, tracing the influence of the

Gothic on the superhero and how both genres work together to reflect the cultural context. He has previous essays published in the Ages of Superheroes series.

Joseph J. **Darowski** teaches English at Brigham Young University. He is a member of the editorial review board of *The Journal of Popular Culture* and has previously edited essay collections on the ages of Superman, Wonder Woman, the X-Men, the Avengers, Iron Man, the Incredible Hulk, the Flash, and the Justice League.

Hollie **FitzMaurice** is a Ph.D. candidate and departmental assistant in the Department of English Language and Literature at Mary Immaculate College in Limerick, Ireland. Her thesis analyzes the parent-child relationship within comic books and its impact on the development of the hero. Her other research interests include popular culture, comics studies, and gender studies.

Charles W. **Henebry** received a doctorate in English literature from New York University in 2003. For the past ten years his scholarship has focused on the world of superheroes. He is the author of seven articles in Greenwood Publishing Group's 2014 *Comics Through Time* encyclopedia and long-form essays in *The Ages of Iron Man*, *The Ages of the Justice League*, and *The Ages of the Flash*.

Peter W.Y. **Lee** is an independent historian specializing in American Cold War popular culture and youth culture. He earned a Ph.D. from Drew University. His work has appeared in many publication including the Ages of Superheroes series. He has published edited anthologies on *Peanuts*, *Star Trek: The Next Generation*, and *Star Wars*, also available from McFarland.

Cathy **Leogrande** is a professor in the Teacher Education Department at Le Moyne College in New York. Her teaching research and publications address issues of race, class, gender, and disability in multimedia and traditional texts. Her focus is in areas of new literacies, using popular culture to provide K–12 teachers the creative skills to teach in inclusive classrooms.

Christopher **Maverick** is a Ph.D. candidate in English at Duquesne University. He holds an MA in literary and cultural studies from Carnegie Mellon University. His primary research interests include race, class, gender and sexuality in contemporary American popular culture, especially in television, movies, professional wrestling and comics.

Carlos D. **Morrison** is a professor in the Department of Communication at Alabama State University. He received a Ph.D. in intercultural communication and African American communication from the Cathy Hughes School of Communication at Howard University in Washington, D.C. His publications and research focus on Black popular culture and communication, the rhetoric of rap music and Black masculinity.

Fernando Gabriel **Pagnoni Berns** is a Ph.D. student and works as a professor at the Universidad de Buenos Aires (UBA)–Facultad de Filosofía y Letras (Argentina). He teaches courses on international horror film. He is the author of chapters in several collections, a book about the Spanish horror TV series *Historias para no Dormir* and the editor of a book on the Frankenstein bicentennial.

Liam T. **Webb** works full time in pharmaceutical regulatory affairs; literary research and writing are his hobbies. This is his fifth essay. He has an MA and has taught at Valley Forge Military College and Northampton Community College. He has published creatively in nine publications and continues to write both academically and creatively.

Index

Afrofuturism 29, 40, 93, 111, 204, 215
apartheid 2-3, 64, 68-69, 71, 74, 113-124, 126
Avengers (comic) 1, 37-38, 42-44 46-61, 73, 81, 94-95, 134, 145, 200
Avengers (team) 3, 30, 33, 37-38, 42-43, 46, 48-53, 55-56, 59, 86, 120, 130-131, 134, 151, 158, 194, 196-198
Avengers vs. X-Men 193-195

Batman 5, 21, 30, 130, 132, 136
Black Leopard 2, 64, 67, 70, 74
Black Panther (comic) 3, 4, 100, 113, 117-119, 122-123, 125, 129-130, 133-134, 137, 139-144, 146, 151, 155, 168-170, 182, 204, 207-217
Black Panther (film) 1, 5
Black Panther Party 2, 36-38, 44, 48, 52, 54, 57-59, 61, 64-67, 108-109, 121, 205-206
Black Power 38, 45, 52, 58, 60, 64, 66, 108, 120, 207-208, 215-216
Blackness 24, 30, 31-32, 66, 71, 73, 93, 204-208, 215-216
Buckler, Rich 2, 82
Buscema, John 67, 81
Buscema, Sal 47, 96

Cage, Luke 113, 132, 150, 214-215
Carmicheal, Stokely 38, 45-46, 108
Civil Rights 23-25, 28, 33, 38-39, 45-46, 56, 65, 101-102, 104-107, 109-111, 116, 120, 124, 152, 163, 205-208
Coal Tiger 12, 25, 205
Coates, Ta-Nehisi 4, 81, 90, 93, 204-205, 207, 209-217
Cold War 13, 23, 40, 94, 96, 115, 126, 150, 206
Cole, Kasper 141-144, 146
Comics Code Authority 20, 85, 163, 207
Communism 23, 58, 115, 119, 126
Congo 2, 13-17, 28-29

Daredevil (comic) 51, 58-60, 74, 146
Daredevil 130, 145
DC Comics 113, 130-131, 144, 209

Deathlok 132, 158
diaspora 28, 117, 187, 215
Dora Milaje 133, 136, 139-140, 143, 182, 188-192, 196, 209, 212

exceptionalism 40, 46, 133

Fantastic Four (comic) 1, 2, 5, 8-9, 14, 16, 18, 21, 25-28, 31, 38, 41-44, 60, 65-66, 69, 71, 80-81, 134, 145, 149, 151, 154-155, 160-162, 206
Fantastic Four (team) 3, 9, 21-26, 29, 31-32, 39, 41-42, 44, 59, 70-71, 120, 130, 134, 145, 150, 151-155, 157-158, 160, 162-163, 164, 196, 205, 209

Gandhi, Mahatma 194, 201
Gillis, Peter 3, 113-114, 117, 119-124
Girard, René 4, 194-202
Golden Age 20, 184
Goodman, Martin 12, 16, 21
Green Lantern 113, 145
Grimm, Benjamin 21, 39, 67-68, 70-72, 154, 157, 161-162, 209; *see also* Thing

Harlem 29, 50, 52-54, 60, 72
Hickman Jonathan 4, 193, 210
Hudlin, Reginald 182-187, 209-210, 216
Hulk 29, 37, 61
Human Torch 21, 70, 153, 159, 160; *see also* Storm, Johnny

imperialism 28, 40, 84, 118, 206
intersectional 3-4, 142, 182-184, 189-190, 192
Invisible Girl/Woman 21, 145; *see also* Richards, Susan; Storm, Susan
Iron Man 43, 59, 84, 130, 151, 193, 209; *see also* Stark, Tony
Iron Man (comic) 57

Jewish 21-23, 32-33, 35-36, 66, 142
Jungle Action 10, 76, 82, 85-86, 88, 94-95, 99, 104-107, 110, 144-145, 207-208, 212

226 Index

Killmonger 76, 82–82, 86, 90, 135, 141, 143, 145
King, Martin Luther, Jr. 24, 32, 38, 42, 45, 104, 109, 116, 194, 201
Kirby, Jack 1, 2 5–16, 20–26, 28–30, 33, 38–44, 46, 52, 65–66, 80–81, 95–96, 144, 206
Klaw 13–14 26, 39–41, 63
Ku Klux Klan 3, 95, 99, 101, 103–111, 115

Lee, Jim 130, 145
Lee, Stan 1, 2, 5–6, 9, 11–16, 20–21, 23–26, 28–33, 38–44, 46, 48–50, 52–53, 55–58, 61, 65–67, 80–82, 206
Lowndes County Freedom Organization (LCFO) 38, 65–68, 206

Malcolm X 29–30, 66, 116
Mandela, Nelson 60, 69–70, 73, 123–124, 126
Marvel Cinematic Universe 1, 64, 182, 221
Marvel Comics 1–2, 6, 8, 16, 21, 23, 31–32, 48, 64–65, 67–68, 82, 113, 125, 129–130, 141, 151, 168–169, 205–206, 217
Marvel Knights 3, 125, 129–130, 141, 145
Marvel method 31, 81, 94
McDuffie, Dwayne 3, 150–155, 157–162
McGregor, Don 2 77, 80–82, 84–86, 88, 90, 92, 94–96, 99, 109–110, 140, 207–208, 212
Mephisto 138–140, 209
Mr. Fantastic 21, 159, 193, 196; *see also* Richards, Reed
Munroe, Ororo 150–153, 156, 158, 163, 172, 176

NAACP 38, 103, 107
Namor 4, 156, 193–203
Native American 39, 169
New Avengers (comic) 4, 193–198, 200
Newton, Huey 38, 43, 48, 66–67, 69, 73, 108
9/11 3, 149, 156

Palmiotti, Jimmy 129–131
Panther God 27, 172, 174, 185–186
"Panther's Rage" 2, 76–77, 80, 82–85, 88–90, 92–93, 99, 208
Patriot Act 3, 149, 152, 157
Priest, Christopher 3, 61, 129–131, 133–134, 136–137, 139–144

racism (racist) 25, 32, 40, 42–43, 45, 47–48, 52–56, 58, 65, 71–73, 99, 100, 104, 106–108, 110, 113–116, 122, 152, 160–161, 183, 189, 200, 216
Richards, Reed 21, 23, 25–27, 41, 51, 80, 149–155, 157–161, 164, 197; *see also* Mr. Fantastic
Richards, Susan 151, 153, 158, 161; *see also* Invisible Girl/Woman; Storm, Susan
Ross, Everett K. 1, 125, 135, 137–141, 143–145, 183

Scarlet Witch 59, 61, 73
Seale, Boby 38, 48, 57, 66, 108
Secret Invasion 3, 168–169
S.H.I.E.L.D. 154, 158, 163–164
Shuri 1, 4, 93, 172, 182–192, 196, 198–199, 216–216
Silver Age 21–23, 159
Skrull 3, 168, 170–176
slavery 22, 28, 40, 44–45, 49–50, 108, 128, 212, 214
social justice 3, 99, 216
South Africa 3, 60, 68–70, 113–124, 126
Spider-Man 5, 29
Stark, Tony 154, 156, 158, 161, 163, 196–197; *see also* Iron Man
stereotype 24–25, 27, 33, 39–40, 42, 52, 62, 73, 131, 140, 152, 162, 185–187, 190, 192, 207–208
Storm 113, 143, 146, 150–154, 156, 158, 160, 163, 172, 176, 184–185, 214–215; *see also* Munroe, Ororo
Storm, Johnny 21, 26, 39, 67, 70–73, 154–155, 158; *see also* Human Torch
Storm, Susan 21, 149; *see also* Invisible Girl/Woman; Richards, Susan
Superman 20–21, 25, 30, 145

Tarzan 2, 6–16, 26, 28, 39, 53, 80, 82, 96, 207
Tarzan of the Apes 5
terrorism 70, 200
Thing 5, 21, 39, 70, 72, 153, 159–161; *see also* Grimm, Benjamin
Thomas, Roy 25, 37–38, 43, 46–61, 67–68, 72–74

United States of America 23–24, 33, 44–45, 47, 53, 65, 68–69, 73–74, 86, 96, 99, 101–102, 104, 113, 115–116, 126, 128, 133–134, 136, 140, 153, 156, 161, 168, 191, 205–208

vibranium 13–14, 27, 29, 39, 80, 93, 134–13, 161
Vietnam War 24, 31, 38, 45, 57, 105, 169

War Machine 132, 146
War on Terror 152, 156–157
White supremacy 70–71, 103, 122, 160
whiteness 30, 72, 90, 132, 204
Wingfoot, Wyatt 39–40, 42, 80
World War II 13, 20, 29, 101, 116, 146, 157, 168, 215

X-Men (comic) 13, 16, 145
X-Men (team) 13, 29, 59, 146, 150–153, 172, 194, 196

www.ingramcontent.com/pod-product-compliance
Ingram Content Group UK Ltd.
Pitfield, Milton Keynes, MK11 3LW, UK
UKHW041949140426
5217IPUK00014B/714